The Nigerian Regiment in East Africa

Brigadier-General Cunliffe, C. B., C. M. G.

The Nigerian Regiment in East Africa
On Campaign During
the Great War 1916-1918

W. D. Downes

The Nigerian Regiment in East Africa: on Campaign During the Great War 1916-1918
by W. D. Downes

Originally published under the title
With the Nigerians in German East Africa

Published by Leonaur Ltd

Text in this form and material original to this edition
copyright © 2008 Leonaur Ltd

ISBN: 978-1-84677-464-5 (hardcover)
ISBN: 978-1-84677-463-8 (softcover)

http://www.leonaur.com

Publisher's Notes

The opinions expressed in this book are those of the author and are not necessarily those of the publisher.

Contents

Introduction	9
The German East African Campaign	20
The Nigerian Brigade in East Africa	43
The Action of the Mgeta River	56
The Ngwembe Action	63
Operations During the Rains	80
The Naumann Pursuit	113
The Action of Mkalama	125
The Rufiji Front	135
The Nigerian Brigade in the Kilwa Area	149
The March to the Lindi Area	167
The Battle of Mahiwa	175
The Battle of Mahiwa (2)	190
The Action of Mkwera	211
The Operations of the Makonde Plateau	224
A Digression	234
The Last Phase of the Campaign	248
Envoi	259
An Epilogue	264
Appendices	269
Maps	315

I humbly dedicate this book to
the memory of all Nigerians
irrespective of colour, race, creed and rank
of the empire in German East Africa
from 1916-1918

W. D. Downes

Chapter 1
Introduction

To the average "man in the street" at home the letters W.A.F.F. convey nothing, so it is necessary for me formally to introduce the readers to the West African Frontier Force, for which the letters stand. In British West African colonies there are certain races and tribes that take to fighting as a duck takes to water. These are trained and led by officers and non-commissioned officers specially selected for service in the Tropics, who are seconded for a certain period from their British regiments to the various battalions of the W.A.F.F. This account deals entirely with the Nigeria Regiment of that Force.

It is my hope that, when the reader has finished this book, he will be as convinced as the writer that these soldiers from the borders of the sun-scorched Sahara, from the banks of the Niger and the Benue, from Yorubaland and Calabar, are second to none among the dark-skinned sons of the Empire as fighting men. It will probably interest my readers if I set down for their information a short sketch of the history and doings of this gallant regiment, dating back as it does to the early days of the British Overseas Empire.

On 9th October 1862 the Governor of British West African possessions, Stanhope Freeman, wrote from his headquarters at Sierra Leone to the Duke of Newcastle, then Colonial Secretary, pointing out the necessity of increasing the armed forces of Lagos. Up to this time one hundred men of the West India Regiment formed the garrison. Of these only thirty-six could turn out in aid of the civil power; the rest were either *on guards* or on the sick list. Stanhope Freeman stated in his despatch:

Her Majesty's Government, in accepting the territory ceded by King Docemo, have bound themselves to assist, defend, and protect the inhabitants of Lagos; to put an end to the slave trade in this and the neighbouring countries, and to prevent the destructive wars so frequently undertaken by Dahomey and others for the capture of slaves. With regard to the assistance, defence, and protection to be granted to the inhabitants of Lagos, I should wish to know what steps I should be authorized to take in the event of Lagos people being kidnapped and sold by the people of any of the surrounding towns? It would appear to me that we are bound to rescue them. It is an easy matter if the kidnappers belong to the places on the borders of the lagoon, where the mere appearance of a gunboat is sufficient to force the natives into submission, but in case of the kidnappers being from a town which a gunboat cannot reach, what measures am I to take? Moral influence in these parts depends upon physical force, and therefore the people of the interior do not acknowledge our power, as they say we are very strong on the coast where we have our ships, but we can do nothing on land. If, therefore, the Lagos people should be kidnapped and this Government contents itself with protest, it would not only be failing in its duty towards its subjects, but would also be lowering the British name, for the natives would not attribute the action of the Government either to apathy or forbearance, but to lack of power to hold their rights.

This striking letter was the first move towards the establishment of the W.A.F.F.

In June 1863 the first Hausas were trained as soldiers. Thirty Hausa police of Lagos were armed and drilled that year. This force went by the nickname of *The Forty Thieves,* but why I do not know; nor have I any records of there being more than thirty all told. John Glover,[1] Lieutenant-Governor of Lagos, wrote to

---

1. Lieut. Glover, R.N., first arrived off the West Coast when serving on board the *Penelope*. In 1857 he joined the Niger expedition with Dr Baikie. On the 24th November 1862 he was promoted to Commander, when his services at

the Colonial Office on the 10th June 1863, stating that this force of thirty was the only available force that could be looked upon in the light of an expeditionary force. It was the only force that could be moved out of Lagos in case of trouble within the *territory*. In this dispatch Glover asked permission from the Colonial Secretary to increase this force to one hundred men. He stated:

> They are very apt in their drill and are proud of being soldiers, and have shown on two recent occasions at Epe that they can fight faithfully and well. They require no commissariat nor barracks, and would form the nucleus of a future permanent force should such a force ever be formed. I would take the liberty of suggesting to your Grace that our West India Regiment might be recruited from this force with much advantage to Her Majesty's service.

On the 10th October the same year Lieut.-Governor Glover again wrote to the Colonial Secretary asking for an additional force of six hundred Hausas to be added to the Hausa force of Lagos. These six hundred men were to be a form of militia, and they would come up for drill two months in each year. When their training was over they would return to their farms in the outlying districts, where they would be still guardians of the peace. The hundred armed police already approved would continue as a permanent force. The Lieutenant-Governor states in his dispatch:

> These seven hundred men, with the hundred and ninety-two men of the West India Regiment, will be a force which will make the Government respected both within and beyond the settlement.

sea came to an end. On 21st of April 1863 Commander, or more often known as Captain, Glover was appointed Administrator of the Government of Lagos; in May 1864 he became Colonial Secretary in the same place; and was from February 1866 till 1872 again Administrator and Lieutenant-Governor. In 1870 Captain Glover was actively engaged in suppressing the marauding incursions of the Ashantis in the neighbourhood of the River Volta; when war with the Ashanti became imminent in 1873, Glover volunteered for special service. He arrived at Cape Coast in the early days of September with three hundred trained Hausa soldiers. His troops materially assisted the work of the main forces under Sir Garnet Wolseley.

Governor Freeman was referred to upon the subject, and wrote on the 3rd December 1863 in the following words: "I cannot consider the force of six hundred police as being excessive when it is considered that each man is only called out for drill and training for two months during the year. Only one hundred will be embodied at a time, which number, with the permanent force of a hundred, will be sufficient for the requirements of the Colony in any but the most exceptional circumstances; but to have the power, on an emergency, of sending an armed and disciplined force of seven hundred men to any point in the settlement would be the surest way of guarding against the evils, and perhaps precluding the event, of such an emergency." Governor Freeman had, in fact, suggested the raising of a similar force for Lagos as far back as July 1862. He sums up his reason for asking the Colonial Secretary to advise the Queen to confirm the ordinance for enrolling this force in these words:

> The expense of this establishment is about one-fifth of what a similar number of regular troops would cost the Imperial Government, and the force is more efficient than the West India Regiment, one-fifth of the men of which are usually on the sick list in this place, while there is rarely more than one per cent, of the Hausa men ill; besides this, they require no commissariat, little or no transport, and nourish themselves on the products of the country, which are always to be had. Wearing no shoes, they do not get footsore on long marches, and the simplicity of their dress renders it both convenient and economical.

Thus the original suggestion for raising the first of the Hausa police force came from Commander Glover, who held the post of the first Commandant of this force.

The extra force of six hundred was duly raised and placed under the command of Commander Glover. Glover must therefore be looked upon as the father of the W.A.F.Fs. Little did he know that in fifty years' time the force which he nurtured in its infancy would be called upon to fight a great and powerful European nation in three different theatres of war, namely, Togoland, the Cameroons, and German East Africa, and in each of these three theatres be victorious.

In 1864 an attempt was made in Lagos to raise the 5th West India Regiment out of the Hausas for foreign service, but the attempt was doomed to failure from the first. To begin with, the Hausas of Lagos were very limited in number, their home being a two months' journey inland. Again, the Hausas did not wish to serve overseas, far away from their own country. Governor Freeman wrote a long dispatch upon this subject, dated 6th May 1864, at the end of which he states: "I would therefore strongly recommend that the War Office should not relinquish the scheme for the enlistment of Hausas; but the regiment must be exclusively for African service; and this settlement (Lagos) must be compensated for the loss of the regular force it now has at its command by a nucleus of the detachment of Imperial troops."

This dispatch put an end to any idea of continuing the attempt to raise the 5th West India Regiment in Lagos. Eight months later we find the Lieutenant-Governor of Lagos pointing out once again the absolute necessity of forming a sufficient force locally for the protection of the Colony. On the 9th April 1865 he again wrote to the Colonial Office, using in the dispatch the words: "I consider it my duty to have at my command a sufficient force for the protection of the settlement."

About this time the Yoruba country was just beginning to be opened up, and the Lieutenant-Governor very rightly saw the tremendous possibilities this country held for enriching the Empire, but without a sufficient force he was nearly powerless to open up the country north of Lagos owing to the unfriendly behaviour of the Egba tribe. In 1865 the Egbas suffered a heavy defeat at Ikorodu, having come within range of British artillery. At last the home Government sanctioned the raising of a regular armed force, known at first as the Lagos Hausa Constabulary, and the Hausa *Militia* became a force of the past. This force was destined to see much service both at home and overseas, taking a most active part under Captain Glover in the Ashantee War of 1873-74. The Hausa Constabulary, later the Lagos battalion,

W.A.F.F., became the 2nd Southern Nigeria Regiment in 1905, the Southern Nigeria Regiment in 1911, and re-divided again in 1914 into the 3rd and 4th Nigeria Regiment. In its ranks have served many famous black warriors, from the time of the native officer Yakubu, who was known in 1879 as the father of the Hausas, to Sergt.-Major Belo Akure, the hero of a dozen fights, and Sergt.-Major Sumanu with his five medals, both of our time.

The Calabar battalion of the Southern Nigeria Regiment, descended from the forces of the Oil Rivers Protectorate and part of the Royal Niger Constabulary, later known as the 3rd Nigeria Regiment, prior to 1911 was known as the 1st Southern Nigeria Regiment, but was amalgamated in that year with the 2nd Southern Nigeria Regiment into one regiment under the command of Lieut.-Col. Cunliffe, who became Commandant of the Southern Nigeria Regiment. On the 1st January 1914 the battalion became the 3rd Nigeria Regiment.

The chief actions that the Southern Nigeria Regiment have taken part in since 1899 are: The Ashantee War of 1900; the Benin River Patrol; the Brass River Patrol; the Benin City Massacre Punitive Patrol; the Aro Expedition; the Onitsha Hinterland and Asaba Hinterland Expeditions; various Munshi Expeditions; the Ijebu Ode Expeditions; various Sonkwala and other pagan districts expeditions and patrols.

The Northern battalions of the Nigeria Regiment date back to the days of the Oil Rivers Protectorate and the Niger Coast Protectorate. They were originally an irregular armed police employed by the Royal Niger Company to protect their trade both by land and river. Later they became a disciplined regular force known as the Royal Niger Constabulary. At the end of December 1899 Sir Frederick Lugard took over the administration and constabulary of the old Chartered Company, and on the 1st January 1900 the Union Jack was hoisted at Lokoja in the place of the Company's flag. The Royal Niger Constabulary was incorporated into the West African Frontier Force, and later became the 1st and 2nd Nigeria Regiment.

1900 was to prove a most active year for the Northern Nigeria Regiment, owing to the outbreak of the Ashantee War. On the

15th April the first intimation of the urgent need for assistance reached Sir Frederick Lugard, and within a very short time an expeditionary force, consisting of 25 officers, 27 British N.C.O.s, 4 doctors, 2 nursing sisters, with 1229 rank and file, and 300 carriers, represented Northern Nigeria at the Ashantee front.

When it is remembered that the great South African War had already reduced the supply of Europeans to a minimum, this was a notable effort for a five-months old British possession to perform. There is no doubt that Sir James Willcocks, who commanded the troops in Ashantee, placed special reliance on the Northern Nigerian troops, to judge by the honours list of that campaign. Capt. Melliss was wounded no less than four times in three months, and was awarded the Victoria Cross and promoted to Lieutenant-Colonel. Colour-Sergt. Mackenzie was also awarded the Victoria Cross, whilst Bugler Moma and Private Ojo Oyo both received the D.C.M. In the King's Speech at the opening of Parliament, on the 14th February 1901, reference was made to the endurance and gallantry of the native troops of Nigeria, so ably commanded by Sir James Willcocks and led by British officers. On the 23rd July 1901 Col. Morland became Commandant of the Northern Nigeria Regiment in place of Sir James Willcocks, who had resigned this appointment.

In 1902 Northern troops were sent to assist the Southern Nigeria Regiment in the Aro Expedition, under command of Lieut.-Col. Festing, D.S.O. In 1903 the towns of Kano and Sokoto were captured by Col. Morland's expedition, and formed the subject of mention in the King's Speech at the opening of Parliament on 17th February 1903. Col. Morland advanced on Zaria on 29th January 1903, and in seven weeks had captured both these great towns, had fought four important engagements at Babeji, Kano, Sokoto, and again near Rawia against a Kano army. The hardships during this expedition were very great, and many native soldiers and carriers died of cold and lack of water. During this year there first came into being the Mounted Infantry Battalion, which was later known as the 5th Nigeria Regiment. This year was a year of war for the W.A.F.F., for in addition to the Kano-Sokoto Expedition there were many minor operations, the most important being the Burmi Expedition, in which no less than 18 officers and 520 rank and file were engaged in the final attack. Major March and 12 natives were killed in this engagement, while 7 other officers and 137 natives were wounded.

All was peaceful in Northern Nigeria till February 1906, with the exception of minor troubles in the Munshi country, when without warning a new *Mahdi* (a Prophet) declared himself in the Sokoto district with the most disastrous results. The rising that followed could not have come at a more unfortunate moment. Sir Frederick Lugard, being assured of complete peace in the Protectorate, had sent the whole mobile force on an expedition to the Munshi country in order to punish them for their attack upon the Niger Company's trade depot at Abinsi on the Benue. A mere handful of men remained at Lokoja. At Hadeija, half-way between Kano and Bornu, there was a garrison of a company of infantry, and another company of mounted infantry, but this force could not be used, as the Emir of Hadeija could not be trusted, and therefore the removal of troops from this area would have been most dangerous.

Major Burdon, the Resident of Sokoto, had just left in order to go on leave, and Mr Hillary had taken over the district. The circumstance which distinguished the Sokoto outbreak from all others was the degree of success its leaders gained at the outset. The rising had been planned some months before to take place at Satiru, after the Resident had left Sokoto, and was headed by Mallam Isa (the Preacher Christ). Mr Hillary, on hearing of the trouble at the village of Satiru, sent a messenger after the Resident to recall him, and then resolved to take the whole mounted infantry company, then quartered at Sokoto, to Satiru. When they arrived near the village he rode forward with Mr Scott, the Assistant Resident, who acted as his interpreter. Lieut. Blackwood, who commanded the troops, fearing that the two civil officers had detached themselves too far from the escort, came up at the gallop and formed square with his company. The Satiru people began to charge, but the civil officers were still outside the square. Lieut. Blackwood made the unfortunate mistake of endeavouring to advance the square to the two civil officers—a fatal error with mounted troops. Before the square could re-form the enemy were upon them, the horses took fright, and a general *mêlée* ensued. Messrs Hillary and Scott, together with Lieut. Blackwood and twenty-five rank and file, were killed on the spot, and the remainder of the British troops were routed, but two troopers of the mounted infantry, whose names I am unfortunately unable to give, behaved most gallantly, and regardless of their own lives they nearly succeeded in saving Mr Scott, and later saved Dr Ellis, who was lying on the ground severely wounded. The Sultan of Sokoto, in the meantime, had assembled his own people for the defence of the Sokoto fort and garrison. It was not till 8th March that sufficient troops had managed to concentrate at Sokoto to operate against the people of Satiru. On the 10th March Major Goodwin, in command of six hundred troops, marched out against Satiru. Here he found awaiting him two thousand unmounted men; all very indifferently armed. The rebels fought with the courage born only of religious fanaticism, but all to no purpose. They made several brave charges, and resisted the troops of the Crown in a hand-to-hand fight in the village itself. The fugitives were pursued by the mounted infantry and by Sokoto horsemen, in which the rebels suffered very heavy casualties. This was the last big rising in the North against the Government.

There were several minor operations during 1906 and 1907, the best known of them being the cave fighting at Margki, under command of Lieutenants Chapman and Chaytor. In this action the W.A.F.F. lost ten rank and file killed, two officers and forty rank and file wounded. If the hillsmen had held the caves and tunnels no force on earth without artillery could have removed them, as they were well supplied with unlimited food and sufficient water. In many cases poisoned arrows were shot at a range of from five to twenty yards through rocky apertures in the caves from unseen foes. It took three months' operating to break this unique robbers' den. In the report upon these operations it is written:

I venture to state my deliberate opinion that no military operations have taken place during the last seven years in which troops engaged had such genuine fighting to do under conditions extraordinarily difficult and nerve-trying.

In 1900 up to the outbreak of the Great War in 1914, Nigerian troops, both North and South, have constantly been employed on patrols and other forms of military operations. No other forces of the Crown have seen so much fighting in the same fourteen years. The following account of the doings of the Nigeria Regiment in East Africa is not intended as a serious history of the East African Campaign, but is just a story told by one who had the honour to go through this campaign with the W.A.F.F.—one who suffered and laughed, fought and trekked, worked and rested, starved and fed with this gallant band of black volunteers from Nigeria, for it must be remembered that every Nigerian soldier that went to German East Africa volunteered his services for that campaign. I am sure that if those pioneers of Nigeria, Glover and Freeman, could have seen the regiment, of which they were the founders, at Mahiwa, they would have seen something of which they would have been justly proud. They could have honestly said to themselves, "If we have achieved nothing else in our lives, we have anyhow founded a regiment to be proud of."

I hope that when my readers have read this account, poorly told as it is by an amateur writer, they will in future respect the fighting black man of Africa, for he has at least proved himself a man. We in England owe our negro brother-subject a great debt of gratitude for all he has done for our beloved Empire. Many a native of Nigeria has trekked his last trek and fought his last fight far away from his own land for the sake of the Empire. Ruskin once said war was—

> . . . . an injustice of the ignoblest kind at once to God and Man, which must be stemmed for the sake of them both.

This story has been written for the express purpose of letting the outside world know how nobly the West African soldier has helped to stem this tide of injustice to civilization. The length of a man's life is not told in words, but in actions, irrespective of colour, race, or creed; and until the "Cease Fire" sounds upon all fronts the W.A.F.F. will continue to sacrifice themselves willingly upon the altar of duty, side by side with their different brothers of the Empire, for the sake of that Empire that has given them freedom, justice, and all that makes life worth living. I personally feel it an honour to have been given the opportunity to have served with such gallant troops, who at all times have been brave, chivalrous, and cheerful, in spite of all they have been called upon to undergo. One realizes the truth in those four lines of Kipling after having served in action with these gallant fellows:

Oh, East is East, and West is West, and never the twain shall meet,
Till earth and sky stand presently at God's great judgement seat:
But there is neither East nor West, Border nor Breed nor Birth
When two strong men stand face to face, tho' they come from the ends of the earth!

CHAPTER 2

The German East African Campaign

The German flag was first established on the East Coast of Africa in the year 1884 by Dr Karl Peters, Dr Thehlke, and Count Pfeil. They crossed over from Zanzibar and began to negotiate treaties of annexation with local chiefs, who up to this time acknowledge the suzerainty of the Sultan of Zanzibar. These treaties were endorsed by the Imperial German Government, who backed up Dr Peters by a German fleet. By the two Anglo-German Conventions of 1886 and 1890, the Sultan of Zanzibar was relieved of all his possessions on the mainland, as well as of all the contiguous islands except Zanzibar and Pemba, which in 1890 were definitely declared British Protectorates. At the outbreak of war the German Protectorate of East Africa was divided into twenty-four administrative areas, and in 1914 the white population was estimated at about 6000, coloured population at 15,000, and the native population at 8,000,000. The campaign can be divided into four main phases, each being capable of further sub-division. The first phase may be said to comprise the period from the outbreak of war to the beginning of 1916. The second phase begins with General Smuts' assumption of the command of the forces in the field to the crossing of the River Rufiji by the British troops. The third phase from early January 1917 till the Germans crossed into Portuguese territory. The fourth phase is the campaign continued in Portuguese East Africa.

During the first phase, with one or two important exceptions, the British and Belgians were on the defensive. The second phase was chiefly composed of wide turning movements on the part of the British and Belgian troops, which led to the Germans falling back and being slowly forced to concentrate. The third phase, which chiefly concerns us in this account, was made up of a series of big fights, and a determined offensive on the part of the British. The fourth phase (which is just touched upon in this book) is von Lettow's (the German Commander-in-Chief) escape into Portuguese territory and the operations which ensued.

The main geographical factors are readily discernible from the map. The eastern coast-line is roughly some 600 miles in extent from the Portuguese border to the border of British East Africa. The chief harbours are Dar-es-Salaam, the coastal terminus of the Central Railway; Tanga, at the terminus of the Usambara line; Kilwa and Lindi. German East Africa is about 384,000 square miles in area. The Union of South Africa is about 473,000 square miles. Germany and Austria together are about the same area as the Union. This will give the reader some idea of the size of the country which formed the theatre for the East African Campaign.

The chief strategic feature of the German Protectorate was the Central Railway, which was completed shortly before the outbreak of war, and spanned the country from Dar-es-Salaam to Kigoma on Lake Tanganyika, a distance of 720 miles. Everything at the outbreak of war was highly favourable to the Germans for a prolonged resistance. They had the initial advantage of interior lines; their Central Railway was admirably planned for defensive purposes; on the Great Lakes they had their gunboats, and at the outbreak of war their military forces far exceeded any possible force which could be brought against them on any border from those already on the spot. The very vastness of their territory offered an awkward military problem. Our total forces in British East Africa, Uganda, and Nyassaland were vastly inferior numerically to the troops the Germans could put into the field, and the majority of K.A.R. (King's African Rifles) were, in the early days of August 1914, far away on the Somali frontier, dealing with some native disturbance. A short time previously a battalion of K.A.R. had been disbanded for *economy*. The K.A.R. were hastily recalled; every able-bodied colonist, both British and Boer, volunteered for service—the latter forming a separate commando—and in due course the 29th Punjabis arrived as an advance guard of an Expeditionary Force from India, which it was hoped would readjust the military balance as between British and German East Africas. Meanwhile actual hostilities had been opened by our naval forces under Vice-Admiral King Hall. Dar-es-Salaam was bombarded on 14th August, the object being to destroy the wireless station. A naval force landed for the purpose, and carried out its aim without resistance being offered, subsequently withdrawing.

Late in August 1914 the Germans were observed to be concentrating north, and it was clear that their aim would be to cut the Uganda Railway, which, running from Mombasa, passes through Nairobi and terminates on the eastern shore of Lake Victoria Nyanza, 584 miles from the coast. The railway runs practically parallel with the German border throughout its length, at distances varying from 50 to 100 miles, and presented a highly valuable objective for the German attack. Doubtless the bombardment of Dar-es-Salaam, coupled with the complete uncertainty as to the direction from which the main British attack would come, hampered the German strategy in those early days, when the numerical advantage was so decidedly in their favour.

It may be stated that the German offensive was singularly feeble, and with one or two exceptions quite futile. Their first offensive move was to seize Taveta, a small police post on the British border, east of Kilimanjaro, which later was the scene of one of the first British successes. From Taveta many attempts were made to cross the Serengeti desert, with a view to destroying the railway near Maungu, but the damage done was never very serious, and on several occasions the raiders were captured, with their arms and explosives. On 4th September 1914 a more serious effort was made at Tsavo, near Voi—a place famous for a book called *The Man-Eaters of Tsavo*.

Fortunately the 29th Punjabis had by this time arrived. Several small actions were fought in this neighbourhood, which is all dense bush country. The Germans led a force at least as large as any that could be brought against them. Lieut. Hardingham, who was in charge of an advanced post on the Tsavo river, reported that the enemy's strength was 1000 rifles, with two screw-guns and two machine-guns. The British troops fought with the greatest gallantry in country quite new to them, and after a somewhat severe action the Germans retreated by long marches along the Tsavo road, having sustained considerable losses. The Germans now turned their attention further west, and 400 rifles occupied Karungu, the Customs station on the eastern shore of Lake Victoria, without opposition. From here the enemy's force marched inland to Kisii, 160 miles west of Nairobi, which place they occupied on 11th September. To meet this raid, 240 K.A.R. were sent down the lake, and after landing at Kendu Bay made a forced march on Kisii, where they heavily engaged the enemy. They fought till their ammunition was exhausted, but the Germans, unaware of this, abandoned Kisii; in fact, they retired so quickly that they abandoned four machine-guns and a quantity of ammunition, as well as their dead and wounded. This retreat was chiefly due to the fact that they received the information that a strong British force was about to land at Karungu, and so cut off their retreat. This landing the Germans were able to prevent, but their position was so difficult that a few days later they abandoned Karungu and retired across the border. In the last ten days of September several attempts were made to invade British territory between Lake Natron and the sea, but these were all repulsed without difficulty. At the end of September 1914 the Germans attempted an attack on Mombasa. It was arranged that the German cruiser *Königsberg*, which had been in hiding for some weeks past, should bombard the port, effect a landing and occupy the island, while the land forces took the bridge connecting the island with the mainland. However, owing to Admiral King Hall's activity, the *Königsberg* was unable to show herself in the open sea, but had to remain in hiding in the creeks. The land expedition succeeded in penetrating so far as Gazi, on the coast, but was repulsed during the first week of October, and forced back across the German border.

This brings us to one of the greatest failures of the whole campaign—the first British attack on Tanga. I have been unable to get together many details of this regrettable incident, as no detailed official accounts have been issued on the subject. The *Allahabad Pioneer Mail* of 18th December 1914 gives the following account:

> The British force, which included both British and Indian Regular troops, as well as Imperial Service troops, sailed from Bombay in October (1914), and arrived off Tanga, the place selected for a landing, at daylight on November 2. Tanga being an open town and reported to be undefended by the enemy, it was apparently deemed right to give notice of the intention to occupy the place and to summon it to surrender before commencing a bombardment. This action was largely responsible, as after events proved, for the failure of the attack. The summons to surrender made by H.M.S. *Fox*, one of the two escorting warship, was refused by the German Governor, who, it appears, had already received news of the intended attack and energetically employed the respite thus afforded him in preparing the place for defence and in getting up reinforcements from the interior by rail. All the troops were ashore by 9 a.m. on November 4, and an immediate advance on Tanga was ordered. Some indication of the extreme difficulty of this operation is afforded by the fact that, although the distance to Tanga was only 1¾ miles, it was 2½ hours before our troops came under fire. Artillery support being almost impracticable owing to the density of the bush, it was decided to attack without waiting for the guns to be landed. The guns were accordingly left on board and fired from the deck of a transport in the outer harbour at such targets as could be made out. The advance was begun at noon, and at 2.30 p.m. the troops came under a heavy fire from rifles and machine-guns.

The 101st Grenadiers, making a fine effort to fill a gap in the firing line due to the difficulty of advancing in line through the dense bush, came under exceedingly heavy cross-fire of rifles and machine-guns. They were unable to advance, but tenaciously held their own. The Loyal North Lancashire regiment and the Kashmir Rifles on the right hand meanwhile slowly gained ground and entered Tanga, to the outskirts of which they held on, despite a heavy fire from the houses, which had been loopholed and strongly prepared for defence. Unfortunately the somewhat extended disposal of the troops, due to the thick bush, rendered it impossible to support these regiments at the moment when efficient support might have enabled them to carry the town. Darkness coming brought the action to a conclusion, after which our troops withdrew unmolested to an entrenched position a quarter of a mile in the rear. In view of the extreme difficulty of the country in the vicinity of Tanga, it was judged inadvisable to attempt a second attack without adequate reinforcements. Orders for embarkation were accordingly issued, and this was carried out without any interference on the part of the enemy.

The British force consisted of one regular battalion of the Loyal North Lancashire Regiment, four battalions of Indian Imperial Service troops, and one battalion of Indian Regular Infantry. All these battalions suffered heavy casualties, and after having failed in their attack were forced to retire and give up the unequal contest.

Meanwhile the British forces had prepared an advance upon the German camp on the slopes of Kilimanjaro. The advance was timed to start on 2nd November. The German frontier was to be crossed by two columns working north-east and south-west of the mountain. The Punjabis stormed the position, taking three successive lines. However, the two small flanking parties of the force encountered the enemy in considerable strength and were forced to retire. On 4th November the Germans retired from their camp on the Longido, a commanding feature in the main ridge, which culminates in Kilimanjaro. But the British forward movement had been checked, and no further offensive movement was made during 1914.

The first success in 1915 was gained by the enemy. The late Lord Lucas gave a brief account of the affair in the House of Lords on 22nd April, and so I quote the following from his speech, as it covers adequately the course of the campaign up to the end of March 1915:

> Early in December 1914 it was found necessary to institute operations against the German forces which had penetrated into our territory along the sea coast north of Tanga, and had there established themselves. With the aid of the naval forces on the East African Station these operations were successfully carried out, and by the end of December we had driven the enemy out of British territory. On January 12, 1915, a strong German force, with guns and machine-guns, secretly concentrated against Jassin, and, although every effort was made to relieve it, I regret to say that the post, after expending all its ammunition, was compelled to surrender. I am glad, however, to report that in these operations the Indian and African troops fought with great gallantry. On January 8 an expedition was sent from Mombasa to occupy the German island of Mafia, situated off the coast of German East Africa. This was successfully accomplished with slight loss; the island has now been placed under British rule. On January 9 a small British force attacked and occupied the German port of Shirati, on the eastern shore of Lake Victoria Nyanza. During December and January steps had been taken to arm the British steamers on Lake Victoria Nyanza, with the result that on March 6 the steamer *Winifred* drove ashore and totally disabled the *Muanza*, the only German armed steamer on the lake. On March 1 a blockade of the East African coast was declared, and ample steps have been taken to make the blockade thoroughly effective. On March 12 a German raiding party of about 300 men was attacked near Karungu in the Victoria Nyanza district by a force of mounted infantry and King's African Rifles, and driven, with considerable loss, over the German border. Latterly,

owing to the rainy season, no operations of any magnitude have been undertaken, although there have been several encounters with hostile patrols.

The German account of these operations was as follows:

A strong British force was beaten in a two-days' battle on January 18th-19th near Jassin. The British lost some 200 killed. Four companies were captured. The total losses of the British were about 700 men, 350 rifles, one machine-gun and 60,000 rounds of ammunition. The German losses were 7 officers and 11 men killed, and 12 officers, 2 staff surgeons and 22 men wounded, and 2 missing.

The Isle of Mafia was occupied by British troops on 10th-11th January.

On 22nd January the British light cruiser *Astroea* bombarded the Custom house on the Isle of Kwale, and on the 1st February the plain of Kiyinje, without doing any damage. On 6th February the cruiser bombarded Kissiwami.

The steamer *Adgital*, which had been captured by the British after heavy fighting, was put out of use on 6th February at the mouth of the Rufiji river, where she was engaged in making a reconnaissance.

At Kirfurbira a British detachment of forty men were surprised by the Germans. The British retreated after losing seventeen dead. There were no German losses.

All these events, though on a small scale, served to indicate that the conquest of East Africa would not be another Togoland, but would be a very formidable task. The officer who wrote home in these early days very rightly foresaw what was ahead for the British when he wrote: "We want as many Maxims with trained white gun crews as they can cram into the country. The Germans are simply bristling with Maxims, and use them like artists, and Maxims do 90 per cent, of the damage we suffer. If the Government think we can muddle through this show, they'll find that we'll get badly mauled. We are up against a powerful and determined enemy, who are not to be despised." I do not know the name of the writer of this letter, but should he ever read this book, I congratulate him upon his foresight. I must thank Mr G. H. Wilson of the *Cape Times* for the copy of this letter, as it is most interesting in the light of after events. From the Jassin battle till March nothing of any great importance took place; with the exception of small German raids on the Uganda railway, all was quiet in East Africa.

In March 1915 there was an important operation on Victoria Nyanza. On the eastern shore of the lake, in the Karungu district, a German column under Capt. Hasethausen had managed to penetrate some distance into British territory. On 9th March the invaders were badly defeated and scattered by a force of King's African Rifles, under Lieut.-Col. Hickson. West of the lake our troops were in position along the River Kagera opposed to a German force which had been operating from the lake port of Bukoba. An attack was planned by our General Staff on this force so as to paralyse any further offensive move by the enemy in this area. The following account of these operations will be found in Mr John Buchan's *History of the East African Campaign*. I here quote from his book:

> The plan was to send an expedition by steamer from the British port at Kisumu, on the eastern shore, about 240 miles away, and at the same time to advance our forces across the 30 miles which separated the Kagera river from Bukoba. The expedition sailed on June 20 (1915). It was under the command of Brigadier-General J. A. Stewart, and consisted of detachments of the King's African Rifles, the 2nd Loyal North Lancashires, and the 25th Royal Fusiliers (the Legion of Frontiersmen), together with some artillery. Bukoba was reached on June 25, when the enemy's forces, some 400 strong, were defeated after a sharp action, in which the Arab troops fought bravely on the German side. We captured most of their artillery, and inflicted heavy casualties. As a sidelight on German policy, it may be noted that a Mohammedan standard of European manufacture was found in the house of the German Commandant. This action kept the Uganda borders more or less quiet during the summer.

Lord Kitchener telegraphed to Generals Tighe and Stewart his congratulations on this success. A short time before this successful British raid another important operation had been successfully carried out by the Navy on Lake Nyassa. On 30th May the German port of Sphinxhaven was attacked by a naval force under command of Lieut.-Commander Dennistoun, supported by field artillery and a landing party of King's African Rifles. The town was bombarded from the lake, and the enemy were forced to retire, leaving behind them arms, ammunition, and other military stores. Commander Dennistoun then shelled the German armed steamer *von Wissmann*, and completely destroyed it. This gave us the naval command of Lake Nyassa.

The next important operation was the destruction of the *Königsberg*, which had been hiding in the mouth of the Rufiji river since October 1914. For this information I again quote from Mr Buchan's history:

> When we discovered her, we sank a collier at the mouth of the river, and so prevented her escape to open seas. Early in June Vice-Admiral King Hall, Commander-in-Chief of the Cape Station, brought out two monitors, the *Severn* and the *Mersey*. Our aircraft located the exact position of the *Königsberg*, which was surrounded by dense jungle and forest. On the morning of July 4 the monitors entered the river and opened fire. The crew of the *Königsberg* had made their position a strong one by means of shore batteries, which commanded the windings of the river, and look-out towers with wireless apparatus, which gave them the range of any vessel attacking. Owing to the thick jungle a direct sight of the enemy was impossible, and we had to work by indirect fire, with aeroplanes spotting for the guns. The bombardment of July 4, which lasted for six hours, set her on fire. The attack was resumed on July 11, when the vessel was completely destroyed either as a result of our shelling or because she was blown up by her crew. The fate of this German cruiser, marooned for months far from the open seas, among rotting swamps and jungles, is one of the most curious in the history of naval war.

The *Severn* and the *Mersey* remained out in these waters during the whole campaign.

Unfortunately for us the Germans managed to salve all the *Königsberg's* guns, which later were used with much success against the British in their advance.

On 28th-29th June the Northern Rhodesian Police and Belgian troops, under command of Capt. and Temp. Major J. J. O'Sullevan, were attacked near Abercorn, in N.-E. Rhodesia, at an entrenched position at Saisi. The attack was repelled and the position strengthened. At the end of July the Germans again attacked Saisi in far greater numbers. This time the Allies were greatly outnumbered, but made a most heroic defence of the position. After suffering heavy casualties the enemy (under the command of General Wahle) were driven off, and on 3rd August they retired. General Wahle was on leave from Germany in East Africa when war was declared. He had with him the 18th, 23rd, 24th, and 69th Field Companies; also four other companies whose numbers are unknown, besides the Tabora and Rukwe contingents of 400 Europeans and 200 Arabs. The war strength of a German field company at the commencement of the campaign was 10 officers and European N.C.O.s., 10 European volunteers, and 200 native Askaris. The German strength in these operations at Saisi must have been about 1800 rank and file and about 500 Europeans. O'Sullevan's strength was only 470 native troops with 19 Europeans. His garrison had very little food, and could only get water at night from the neighbouring river. On 31st July the Germans sent out a white flag to O'Sullevan demanding his surrender. O'Sullevan would not consider any terms, so the Germans attacked the position, with the result that they had 40 Europeans and 50 to 60 Askaris killed. It was estimated that the Germans fired about 216 shells and at least 90,000 rounds of ammunition into the British perimeter. The whole operation was most creditably carried out by the defending forces. Capt. O'Sullevan was promoted to the rank of Major and awarded the D.S.O. in connection with his services in this engagement. During the rest of 1915 there were only minor operations, such as occasional German raids in the direction of the Uganda railway, small skirmishes along the Uganda border, and small engagements on the lakes. In August the enemy made one more determined attack on the Uganda railway, which was also repulsed. This brings us to the end of the first phase of the campaign.

Gen. Sir H. Smith-Dorrien and his staff had arrived in South Africa at the end of 1915, but most unfortunately for the rapid completion of this campaign that gallant officer fell sick at Cape Town and was unable to take over the appointment of Commander-in-Chief in East Africa. Gen. Smuts was therefore appointed in his place, and sailed from South Africa on 12th February 1916 in command of an Imperial Service contingent raised in South Africa for service in East Africa. On the same day Gen. Smuts assumed command of His Majesty's Forces in German East Africa. The situation in East Africa at this time is well explained in Gen. Smuts' dispatch published in July 1916. From this we find that the German forces in February of that year were estimated at 14,000 native rank and file, 2000 Europeans, 60 guns and 80 machine-guns, though the number of machine-guns and native rank and file was under-estimated. This was subsequently proved by the known casualties and surrenders of the enemy, added to the number which escaped into Portuguese East Africa. The enemy at the time were occupying considerable tracts of British territory. I quote now from the official dispatch:

> At Taveta they had established a large entrenched camp with an advanced position at Salita and an entrenched camp at Serengeti, and an outpost at Mbuyumi. At Kasigau they maintained a garrison of 500 to 600 rifles, with the object of delaying our concentration by blowing up the Uganda railway and the Voi-Taveta railway. In the coastal area they maintained a considerable garrison on the Umba river, and actually patrolled thence to the vicinity of the Uganda railway, Mwele, Mdogo, and Gazi. At numerous points along the 600 miles of land frontier the opposing troops were in touch, and the result was that Gen. Tighe had to disseminate widely his small force, and was unable to keep any large reserve in hand to meet a sudden call.

Gen. Tighe had been put in charge of the preliminary operations before the arrival of Gen. Smuts and his staff, and to prepare for the offensive operations that were to follow. Thus Gen. Smuts was able to begin his offensive immediately on his arrival in British East Africa. Only five weeks remained to Gen. Smuts before the rainy season commenced in the Kilimanjaro district. A few days before the arrival of Gen. Smuts, Gen. Tighe had reconnoitred the German position at Salita with three battalions of the 2nd South African Brigade. The enemy were found to be strongly entrenched. The general plan of attack on this position and how it was carried out I give here word for word from an unpublished article by G. H. Wilson of the *Cape Times*:

> The plan was broadly to avoid frontal attacks against strongly held positions. The 1st Division, based on Longido, was to cross the waterless bush between Longido and the Engare Nanjuke river, occupy the latter and then advance between Meru and Kilimanjaro to Boma Jangombe. Hereafter it was to march to Kahe and cut the enemy's communication by the Usambara railway. The 1st South African Mounted Brigade, 2nd Division, was to advance through the gap between Kilimanjaro and the Pare hills against the enemy's main force, which was concentrated in the neighbourhood of Taveta and at Salita. The enemy's total force in the Kilimanjaro area was estimated at 6000 rifles, 37 machine-guns and 16 guns. The movements of the various divisions were so coordinated in accordance with a carefully drawn up time-table.
>
> Limitations of space compels a mere résumé of operations which resulted in the clearing of the Kilimanjaro area, and only just fell short of bringing the whole campaign to a triumphal conclusion within a fortnight of the arrival of Gen. Smuts on the scene of action. The map will show the general character of the plan, and how it was carried into effect. The 1st Division, under Gen. Stewart, duly advanced on its great outflanking project, being given two clear days' start. At 2 p.m.

on 7th March it had reached Gereragua. On the 9th it halted to reconnoitre and allow supplies to come up. On the 10th, in Gen. Smuts' words:

> Gen. Stewart considered it necessary to halt and reconnoitre for a road further west. On the 13th he was at Boma-Jangombe. On the 14th he joined hands with Gen. van Deventer in New Moschi. But he arrived too late. The enemy, after being driven from their position at Salita and Taveta, as will presently be described, had effected their retreat on the Kahe and the Ruvu river position. The splendidly conceived plan had just failed of the reward which was justly its due. Had the 1st Division been able to keep to the allotted time-table, military opinion in East Africa holds that although the movement demanded the greatest energy and decision, it was well within the capacity of Gen. Stewart's troops, and there can be little doubt that the course of the campaign would have been very different—the greater part of the German forces, including the whole of the staff, would have been caught in Gen. Smuts' skilfully flung net, and the war in East Africa might have been at an end in a month.

Though these operations were only a partial success, they cleared the whole Kilimanjaro area of the enemy within a fortnight of the beginning of the British offensive.

In the meantime the 1st South African Mounted Brigade and the 3rd South African Infantry Brigade—both under Gen. van Deventer—were operating against the enemy's position at Taveta and Salita, and were endeavouring to turn the position from the west. These operations resulted in the enemy abandoning the Salita position on 10th March. The Taveta position was occupied a few days later after a hard fight. From here the enemy retreated to Latma Nek towards the south-west, and along the Taveta Moschi road to the west. The fighting at Latma Nek was most obstinate. The enemy held strongly prepared positions on the slopes of densely wooded hills. Portions of these hills were taken and retaken several times in the heavy fight of 11th March. The Rhodesians and King's African Rifles gallantly pressed home an assault on Latma Ridge, but were unable to make the ground good. Gen. Tighe ordered a night attack by the 5th and 7th South African Infantry. Col. Byron, the commander of the 5th South African Infantry, gained the Nek himself with eighteen men by midnight, but finding it impossible to hold his ground, was forced to retire. The 7th South African Infantry had in the meanwhile secured a firm hold north and south of the position attacked by Col. Byron, and maintained it until reinforced the following morning, when the enemy were seen to be retiring. The enemy's strength in this action was between 1500 to 2000 rifles. Fifty of their dead were found on the position. From here van Deventer advanced west and occupied Moschi without opposition, the enemy having retired south-east towards the Kahe. Much might be written here if space permitted of all the hardships encountered by white troops in a tropical climate. Before this campaign many men that took part in it did not know what it was to be ill. After a few weeks thousands of these once healthy men returned to the Union broken in health, not to know for months after leaving East Africa what it was to be really healthy and free from pain. Many never will get over their experiences, whilst again many a strong and healthy man never returned to his native land, but fell a victim to malaria, dysentery, black water, or enteric contracted in German East Africa. I do not know a more pitiable sight than a man that one has known as once a strong and powerful athlete, brought by sickness and privation to a poor and wretched thing of skin and bone—date's caricature of a man. Malaria takes many forms. Sometimes just a shiver; next a splitting head and feverish body; other times severe vomiting followed by aches and pains all over the body, and burning heat. Thus in the East African campaign, where sickness was as bad an enemy as the Germans to the soldier, the hospitals played a most important part. Malaria was at all times the chief enemy of the white soldier and the Indian. However, the ration question had much to do with the poor condition of many, thus making them an easy prey to malaria. I have talked to several men who were with Gen. van Deventer during his advance, and all tell me that frequently they had to go all day without any rations, and depended entirely on mealy cobs picked from local farms through which they passed. In these early days of the campaign the white soldier carried his pack and full kit—the same as if he were in Europe—but mosquito nets were an unknown part of the men's equipment, whilst the daily dose of five grains of quinine was not thought to be as necessary a daily ration as bully beef and biscuits. Much had to be gone through first before the soldier's condition was to any great extent improved. I do not think that any army could have suffered more than the first white troops that arrived in East Africa early in 1916. About 80 per cent, of the regiments was, after a few months, no longer fit for active service.

On 18th March a general advance towards Ruvu was commenced. On 20th March Gen. Sheppard, in command of the Indian Brigade, had his camp at Store attacked by an enemy force of about 700 men. The enemy were repulsed. On the 21st March van Deventer occupied Kahe station and Kahe Hill. As soon as this was completed Gen. Sheppard, with the 2nd East African Brigade and the 2nd South African Brigade, pushed on to Ruvu river, and at dawn on the 22nd March, after severe fighting in dense bush, the enemy crossed that river, abandoning a 4·1 naval gun after they had blown it up. Gen. Smuts in his dispatch summed up his operations in the following words:

> The result of these operations from the 18th-21st March was to drive the enemy out of the country north and along the Ruvu river. Aruscha had meanwhile been occupied by our mounted scouts, who drove off an enemy's company in a southerly direction, and thus the conquest of the Kilimanjaro-Meru areas, probably the richest and most desirable districts of German East Africa, was satisfactorily completed. After his advance the British force had to be organized before any further advance could be made. The Ruvu river was held by a chain of outposts.

The enemy had by this time split up into two portions: one had retired towards Tanga, and the other had marched south-west towards the Central Railway through Kondoa Irangi, making for Kilimatinde and Dodoma.

In the middle of April van Deventer started his march to Kondoa. During this long advance this general did not trouble about his supply column and transport, but lived as far as possible upon the country. European troops were thus forced to live on mealies, sugar-cane, sweet potatoes, cassava, etc., and in consequence suffered greatly from sickness.

Van Deventer arrived at Kondoa by way of Kassile on 15th April, but with a very weak force. If the Germans had made a determined resistance to the advance about this date he would have found himself in a very dangerous position. But the luck of war was on his side, and the enemy, thinking they were opposed to a strong force, fell back towards the Dodoma and Kilimatinde district. The British force in this area was not more than 500 strong, with an ever-increasing daily sick return. Reinforcements were sent to Kondoa as quickly as possible from the north, and by 9th May the position was consolidated. Thus the Germans lost a golden opportunity; they did not discover their mistake till too late. On 9th May Col. von Lettow Forbeck, the German Commander-in-Chief, arrived on the scene, and immediately attacked the British position. For three days they continued the attack; the German Askaris, as they did frequently at later dates, attacked with the greatest gallantry, and again and again advanced to the assault, each time suffering very heavy casualties, but at every attack they were repulsed. The 11th battalion of the South African Infantry had to stand the brunt of the fighting during these three days. This battalion did most excellently, for it must be taken into account that they had just finished a twenty-four days' forced march in order to reinforce van Deventer. In their attacks the Germans lost 150 killed and a very large number of wounded. They eventually retired, leaving Kondoa Irangi in the hands of the British.

In the meantime, on the Northern Front the British forces were established at Kahe, with posts along the Ruvu. In this formation they remained until the end of May, when the advance was re-commenced. Columns under Brigadier-General Hannyngton and Major-General Hoskins pressed steadily south. On 15th July Gen. Hannyngton had taken Korogwe, on the Tanga railway. Generals Hoskins and Sheppard moved from here on to Handeni, a strong enemy position 60 miles due west of the mouth of the Pangani river. Gen. Sheppard manoeuvred the enemy out of their position without fighting an action. However, on the following day the 5th South African Infantry took part in a sharp action, in which they suffered many casualties. This battalion's advanced guard walked into a skilfully prepared trap whilst marching along a narrow bush path. Fighting continued till dark, when the Germans retired. Handeni was occupied on 19th June, and by 24th June British troops were 40 miles south of that place on the Lukigura river, on the western side of which the enemy had taken up a position in the dense bush. The British delivered a frontal holding attack on the morning of the 24th June, while the main attack was delivered later against his left flank and rear. The attack was most successful, and the British, whose casualties were extremely light, captured eleven Europeans, a pom-pom, two machine-guns, and a quantity of rifles and ammunition. On 7th July the British marched into Tanga without serious opposition, but before the Germans evacuated the town they blew up the water-works and did as much damage as they could in the time. The capture of this place brought the whole of the Tanga railway into the hands of the British. From Tanga the enemy fell back on to Korogwe and Handeni. Sharp fighting took place at the former place on 15th July. On the same day Gen. Hannyngton attacked Sakarre Hill, and captured a strong enemy position, together with a Hotchkiss gun.

August saw a good many small engagements take place, chiefly carried out by South African mounted troops against small detached parties of the enemy which had been menacing Gen. Smuts' lines of communication.

On 5th July Gen. van Deventer resumed the offensive towards the Central Railway. The advance was made by three roads, and everywhere met with success. On the central line an entire German camp fell into British hands, whilst on the eastern road large quantities of German supplies and ammunition were seized. On 29th July Dodoma—a big station on the Central Railway—was occupied by van Deventer's troops. Kilimatinde and Kokombo, two other important railway stations, were captured. At Tschungi, also on the Central Railway, the enemy were again encountered, but after a hard fight they fell back on to Mpapua or Mpwapwa, 10 miles further east along the railway.

During August the British force from Tanga, cooperating with the naval forces, occupied in succession Sadoni, Pangani, and Bagamojo—all three places being coastal towns. At 9 a.m. on the 4th September Dar-es-Salaam surrendered to the same force. The capture of Dar-es-Salaam was most important, both from a strategical and political point of view, for in addition to being the capital of German East Africa, it was the terminus of the Central Railway and an extremely good seaport. A few days before its fall Morogoro was captured by van Deventer's force. The capture of this place was followed two weeks later by the fall of Tabora. This placed the whole of the Central Railway from Tanga to Dar-es-Salaam in the hands of the Allies, together with the entire territory north of this railway and east of a line drawn from Tanga north to Muanza on Lake Victoria. Tabora was taken by the Belgian forces on the 19th September after very heavy fighting. During August Gen. Botha made an official visit to East Africa.

I have now reviewed briefly the advance of Gen. Smuts' force from British East Africa to the line of the Central Railway. There were two other forces distinct from Gen. Smuts'—Gen. Northey's and the Belgian contingent. The former force was based on Nyassaland and Rhodesia; the latter on the Belgian Congo. During 1914 and early in 1915 the Rhodesian border was constantly being threatened by small raiding parties. At the outset of the campaign the British forces available to defend this border were very small, but had most gallantly held a 200-mile frontier for all these months.

Gen. Northey had accompanied Gen. Sir Horace Smith-Dorrien from the United Kingdom to Capetown, arriving at the latter place on Christmas Eve, 1915. Gen. Northey was a regular soldier, and had seen much service in France during the early weeks of the war, where he had been badly wounded. After a few days spent at Capetown and Pretoria he left for Rhodesia. On 23rd January he was at Beira, where he had a consultation with the Portuguese governor, and on 19th February he reached Karonga on Lake Nyassa. Up to May 1916 his time was spent in reorganizing and distributing the forces along the border, converting the garrisons between Lake Nyassa and Lake Tanganyika into mobile columns, and arranging for supplies and transport. A proof that the administrative services of these forces were extremely good is found in the fact that never on one day did Gen. Northey's troops go without their rations. I here quote from Gen. Northey's dispatch, dated 10th March 1917:

> Arrangements were made by which we were able, in a few months, to deploy, feed, and ammunition columns operating 100 miles north of Bismarckberg, east of Irangi, and 50 miles east of both Lupembe and Songea. The distances by road from Bismarckberg to New Langenberg, thence to Irangi, and from Irangi to Songea, are each about 200 miles. None of the roads are more than improved native paths; the country is bad—hilly and mountainous, much of it being dense bush and very unhealthy.
> It must be remembered that up to our own frontier all supplies had to be brought either through Rhodesia, some 600 miles from the nearest railway, by native bearers, or from Chinde up the Zambesi through Nyassaland and up the lake, a distance of 700 miles, with constant transfers from a sea-going ship to a stern-wheeler, railway, motor, carriers, and lake steamer.
> In addition to the troops of the columns, many thousands of carriers had to be fed, and it must be borne in mind that each carrier eats the equivalent in weight of his own load in three weeks.
> This colossal task was considerably helped later by the arrival of light motor lorries. ... In six months 450 miles of

motor road were made, and from Mwaya to the Poroto hills, just north of New Langenberg, the road-level varied from 1500 to 8000 feet above sea level.

On 25th May we attacked the enemy all along the frontier, and by the end of July had cleared him out of the whole of the New Langenberg and Bismarckberg districts, occupying about 20,000 square miles of their rich and fertile country, and captured many prisoners and much war material. During August and September we made a complete wheel to the eastward, pivoting on the north end of Lake Nyassa and driving our enemy, who had now been reinforced, from the north eastwards from the districts of Irangi, Ubena, and Songea, the occupation of Irangi being synchronized with the arrival of Gen. van Deventer at Kilossa.

From October to February the troops under my command had some hard fighting. In addition to our original opponents we had to deal with Major Kraut (the late adversary of the 2nd Division) on our right, while the Tabora forces under Gen. Wahle, ordered to join Kraut, came down on our left, and across our lines of communication. Kraut, in his attempt to block Colonels Hawthorne and Murray, suffered very heavily on the Ruhudje river, and the Tabora forces lost about half their numbers in getting across.

Between 30th October and 26th November we inflicted over 600 known casualties on the enemy.

Gen. Northey's force at the commencement of his offensive was organized in four columns. His force included the 1st and 2nd South African Rifles, the 1st King's African Rifles, the Northern Rhodesian Police (native), the British South African Police (Rhodesians), and some naval guns.

In August 1914 the Germans had opened hostilities against the Belgian territory by bombarding Albertville on Lake Tanganyika, the terminus of the Belgian-Congo Railway. At the time the Belgians were not able to take the offensive against the Germans.

At the beginning of 1916 the Belgians began to assemble on the extreme north-west border of German East Africa. This force was under the command of Gen. Tombour; his sphere of operations was from Ujiji on Lake Tanganyika to Tabora, a distance of 250 miles; from Lake Tanganyika to Lake Kivu; from the Belgian Congo to Victoria Nyanza; from Muanza to Tabora.

In April the Belgians advanced in two columns, and by the end of May had made a big advance eastward towards Victoria Nyanza. On 12th August a Belgian brigade occupied St Michael south of Lake Victoria, having thus completed an advance of 312 miles. During this advance the Belgians had defeated the enemy in five engagements, the actions of 3rd July and 13th July being very successful, and costly to the enemy. At St Michael the Belgians established touch with the British who had occupied Muanza, and had advanced south along the main Tabora road. The Germans took up a strong position 50 miles south of Muanza. In the meantime another Belgian column closed Lake Tanganyika and seized Ujiji, the western terminus of the Central Railway. By 29th July this column had advanced east for 62 miles along the railway. The enemy stubbornly resisted this advance, and many sharp engagements were fought, in which the Germans lost over a hundred killed. The Belgians captured two 4·1-inch naval guns off the *Königsberg*. Another of these guns was taken at Muanza.

The German force south of Muanza, fearing that their line of retreat was in danger, fell back on Tabora, on which place the Belgian columns from the north, south, and west were converging. At Usoke a three-day battle was fought from 9th September to 11th September by Col. Molitor's Belgian column, the main German force retiring on Tabora. The enemy, seeing that their position was desperate, began a hurried evacuation of the town, whilst they held the ever-increasing force of the Belgians at bay for a week. On 19th September the Belgians entered Tabora. In the advance on this place the Germans lost at least 50 Europeans and 300 native soldiers killed, in addition to 100 unwounded European prisoners, the Belgian losses being not nearly as heavy. On entering Tabora the Belgians released 189 European prisoners of war or interned civilians of the Allied Powers. In these operations the Belgians had conquered a territory nearly four times as large as Belgium in Europe. Of a portion of the German forces that retired from Tabora we shall hear more later, as the Nigerian troops were destined to come in contact with them north of the Central Railway during June 1917 (see Chapter 7).

The completion of these operations placed the whole of the Central Railway in the hands of the Allies from terminus to terminus. From the line of the railway the Germans fell back towards the Rufiji river.

For two months there was very little activity to be noted on either side. The British position was consolidated, the brigades re-organized, the Central Railway almost relaid, and food dumps established.

The British column from Morogoro had pressed forward to Tulo, and later to Duthumi. There was sharp fighting near the latter place on the 16th September 1916, in which both sides suffered several casualties.

In the middle of December Gen. Beves, of the South African Infantry Brigade, left Morogoro for the Duthumi front. On the 11th December the first Nigerian troops landed in German East Africa.

CHAPTER 3

The Nigerian Brigade in East Africa

Before going any further it is necessary to leave East Africa for a time and turn to Nigeria itself. The following few remarks on the formation of the Nigerian Brigade are not intended to reflect badly on any individual, for at one time it was never expected that Nigerian troops would be called upon to take part in operations away from the West Coast of Africa. There are a number of things to be taken into account to answer for the state that the Brigade found itself in when it sailed for East Africa. That it was able, in spite of all, to give a good account of itself within a few days of disembarking only speaks the better for the West African as a fighting man.

Most of the Nigeria Regiment had taken part in the Cameroon campaign, which did not officially come to an end before the 31st March 1916, but by this date the greater part of the Nigeria Regiment had returned to their different peace stations in the Protectorate and Colony. That the regiment had done most excellently during that campaign is proved by the fact that in a comparatively short period of eighteen months the German Cameroons had been completely conquered and the German flag removed from the whole of the West Coast of Africa.

Prior to this, it never had entered the heads of the average European living in West Africa that the services of the W.A.F.F. would be required in any other theatre of war. In May 1916 it was first rumoured that troops might be sent away from the

West Coast to take part in the German East African campaign. In June the Gold Coast Regiment of the W.A.F.F. sailed for East Africa, arriving there in time to take part in the operations of July and onwards, already referred to in the previous chapter. I would like to write more upon the wonderful work performed by this regiment, but am sorry that the doings of the Gold Coast Regiment cannot form any part of this chronicle, for the reasons both of time and space. Their gallantry is beyond praise, and the Protectorate of the Gold Coast must be indeed proud of possessing such a regiment.

The Gold Coast has set an example which other British dependencies of Africa should be proud to follow, from the point of view both of its regiment and of the co-operation and assistance rendered by all in that Colony so that their troops might want for nothing. The Gold Coast Regiment has suffered most heavily both in officers and men. The gallant Capt. Butler, who was awarded the V.C. for his services in the Cameroon campaign, is unfortunately amongst the many of that regiment that will return no more. He was killed on the Ruvu river, not long after the arrival of that regiment in East Africa. The Gold Coast Regiment volunteered for service overseas soon after their return to the Gold Coast from the Cameroons. Their services were promptly accepted by the Imperial Government. In July 1916 the establishment of most of the Nigerian infantry companies was reduced. Time-expired men, at the close of hostilities in the Cameroons, were permitted to take their discharge.

From these and from many other signs the average man in Nigeria deduced that as far as Nigeria was concerned that country would not be called upon to make any further sacrifice for the Empire.

About this time the military authorities in East Africa had decided that the use of European troops in that theatre was most wasteful owing to the heavy sick returns; thus native troops were badly needed to replace the white troops. The Gold Coast Regiment had already made its name, and the fact was proved that, as far as that regiment was concerned, West Africa could produce excellent fighting material. The authorities therefore turned their eyes towards Nigeria, where the soldier was enlisted from very similar people to those that filled the ranks of the Gold Coast Regiment.

It was not till the end of August 1916 that instructions were issued for raising a Nigerian overseas contingent. One of the chief conditions laid down in these instructions was that the men serving in the Nigeria Regiment should be called upon to volunteer for service overseas. The result of this call for volunteers was most gratifying in the northern provinces. In some cases companies volunteered to a man, when only between 50 and 60 per cent, were required from each company; but in the south matters were not nearly so good, as there volunteers were not forthcoming nearly as well as was expected. The men of the two southern battalions cannot be blamed for lack of courage or of a proper sense of duty. A certain native N.C.O., when asked by me why the men of the south were not coming forward in the numbers required, explained the case very clearly when he stated that black soldiers would go anywhere where they were ordered to go; but a man was a fool to leave his wife and family, home and comfort, for war and discomfort. If the white man required the black man's services he had only to order, and the order would be obeyed; but when it was left to a man, soon after the completion of an eighteen months' campaign, to choose between wife, children, good food and a comfortable home, and shortage of food, rain, marching, fatigue, and hard work in a foreign country, it was hardly to be expected that many would choose the latter in preference to the former. To my mind it is a wonder that so many men volunteered for further active service, far away from their own homes. To the native mind it was quite impossible to follow any reason in asking a man, who was required for certain work, to volunteer for that work when it would have been so much easier to give an order for that work to be done; for as the sergeant just referred to said, "Are we not all soldiers?"

In the original scheme it was intended that 52 men should be allowed to volunteer from each company in Nigeria. These companies were to be linked together in pairs, and then re-numbered 1 to 16 inclusive, so that in each company there would be 104 trained soldiers. The balance of 26, to make up the strength to 130 rank and file, was to be taken from reservists and recruits who were willing to go on active service. The scheme of linking the companies together was not good at first, as native soldiers do not like serving under N.C.Os of another company. It therefore took some time to get the companies to have the necessary cohesion required to make a really good fighting machine. Further, the company commanders in many companies did not know the N.C.O.s. and men of the company, as these officers were transferred in many cases from companies they knew to these mixed service companies.

The concentration of the overseas contingent commenced on the 1st October. It had been decided that the Nigeria Overseas Contingent should consist of four battalions numbered 1, 2, 3, and 4, commanded respectively by Lieut.-Col. Feneran, Lieut.-Col. West, Lieut.-Col. Archer, and Lieut.-Col. Sargent, and in addition there was to be a 4-gun mountain battery under the command of Major Waller, D.S.O. Each battalion was to have four companies, numbered consecutively throughout the Brigade from 1 to 16. The Brigade was to be commanded by Brig.-Gen. Cunliffe, C.B., C.M.G., with Lieut.-Col. Mann, D.S.O., as Brigade-Major, and Captain the Hon. J. Crighton as Staff Captain. The total number of the force was 125 officers, 70 British N.C.O.s., 2402 native rank and file, and 812 machine-gun and battery-gun carriers. This force later received substantial reinforcements.

Mobilisation was completed by the end of October, with the exception of the rifles. Up to this time, except for a few companies of the northern battalions and three companies of the southern battalions, all the men had been armed with the old long rifles. The short rifles did not arrive till the transports arrived from England, and these were not handed over to the men till they had actually embarked. Thus the Contingent found itself actually embarking for active service in possession of rifles which most of the men had never used before, with the result that during the voyage the rank and file had to learn the use of an entirely new weapon.

A great many of the younger officers and British N.C.O.s. of the Contingent had never served with native troops before; yet many of these turned out to be most useful members of the Brigade after a few months of active service.

On the 15th November H.M.T. *Berwick Castle* sailed from Lagos roads with the 1st and 4th Battalions on board. For some reason or other the Deputy-Governor, Mr Boyle, C.M.G., and other high officials were unable to give these battalions a send-off, which fact was rather a disappointment to all on board, for this ship contained the very first Nigerian troops ever to leave Nigeria for an overseas campaign. The 15th November 1916 was therefore a red-letter day in the history of the Colony and Protectorate. The H.M.T. *Seangbee*, with the 2nd Nigeria Regiment, two reserve companies, and the battery gun-carriers on board, followed on the 16th November. On the 27th November H.M.T. *Mendi* left Lagos for Calabar. She had on board the Brigade Headquarters and the Nigerian battery. At Calabar she picked up the 3rd Nigeria Regiment, where that battalion had a most enthusiastic send-off. There had been a farewell service conducted by the Rev. Mr Wilkie on the previous day, which was attended by all the officers and British N.C.O.s. The whole European population was on the wharf to see the *Mendi* off. The Governor-General, who had only just lately arrived from England, was able to see the *Mendi* off at Lagos in person, and though there was not a big gathering of Europeans present with him, the native population turned out in large numbers. The H.M.T. *Malukuta* left Lagos also on the 27th November, with the telegraph section and the remainder of the personnel of the Brigade on board. All four ships travelled to East Africa independently. I, personally, was on board the *Berwick Castle* with the 4th Battalion. Most of the men on board had never been on the sea before, except just round the coast of Nigeria from one port to another, when they were not once out of sight of land. Quite 40 per cent, of the native rank and file had never seen the sea before. Great was their astonishment, therefore, when they found that for two weeks on end they were out of sight of land. They were constantly asking how the white man knew the road, and how the *jirigi* (canoe) was able to walk so far without rest; for to the black man of Nigeria everything that moves upon its own internal power is a *jirigi*, be it a motor, locomotive, ship, or aeroplane, the last-mentioned being always called a *jirigi bisa*, which literally means a canoe that lives in the air. The log lino over the stern of the ship was said by the natives to be the wire communicating back to Lagos from the ship, by which we were able to find our way. Great was the consternation of all when the log cord was cut by a bullet one day when musketry instruction was being carried out over the stern of the boat!

Much time was spent on board instructing the men in the use of the short rifle, empty barrels being thrown over the stern to act as targets both for machine-gun and rifle fire.

Sleep in the afternoon was often a little difficult at the after end of the good ship *Berwick Castle*, owing to rifle fire being carried out on one side, machine-gun fire on the other, and bugle practice by all the buglers of both battalions in the centre. These were the main disturbing elements, but there were lesser troubles to compete with, such as the armourer-sergeant hammering on what sounded like a tin tray, and the musical element holding concerts in the after dining saloon. Whatever can be said against the old tub, it was packed full of some of the best fellows it was possible to find in even the good old days of "before the war." They took all these discomforts as a joke; the voyage was therefore one long laugh. The old steward, usually called "Asquith" by his friends, once said that he had been at sea for over twenty years, but never travelled with such a light-hearted lot in all his life. By the way, Asquith was not so named after his political convictions, for he always said "he did not hold with any of them wait and see crowd," but rather his remarkable likeness to the famous politician. The likeness, I am sorry to say, was a little bent after the worst of three falls with a drunken fireman at Durban.

All four ships stopped for a few days at Durban. The people of this place were most kind and hospitably inclined towards the Nigerians, notwithstanding the fact that they had for months past been inundated with troops of all kinds. The men were taken to the local Zoo, picture palaces, and other places of amusement, and thoroughly enjoyed their first taste of civilization as known in Europe. Whilst at Durban the men were taken for a route march, which unfortunately for all, led past a whale house. I do not know if my reader has ever been to a blubber factory, but if he or she has not, my advice is, "Don't!" you are better off in remaining innocent. Without going into harrowing details, "the stink was 'orrible," enough to make the most hardy *stink-fish lover* wish to be a little sick—which, by the way, many of the delicate Nigerians were forced to be. On returning from the march many of the officers were asked by their dusky warriors if this was the place where the white man made the *bully beef!* (the rationed canned beef).

The visit to the picture palace will be talked of for many years to come, for the negro still wonders if Charlie Chaplin is typical of the white man at home, and if his antics with feet and crook stick are usual in London and other great cities; but then all white men are mad; for if they were not mad, they would stay at home in comfort—at least, so thinks the Nigerian native. The men stood up in their places and shouted at the top of their voices when that wonderful little man managed, simultaneously to hook by the neck and kick in the stomach, a fat rival, who aspired to the company of a charming, though rather eccentric, young lady.

The monkeys in the Zoo never failed to please their black soldier cousins. To me there is nothing more amusing than to watch a black man with an ape, making faces at each other; one then realizes that there must be something in Darwin's theory.

The voyage was fated to be the last to be performed, without mishap, by the *Mendi,* for after leaving East Africa she returned to South Africa, and took on board a large number of native coloured labour for France. She had completed her voyage to the United Kingdom, but when crossing to Havre she collided with another vessel in a fog off the Isle of Wight on 21st February 1917. Ten European officers and N.C.O.s and 615 South African natives lost their lives. Only 10 European officers and N.C.O.s and 191 natives were saved. She was a well-known Elder Dempster liner, and as such had carried her load of palm oil and officials between Liverpool and Lagos or Forcados, for many a long year. Every Nigerian was distressed when later they heard of her tragic end. Both the *Berwick Castle* and the *Seangbee* left Durban on the 3rd December, arriving respectively at Dar-es-Salaam on the 11th and 10th December. When anchored off Dar-es-Salaam the Brigade was first introduced to aeroplanes, several of which were flying around the harbour. Words will not describe the wonder of the men at this white man's *Ju-ju!* At first they declined to believe that any man could possibly be inside them; they were more inclined to believe that they were some great flying mammal, not known in their own country.

At the end of this book will be found a list of all the troops operating in East Africa at the time of the arrival of the Brigade in that theatre.

The move to the front was commenced almost at once by the 2nd Nigeria Regiment, who left for Mikesse on the 12th December, followed by the 1st Battalion on the 13th, and two companies of the 4th Battalion on the 14th; the remainder of the 4th Battalion left two days later.

The *Mendi* arrived at Dar-es-Salaam on the 19th December, the troops from her left that place so quickly after their arrival, that many officers and British N.C.O.s. had hardly time to separate the kit that they would require up country from that they wished to leave behind at the base.

When at Dar-es-Salaam we heard that Gen. Smuts was shortly to commence a big offensive, which everyone at that time believed would end the whole campaign. The journey to Mikesse—a distance of a hundred miles from Dar-es-Salaam—is most interesting from an engineering point of view. Only a few months previous to our arrival the Germans had done all in their power to damage the permanent way and rolling stock before thy were forced to retire south of the Central Railway. As usually happens on a military railway in an enemy's country, there was not too much rolling stock, with the result that the men were most shockingly overcrowded. The iron cattle trucks became veritable ovens in the heat of the day—these being the only accommodation for all troops. As for a first-class coach, I can truthfully say I never saw one in East Africa. The men, in consequence of the overcrowding, longed for the comfort of the rounded iron roofs of their wagons. During the day six men from each coach were given permission to climb on to the top. Several local carriers, commonly called *hapanas* by the Nigerians, travelled on the roof of the 3rd Nigeria Regiment's train during the whole journey, for fear that if they travelled inside with the soldiers, the latter would eat them! Those who have only travelled on home railways, including those of the Isle of Wight and Ireland, sometimes grumble at the un-punctual nature of their own lines, but for unpunctuality personified I commend them to the Central Railway of German East Africa. The train I travelled in on this occasion was twenty-four hours late—not bad for a 120-mile journey! There can be no slowness like the progression of those troop trains. They started late, they came to a standstill before they reached every culvert or bridge; these they passed over going dead slow, only to halt again on the other side. They stopped at every station, waiting whilst the Babu station-master calls up on the telephone the stations east and west of him. If the train was lucky, it was permitted to proceed to a certain siding in between two stations, and there rest for an hour or so, waiting for another train to pass it. The engines ran out of water miles away from the nearest station, so that a number of men had to be detrained to carry water up by hand, in any old available tin, to the engine from the nearest stream. They stopped to take on wood for fuel; they stopped to generate steam in sufficient quantities to take them up the slightest gradient. They were the most wonderful, if somewhat annoying, means of travelling to be met with on earth. Almost every gully passed over on this journey had a derailed truck or engine lying overturned at the bottom. In one place a deviation had been made, at what had once been a fine bridge. The Germans, before retiring, blew up the centre span, and then drove train after train into the deep valley, so that one train lay on top of another, till the pile of wreckage was flush with the old bridge level. The Germans had damaged almost every bridge and culvert between Dar-es-Salaam and Mikesse. The Indian Pioneers had done the most wonderful work on this line, which they nearly had to relay;

they had built temporary bridges, cleared the line of wreckage, and reopened the line in record time. Rolling stock had been imported from India to replace the German stock, which was chiefly lying in the many dongas and at the bottom of high embankments all along the line. On 22nd December Gen. Cunliffe and his staff left Dar-es-Salaam for Mikesse, proceeding thence by motor to Tulo and later to Duthumi. The latter place was Gen. Smuts' headquarters.

On arrival at Mikesse each battalion or detachment of the Nigerian Brigade was ordered forward to Ruvu-top camp. A few words might be said here in passing on this our first march in German East Africa, for it was a most miserable undertaking. No troops in these days were allowed to leave Mikesse except early in the morning or in the evening, so that they should not march in the heat of the day. The first march out was about twelve miles, but owing to the heavy rains the condition of the road from the very first was terrible. The country passed through was hilly and only thinly wooded. Water along the road was not procurable. The weather was extremely hot, and both Europeans and natives were over soft after the long sea voyage. The road was packed with other troops and guns all going the same way as ourselves, whilst very large motor supply convoys and motor ambulances were constantly passing through the ranks of the marchers. The road being un-metalled became very quickly cut up with all this traffic, and at the end of the twelve miles everyone was too tired even to talk. Added to the troubles of the day it rained heavily that night, yet by 5 a.m. on the following day we were all on the road again. Soon after our reaching the bivouac, Gen. Beves' Brigade arrived from Morogoro and encamped a mile from us. It was therefore necessary for us to get on the road as early as possible so as to be clear of this brigade, which was also on its way to Duthumi. The country passed through the second day was more interesting than the first march—with its wealth of forest, wonderful colouring, and rushing streams,— and we were also in better condition for a march. About 11 a.m. we arrived at the Ruvu camp, where we met the 1st and 2nd Nigeria Regiments. Here the Nigerian soldiers first mixed with their brothers-in-arms from India, South Africa, and the United Kingdom. The South Africans always call all African natives *boys*, regardless of their age. This led to a certain misunderstanding, for a *boy* is looked down upon by Nigerian soldiers, who regard all boys, or *boy-boys* as they are commonly called in the barracks, as menials. A Nigerian water-party under the command of a native sergeant was asked by a South African motor driver to give him a hand with his car, but he unfortunately called out to the sergeant, "Hey, boy, give us some water for my car," with the result that the sergeant was infuriated, and, ordering his party back to camp, declined to help the driver in any way. Should this be read by any South Africans, I hope this will explain away any discourtesy they may have met with from Nigerian soldiers. They really must not call soldiers of His Majesty, be they black or white, by the term *boy*, as it is most resented by black soldiers generally, and therefore the cause of much annoyance to their officers. This seems a little matter, but it really is much more important than it first appears.

At Ruvu the Nigerian Brigade got the nickname, by those who were envious of them, of the *bed and bath brigade*. This title needs a little explanation. Up to date no troops in German East Africa had been allowed any kit except the active service kits as used in Europe. The Nigerian Principal Medical Officer maintained that Europeans in the tropics must have a certain amount of kit if they are to keep fit. This had been very conclusively proved in the Cameroon campaign. The result was that the Nigerian Brigade held out from the very first to be allowed at least two loads, not including food, per European. This was finally agreed to by the Commander-in-Chief. Therefore a bed-load and a tin bath, filled with kit, was carried by almost every European in the Brigade. Hence the second line transport was made up largely of beds and baths. The sight of all these beds and baths greatly amused the South African troops, and many were jealous of this privilege. Thus the name stuck to us for many months after our arrival. But the *bed and bath brigade* was able later to show that these same West African troops were men who were not afraid to fight, and were therefore not to be despised as being just so many *kaffirs*, led by officers who thought so much of their comfort that they could not be separated from their beds and baths. I hope my South African readers will read, mark, learn, and inwardly digest these last two paragraphs, for in these matters South Africans and West Africans did not see eye to eye.

An elaborate camp was being laid out for the Brigade at Ruvu, as it had been given out that the Brigade would concentrate there and would be some days in camp. But this was not to be. The 1st, 2nd, and 4th Battalions were ordered forward to Tulo on the 22nd December. The first march to Summit camp was fifteen miles, but it was a most trying up and down hill march in the most tropical weather. On the 23rd Tulo was reached after a thirteen-mile march. A cheerful Christmas Day was spent here by these three battalions.

The language question was at all times difficult in German East Africa. This federation of languages included English, French, Dutch, Flemish, Hindustani, Swahili, Hausa, and other West African languages, and Arabic. From time to time a German batch of prisoners was added to the Babel.

On the 29th December the 3rd Nigeria Regiment joined the Brigade at Tulo. All the officers belonging to battalions other than the 3rd Battalion that had come round on the *Mendi*, rejoined their own units on this day. Every afternoon for the past week it had rained extremely hard, so everyone in the 1st, 2nd, and 4th Battalions was glad of the rest in good grass huts at Tulo, but the 3rd Nigeria Regiment and guns had a most unpleasant march from the rail-head, as it rained incessantly during their journey.

At 5.30 p.m. on the 29th the 4th Nigeria Regiment marched six miles south along the main road and bivouacked for the night. The march was continued at dawn the following day to Duthumi—a distance of seven miles. The 1st Nigeria Regiment had completed the same march on the 29th. On the 28th Gen. Cunliffe took over the command of the forces at Duthumi, consisting of the Cape Corps, the 2nd Rhodesian Regiment (Europeans), the 30th Punjabis, the African Scouts (which later became a battalion of King's African Rifles), and the 1st and 4th Nigeria Regiment.

On the 30th December the Nigerian battery arrived at Duthumi. On the same day the 4th Nigeria Regiment took over the advanced line of trenches and dugouts from the Cape Corps. This desirable site was known locally as *Shell camp*. At this place we arrived at twelve noon. Shell camp was about a mile and a half from the German position on the Mgeta river. For five weeks before this British troops had lain passively in this water-logged camp under an irregular, but very accurate, fire from a 4·1 naval gun off the *Königsberg*. The range of this gun was about eight miles. It was so carefully hidden in the bush that our aeroplanes could not possibly spot it, and it therefore had everything all its own way, as none of the British guns up at this front, up to date, had a range of more than four miles. On the 28th December two 4·1-inch British naval guns were brought into action against the *Königsberg* gun. By the time the 4th Nigeria Regiment took over this position this gun had been removed, but there was still a 4-inch Howitzer in this area that gave trouble from time to time. The Cape Corps had a good many casualties at Shell camp from both gun and rifle fire, and on the 29th December three of their men were killed whilst patrolling in this neighbourhood. We were therefore justified in feeling that we had at last arrived at a battle front.

On the 30th December the 2nd Nigeria Regiment joined Col. Lyle, who commanded a Kashmiri battalion. This column, consisting of Kashmiris and Nigerians, left Tulo on the same day on a special mission.

This brings us to the eve of a general advance, which for want of a better name is called the action of the Mgeta river.

CHAPTER 4

The Action of the Mgeta River

On 31st December Col. Lyle was at Kiruru; Gen. Beves with the South African Brigade at Kissaki, Gen. Sheppard with an Indian Brigade at Dakawa-Kissaki, and Gen. Cunliffe at Duthumi. The 3rd Nigeria Regiment in reserve remained at Tulo. The object of the coming advance was to drive the enemy from his entrenched positions on the Mgeta river, and seize the fords of the Rufiji before the enemy could consolidate in a new position. On the 31st the 4th Nigeria Regiment moved to a more forward camp known as the *Old Baluchi* camp.

This was the most forward position occupied by British troops facing the Mgeta river at this date. During the day a battery of field guns arrived at the Old Baluchi camp. In the afternoon 13 company, under the command of Capt. Green, was sent forward to make a reconnaissance and improve the forward lines of communication. Whilst so employed a few shots were exchanged, with the result that two privates of this company were wounded. Thus the first blood of the Nigerians was drawn.

This little trouble was brought about by a certain gentleman named Private Jack Warri, who, being inquisitive about a certain grass hut that he discovered close to the Mgeta river and out in the open, put his head through the window to ascertain who the occupant might be. Slightly to his surprise, but still greater to the consternation of the occupants, he found three German Europeans sitting round an improvised table having an afternoon meal. The Boches were not pleased at the interruption, and much shooting was the result, but the innocent always get punished for the guilty. Jack Warri escaped without a scratch, but two of his friends were punctured.

On 1st January 1917 the main operations commenced. The enemy's position lay on both banks of the Mgeta river, and was separated from the British lines by a belt of swamp and bush two or three miles in width. The front trenches of each opposing side lay in swampy ground. At 7.45 a.m. the 1st Nigeria Regiment took over the 4th Nigeria Regiment trenches, and the 4th Nigerians advanced a thousand yards south-east under cover of the thick bush, and there dug in.

At 10.30 a.m. the British howitzers and naval guns opened fire on the enemy's trenches on the north bank of the river; at 11.30 a.m. the 4th Nigeria Regiment was ordered to advance to the attack with three companies in the firing line and one in support—the 1st Nigeria Regiment being in reserve. This operation was carried out more for the purpose of attracting the enemy's attention than of driving him out of his trenches. The Baluchis on the right near Dakawa had been heavily attacked by a very strong force that delivered three bayonet charges against them. The Baluchis' casualties had been heavy, thirty-five being killed in the action, but they had prevented the enemy breaking through, and in fact had driven him back with heavy losses. It was of the utmost importance that the enemy in this area should not be reinforced, and therefore the 4th Nigerians were ordered to carry out this attack in order to pin him to the ground, or force him to retire, but in any case to prevent him reinforcing his left. The attack was originally ordered to take place at a much later hour, but this German attack on the Baluchis forced Gen. Cunliffe to accelerate his programme. Immediately the 4th Nigerians advanced they became engaged from their left flank, but the enemy retired almost at once. After this the 4th Nigerians were not engaged again for some time, but when within a short distance of the Mgeta river, progress having been slow, our advance was held up by the enemy across the river who were able to direct a heavy rifle and machine-gun fire on to the advancing troops, whilst they were crossing an open *vlei*.[1]

---

1. Grass-covered plain, sometimes swampy.

At 3 p.m. the whole line retired 600 yards from the river, and a quarter of an hour later the British again opened fire on the enemy's position south of the river. After half an hour's heavy shelling the enemy were reported by aeroplane to be retiring. During this retreat the same plane dropped bombs on the retiring enemy's *safari*.[2]

About 4 p.m. three companies of the 4th Nigerians succeeded in crossing the river and establishing bridgeheads at the two bridges left intact by the Germans to the east of the Duthumi-Kiderengwa road. No further advance was possible on this day, as the troops were exhausted, having been without food since the previous day.

The artillery in this section did excellent work, and it was thanks to them that the 4th Nigeria Regiment had so few casualties in this frontal attack. The guns were controlled from the top of a hill close to the camp of Duthumi. Here was a wireless station in addition to a signal and air line section of R.E. The burning of some huts on this hill was the signal for the commencement of the offensive, timed to start at 7.30 a.m.

During the advance of the 4th Nigeria Regiment, Lce.-Cpl. Suli Begaremi of 16 Company received four bullet holes through his clothes from a German machine-gun. On his own initiative he crawled back and reported that he could point out to the guns where this machine-gun was in hiding. Nothing daunted he went forward again with the forward observing officer and gave the exact position of the gun to him, with the result that the British guns opened fire on to the spot, forcing the machine-gun to retire, and thus permitting the infantry to advance without being fired on again. For this Lce.-Cpl. Suli Begaremi was afterwards awarded the Military Medal.

At the end of the advance the 4th Nigerians took up a position south of the Mgeta river, covering the bridges. The night was quiet with one exception. When a certain officer was going round the sentries about midnight, one of them must have thought he had seen the devil, for he opened his mouth wide and let forth one great scream of terror. The result was pande-

---

2. A string of porters carrying loads.

monium let loose. Every one jumped up from where they were lying, thinking the Germans had arrived. Some of the officers were sleeping on camp beds along the main path; a crowd of men fell over them, with the result that officers and men rolled together in the dust. A certain British N.C.O. suddenly wakened up in this abrupt manner made certain that his orderly was a German, and fired point blank at him with his rifle, but luckily missed him. This *jolly* lasted for about five minutes, in which time everything was upset and everyone was waked up. That sentry was the most *popular* man in the camp for the next half-hour, till sleep once again descended upon the camp, and all alarms were forgotten in the land of the unreal, where mind and matter have no part, and where all is peace to a tired soldier after a long day.

We must now return to the doings of the 2nd Nigeria Regiment. At 5.30 a.m. on the 1st January Lyle's column advanced on Kiruru. Two companies of the 2nd Nigeria Regiment formed the advance guard. At about 1 p.m. these companies engaged the enemy who were retiring from the Mgeta river. Some sharp fighting ensued, in which the enemy were roughly handled and were forced to retire in haste, leaving behind them a large amount of stores and ammunition. A party of the advance-guard, under the personal leadership of Capt. Gardner, charged with fixed bayonets a party of Germans that were forming the escort to the 4-inch howitzer, already referred to, which was being man-dragged back from the river. The result was that the howitzer was captured together with three Europeans and some natives. For this act of gallantry Capt. Gardner was afterwards awarded the Military Cross. Near to where the howitzer was captured one German European and many natives were killed.

After this action the advance guard was reinforced by another company of the 2nd Nigeria Regiment. These three companies then commenced to dig themselves in across the road, but before this was completed they were attacked by a strong enemy's force at 3.30 p.m. A sharp action was fought, but the enemy, being unable to break through and recover their lost gun, retired at dusk. The 2nd Nigeria Regiment was most fortunate, for notwithstanding the fact that two sharp engagements had been fought this day, the battalion's casualties were only Lieut. J. Dyer wounded, two native soldiers killed, and one other wounded. There is no doubt that the Germans lost heavily in both engagements, for on the following day the bodies of over twenty German soldiers were found and buried. That there were many unburied in the bush in this neighbourhood was certain—to judge by the stench a few days later. On the 2nd January the 2nd Nigeria Regiment remained in the position they had held the previous day. A German patrol came close to them but returned without firing a shot. This introduction of the Germans to the Nigeria Regiment was never forgotten by the former, who on every possible occasion did their best to avenge the heavy losses they suffered on this day at the hands of the Nigerians; also they did not think it fair of the Nigerians to use matchets[3] as a lethal weapon, for many a good-looking German this day had suffered from a tap on the head from one of these weapons.

On the 2nd January the 1st and 4th Nigeria Regiments moved to Kiderengwa. Later in the day the advance was continued to Tsimbe in order to get in touch with Lyle's column. When this was achieved, this force returned to Kiderengwa. Near to this place there was a large German camp which had only been evacuated the day before. Evidently the Germans had kept Christmas Day here, for in several huts manufactured Christmas trees were found. On the ground near here were found many complete clips of German ·311 cartridges, in which every bullet had been reversed, so that the bullet would enter base first and thus make a wound similar to a dum-dum bullet. This was our first introduction to the German methods of warfare in East Africa, but we were yet to learn much more of the ways of war as practised by the Boche in German East.

On the 3rd January both the 1st and 4th Nigerians returned to the old Baluchi camp. This return to comparative comfort was most unexpected, but was forced upon Gen. Cunliffe on account of lack of transport and the difficulties of getting supplies for-

---

3. A long and heavy knife used for cutting bush and felling small trees. It is carried in a leather case suspended from the belt by all rank and file of the W.A.F.F.

ward. On the same day Lyle's column advanced towards Beho Beho at 5.30 a.m. By 10.30 a.m. they were in touch with the enemy's rear point. Again the 2nd Nigeria Regiment formed the advance guard. By 2 p.m. the vanguard was in thick bush country and was suffering casualties from the enemy's snipers. At last the 2nd Nigeria Regiment's point was completely held up by a strong German position held by about two hundred rifles and three machine-guns. The advance guard deployed, and got within 400 yards of the position, but was unable to advance any nearer. A heavy fire was kept up on both sides till dark. The 2nd Nigeria Regiment was therefore forced to dig in and hold their ground. Lieut. Strong was killed in this advanced guard engagement.

On the 4th January Lyle's column was still held up. Intermittent firing continued on both sides all the morning. About noon very heavy firing was heard from the south, which was no doubt Gen. Sheppard's Brigade in action, *en route* to the Rufiji, having pressed forward along the main Kissaki-Kibambawe road. Gen. Sheppard's Brigade had to engage in a series of actions against a strong German rearguard. In one of these actions Capt. Selous, D.S.O., the famous African traveller and hunter, and the original Allan Quatermain of fiction, was killed whilst commanding a company of the Royal Fusiliers (Legion of Frontiersmen). The sound of this firing doubtlessly led to the withdrawal of the Germans who were opposing Lyle. About 2 p.m. the 2nd Nigeria Regiment occupied the German position. Col. Lyle, as soon as he had discovered the enemy had withdrawn, received orders to advance to Beho Beho and there join Gen. Sheppard's Brigade. That night it was reported that the Germans were everywhere retreating in haste to the Rufiji river. Between the 1st and 4th January the right flanking column of Gen. Sheppard's Brigades had been most of the time heavily engaged. The Baluchis in particular did most excellent work and inflicted heavy casualties upon the retreating enemy, but unfortunately suffered heavily in return.

On the 4th January the 1st and 4th Nigerians with the Nigerian battery were withdrawn to Duthumi, where the 3rd Nigeria Regiment had meantime arrived. With the withdrawal of the enemy from the Mgeta river the first objective had been gained.

Nigerian casualties in this four days' action were slight when it is taken into account what had been achieved. Besides the casualties already mentioned the Nigerian Brigade had twenty-nine natives killed and forty-nine wounded. On the 5th January the 2nd Nigeria Regiment left Beho Beho at 5.30 a.m. and marched south towards the Rufiji. On the 6th January a few Indian soldiers crossed the river during the night and formed a covering party to the 30th Punjabis that had crossed the river at dawn on the 7th January. The crossing was aided by the covering fire of British artillery.

It is now necessary to go back a few days and follow the doings of Gen. Beves's South African Brigade. This Brigade left Duthumi on 30th January, and did not take part in the Mgeta river action. Gen. Beves's object was to make a wide detour to the east, and cross the Rufiji river at a point about 30 miles up-stream above the crossing by which it was expected that the enemy retiring from Mgeta would cross. This Brigade had some very hard marching, and had little rest for several days, during the 70-mile march. Without opposition Gen. Beves succeeded in crossing the river at Kipenio, where he took up a position on the south bank.

On 10th January the 1st and 3rd Nigeria Regiments and the Nigeria battery left Duthumi under the command of Gen. Cunliffe in person. The 4th Nigeria Regiment was kept at Duthumi as a reserve. The Rufiji was reached and crossed by this force at Kipenio on the night of the 15th January.

At the end of the dry season the Rufiji river is about 300 yards wide, and was crossed by a swinging bridge, constructed and worked by the Faridkhot sappers and miners. This march of the 1st and 3rd Battalions was almost as trying as the march from Mikesse. There was no water at all at Kissengwe, the camp after Kissaki, and *giggers* (Ford light motor cars) had to be sent back to Kissaki, 9 miles, carrying relays of *châgls*,[4] and some companies did not get watered till late in the evening. When the 3rd Nigeria Regiment was crossing the Rufiji on this occasion Pte. Awudu Elo, of this battalion, won the Meritorious Service Medal for gallantry in life-saving.

---

4. Indian water carriers.

Chapter 5
The Ngwembe Action

This brings us to another phase of the campaign. By the 15th January a strong British force was on the south bank of the Rufiji at Kipenio. From the 7th to the 14th January the 2nd Nigeria Regiment remained in position on the north bank of the river at Kibambawe. Desultory firing took place on both sides during these few days. On the 14th January Gen. Smuts arrived at Kibambawe, and on the following day one company of the 2nd Nigeria Regiment crossed the river in the evening without any opposition. However, one of the boats used for the crossing was upset and bitten in two by an infuriated hippopotamus, but fortunately this accident did not result in any casualties. On the 17th January the remainder of the 2nd Nigeria Regiment crossed the river after dark at about 9 p.m. This battalion now concentrated on a sandbank across the main stream, but cut off from the mainland by a swamp and a small backwater of the river. The General Headquarters Staff ordered the 2nd Nigeria Regiment to advance from this position at 4 a.m. on the 18th January, in the formation of each company in lines of sections. A machine-gun was to be on each outer flank of each company. On looking at the formation in which the advance was to be carried out, in the light of after events, it is doubtful if this was the best formation for the time and place. The chief objection to it was the possibility that if attacked the sections would lose touch in the dark and swamp, and would fall back upon each other, and so cause confusion. Again if the 2nd Nigeria Regiment had been attacked, only the equivalent of one company, and less than half the machine-guns of the battalion could come into action at a time; all the remaining companies and guns of the battalion being useless. Owing to a difference of opinion as to the soundness or likely success of this operation, between the General in command of the whole force and Colonel West, the former directed Major Uniacke to take over command, and the latter left the Battalion and Brigade, and returned to the United Kingdom. Major Uniacke continued in the command of this battalion during the remainder of the campaign.

When the 2nd Nigerians next advanced it was pitch dark. The advance through the swamp in the dark was very difficult and most trying to all ranks. Luckily no opposition was met with; in fact, not a sign of the enemy was seen till 8 a.m., when a few scouts were observed. At noon the Cape Corps arrived to reinforce the 2nd Nigerians. By the evening of this day most of Gen. Beves's column had arrived.

On the 17th January the Nigerian force at Kipenio left for Mkindu, where an enemy's force was reported. All baggage was left behind at Kipenio. This column bivouacked for the night at some water holes. During the night a certain amount of firing took place, which resulted in one European being wounded and one native soldier being killed. On the 18th the march was continued at 3.30 a.m. At 7 a.m. *the point* reported that they were close to the enemy's position at Mkindu. Mkindu is a low table-topped hill about half a mile square in area. It is faced by an abrupt escarpment on the north, west, and east about 50 feet high, whilst it slopes gently away towards the south. The Mkindu stream flows close to the hill on the north side and passes round the western end of the hill. The hill itself is covered with bush and trees and was a fine position for a defending force to hold. The column was halted whilst two companies of the 1st Nigeria Regiment under Major Badham were detached, with orders to cross the Mkindu stream higher up on the right and attempt to outflank the enemy. As soon as Major Badham had moved off he became engaged, and a sharp action was commenced. The enemy's position was a strong one, and as usual the machine-guns played an important part, but the enemy were afraid of being cut off from their main body, which had fallen back some miles towards Ngwembe. They therefore gave up a strong position without a determined fight and withdrew south. By 11 a.m. the 1st Nigeria Regiment occupied the position. Major Badham's casualties were light, and consisted of Lieuts. Newton and Young wounded, one native soldier killed, and seven others wounded. Mkindu was destined to be the home of the Nigerian Brigade for many weeks to come.

In the meantime the Germans at Kibambawe, who were being opposed by Gen. Sheppard, retired when they found that the Nigerian force occupied Mkindu, as this force threatened their line of retreat.

On the 19th the 2nd Nigeria Regiment, the Cape Corps, and two guns of the Kashmir battery—all under the command of Lieut.-Col. Morris (Cape Corps)—marched to Mkindu, arriving there about 10.30 a.m. In the evening of that day heavy firing was heard from the direction of Kibongo, to which place the Germans, who had held Mkindu, had retired. At the same time a British aeroplane which had been engaged in bombing the enemy's position seemed to be in trouble, and suddenly crashed to the ground half-way between the enemy position and the Nigerian advanced post. Both sides tried to get the machine, which had been brought down by having the petrol tank punctured by an enemy bullet. The machine was eventually brought into Mkindu in a very damaged condition. The pilot was none the worse for his fall, and walked into the Nigerian camp shortly after the action. A curious incident occurred on this day to a wounded and sick convoy, when on its way back from Mkindu to the river. It serves to illustrate what the wounded frequently have to put up with in German East Africa. As the convoy neared the river it was suddenly greeted by a very heavy rifle fire, which everyone took to be the enemy. Lieut. Mills, who was in charge of the convoy, was placed in a very awkward dilemma, as he had with him some very serious cases, including Lieut. Newton, who was suffering from a dangerous stomach wound. After a little while Lieut. Mills came to the conclusion that it was not the enemy firing, but the Baluchis, which turned out to be the case. He immediately showed great presence of mind by cutting out a red cross from a hammock curtain and deliberately walking over to where the sound of the firing was coming from. The whole of the white men, other than the stretcher cases, and a few of the walking cases of wounded natives, thinking that Lieut. Mills was surrendering to the enemy immediately cleared out into the bush. One *very serious case* that was being evacuated by stretcher, as it had been stated that the patient could not possibly walk, was seen to get up and run like a greyhound as soon as the firing commenced, which proves the truth of the old saying "all that glitters is not *gold,*" and that "all are not dying men who are evacuated." He was what would be commonly called in East Africa a "lead swinger."

When Lieut. Mills was seen by the Baluchis the firing was stopped and the Baluchis came out of their trenches. The whole trouble was caused by the fact that no notice of any sort had been sent back to inform our troops of the probable arrival of a sick and wounded convoy; and even the hospital authorities had received no warning of the convoy leaving Mkindu. As all the stretcher-bearers had bolted as soon as the firing commenced, thinking that the Germans were upon them, the Indians had to send out carriers to bring in the stretchers. However, all's well that ends well, and luckily the convoy received no further casualties, in spite of the heavy firing that had been directed at them. But it was very hard on some of the seriously wounded cases, who had to get up out of their stretchers and crawl into the bush.

On the 20th January the 2nd Nigerians, the Cape Corps, and the two Kashmir guns moved forward from Mkindu at 4 a.m., the Cape Corps leading. At 9.15 p.m. the previous evening the 1st Nigerians and a section of the Nigerian guns, all under Lieut.-Col. Feneran, left camp with the object of making a night march and taking up a position in rear of the enemy at Kibongo. The night was dark, and the country difficult, owing to the bush and dongas that had to be traversed. It was broad daylight before Col. Feneran gained his objective.

Col. Morris was therefore delayed so as to give Col. Feneran sufficient time. Almost directly he commenced his advance he came in touch with small parties of the enemy who fell back after firing a few shots. He advanced two and a half miles from Mkindu before he was seriously held up. At 9.30 a.m. Col. Feneran informed the Brigade Headquarters at Mkindu that he had been unable to find a good position for a camp. He also stated that, from information he had received, the enemy in this neighbourhood had been greatly reinforced from Mawa, and were now quite thirteen companies in strength. About the same time it became evident that Col. Morris was not strong enough to advance further on this frontal attack. Col. Feneran was therefore ordered to deliver an attack against Kibongo and thus threaten the enemy's left flank. These tactics were most successful, and by 3 p.m. Col. Morris was able to continue his advance. By 4 p.m. the two columns were in touch with each other. The Cape Corps had a sharp fight about this time, which was altogether successful. Soon after Kibongo was occupied by them, the enemy retired south towards Ngwembe. The Cape Corps did exceptionally well this day, and were later thanked on parade for their work by Gen. Cunliffe. Once again luck was on our side. Taking into account the determined nature of the day's fighting, the British casualties were slight, being only one officer killed and two wounded, and eight native soldiers killed and fourteen wounded. The number of the enemy's casualties could not be ascertained, but one European was captured, and 170 cases of 4-inch howitzers' ammunition was later found buried in the old German camp. This ammunition would subsequently have been most valuable to them. The 1st Nigerians remained at Kibongo; the Cape Corps, all guns, and the 2nd Nigerians returned to Mkindu, which place had been held all day by the 3rd Battalion. On the 22nd January the 3rd Nigeria Regiment tried to get in touch with the enemy south and south-east of Kibongo. There was a small patrol engagement which resulted in the capture of one German-European and three Askaris, for which Col.-Sergt. Russell of the 3rd Nigeria Regiment was awarded the D.C.M. In the meantime the 4th Nigeria Regiment had left Duthumi on 19th January for Kibambawe *via* Beho Beho. The weather during this march was terribly hot, the path dusty and bad beyond words, and water very scarce. To add to the general discomfort of the march, the carriers were of most miserable physique. They fell out continually, and at the end of every day's march a considerable number were added to the sick list as being medically unfit to carry their load.

Whilst the four battalions were at Duthumi a certain amount of shooting and hunting was indulged in. The country all round simply teemed with game of every kind. One huge *vlei* in this district resembled a private park more than virgin bush, so plentiful was the game wandering about upon it.

The 4th Battalion arrived at Kibambawe on the morning of the 21st January and immediately commenced to cross the river. One company had to be left behind for a day to escort stores, etc., to the front. The remainder of the battalion arrived at Kibongo on the 22nd, having passed through the main Nigerian camp at Mkindu *en route*.

On the morning of the 24th January Capt. Green left his company, handing the command over to Capt. Barclay, in order to take up the duties of *second in command* of the 2nd Battalion. Early in the morning a section of the guns of the Nigerian battery arrived at Kibongo from Mkindu, while the 3rd Nigerians were in camp about 400 yards south of the 4th Battalion. Soon after the arrival of the guns they left with the 3rd Battalion and their baggage, with the intention of first making a reconnaissance in force of the German position at Ngwembe. Later they were ordered to attack the German position there, which was reported to be held by two companies only. The guns were escorted by 16 Company of the 4th Battalion, the whole detachment being under the command of Lieut.-Col. Archer. The enemy were encountered in strength about 7 miles from Kibongo, and Major Gard'ner, with two companies of the 3rd Battalion, was dispatched in order to get round the enemy's right flank. I will now quote word for word from my own private diary, which, being written at the time, will give the best account of the action that now occurred.

> Our point came in touch with the German position at 11 a.m., about 1 mile from the objective (the water holes at Ngwembe on the Nyandote Road); 15 Company of the

4th Nigeria Regiment had in the meantime moved over to the 3rd Nigeria Regiment camp at Kibongo and received orders at midday to reinforce Lieut.-Col. Archer's force.

Capt. Milne-Home's company of the 3rd Nigeria Regiment was advance guard. Soon after 11 a.m. this company was driven back from the line on which they had deployed when the action was opened, then 50 yards from the objective, and fell back about 200 yards. Major Gard'ner, second in command of the 3rd Nigeria Regiment, was ordered to take Capt. Cooke's and Capt. Dudley's companies and drive the enemy out of his position by making a left flank movement. After a heavy fight of one hour's duration, they successfully captured two machine-guns and one European, having also inflicted heavy casualties on the enemy, thirty dead being counted between the two gun positions. After this success Major Gard'ner was continuing with the advance when he was heavily counter-attacked. He himself was wounded, and both Capt. Cooke and Capt. Dudley, with Lieuts. Ewen and Harrison were killed. The two companies became disorganized and fell back in disorder, but managed to get back the two captured enemy machine-guns, but in the counter-attack these companies lost three of their own machine-guns. About the time that Major Gard'ner moved out to the left flank, the baggage and baggage-guard reached the main body. It was not long before the enemy realized that Major Gard'ner's flank attack had failed and that his two companies had been disorganized, and they took every advantage of the occasion. They opened a heavy fire, and pressed on with their counter-attack. These disordered companies retired through the bush, and did not strike the road till far behind the main body. As soon as Col. Archer realized that his flank attack had been unsuccessful he wired back for reinforcements. 15 Company left to reinforce at 1.45 p.m., but they had a 7-mile march to complete before they could be of any use. They did not meet Col. Archer till 4.15 p.m. By this time he had commenced to withdraw. Capt. Maxwell, commanding 15 Company, was ordered to turn back the way he had come and dig in at a small stream 3 miles in rear. This movement was done so hurriedly that the company had no time to reform. After retiring for about ten minutes, the company carriers that were now in front of the company met the advanced guard of the 4th Nigeria Regiment under Lieut.-Col. Sargent, that was hurrying from Kibongo to reinforce the 3rd Nigeria Regiment. In the confusion that followed these carriers got out of hand and made for the bush; they were not seen again that day. Col. Sargent had with him most of the battalion baggage, but only one company. The remaining company of the 4th Battalion had to remain behind to help garrison Kibongo. At about 4.30 p.m. Col. Sargent met Col. Archer. The latter stated that he would take up a position with his battalion at the stream, already referred to, and would there dig in for the night. This, for some reason or other unknown to the writer, he never did, but continued his retirement to Kibongo.

Col. Sargent immediately ordered No. 15 Company to again advance. Major Roberts (second in command of the 4th Nigeria Regiment) was put in command of half 13 Company and 15 Company, with instructions to form a rearguard, and cover the retirement of the 3rd Nigeria Regiment.

By 5 p.m. these six sections were in position, the whole of Col. Archer's force having passed through them with the exception of one company, the section of the battery with its escort of 16 Company being the last to retire. No sooner had the guns passed through this party than the enemy opened a very heavy fire with rifles and machine-guns, and delivered a counter-attack. Col.-Sergt. Lamb of 13 Company was killed at the first burst of this fire. In Lamb's death the Nigerians lost one of their best British N.C.O.s. He was a man of unlimited pluck. He had seen service in two other theatres, and had been awarded the D.C.M. and a bar for his services in Gallipoli. At the first sound of this firing all the carriers of both battalions stampeded. The confusion was added to by a few of the enemy working round both flanks and sniping at the already demoralized carriers. No. 10 Company of the 3rd Nigerians, under Capt. Robinson, had up to this time been the rearguard. They now became part of Major Roberts' force. The firing line was now built up on each side of the road. Major Roberts held this position for half an hour, when he was at last forced to retire owing to the enemy having worked round his right flank and opening a machine-gun fire from the right rear into his firing line. No sooner had the two sections of 13 Company (that had up to then been in advance of the main firing line) turned about and commenced the retirement, than Capt. Barclay was shot through the back. He died of wounds an hour or so later, having only commanded his company for a few hours.

The description of this action would not be complete if the doings of a machine-gun carrier of 13 Company were not recorded. Gun-carrier Awudu Katsena, a Munchi by birth, was during this action carrying Capt. Barclay's field glasses, haversack, water bottle, etc., when his master fell mortally wounded. There was not a single soldier near to help him get his master back to a place of safety. The Germans were by this time advancing very rapidly on each side of the path on which Capt. Barclay was lying. Awudu Katsena picked up a rifle that was lying beside a dead soldier, and whilst kneeling over his mortally wounded master, opened a rapid fire upon the oncoming enemy. In the ordinary course gun-carriers are not expected to know anything about the use of a rifle; they are, to all intents and purposes, non-combatants. So rapid and effective was his fire that the enemy were momentarily checked in their advance. These few moments were sufficient time for a party of 13 Company to arrive back and get Capt. Barclay away. For this most plucky act Awudu Katsena was later awarded the Military Medal. (See also reference to this gun-carrier at the Battle of Mhiwa, Chapter 12.)

To return to the diary account:

During the first 200 yards of 13 Company's retirement these two sections were under continual heavy fire from both rifle and machine-guns. The men behaved wonderfully well and carried out this most difficult manoeuvre in perfect order, and their discipline was beyond praise. Luckily the enemy's fire was wild and inclined to be very high, especially the machine-gun fire, the bullets from which frequently struck the branches of the trees above the heads of the retiring troops. Lieut. Hilton assumed command of the rear *point* after Capt. Barclay was wounded. The bush was so thick that in spite of the fact that the enemy were within 50 to a 100 yards of Lieut. Hilton, he did not see a single German soldier.

This is typical of the fighting in East Africa. Several times in my own experience a considerable force of the enemy were quite near to me, yet I was unable to see a single man to fire at. The consequence was that a heavy fire had to be kept up in the direction of where the enemy were thought to be, with the hope that a few bullets would find a billet.

Throughout the action the Nigerian guns under Major Waller were unable to come into effective action, owing to the nature of the ground and the heavy and accurate machine-gun fire of the enemy.

Pomeroy was wounded about twelve noon, during the advanced-guard operation; Thompson was wounded during Gard'ner's flank attack in the morning; Winter was wounded at 5 p.m. during the German counter-attack. Jeffries was captured in the retirement of Nos. 9 and 12 Companies, with Gard'ner, whom he was at the time helping to *dress*. Col.-Sergt. Speak was wounded and captured in the first advanced-guard withdrawal. Sergts. Wroe and Woolley were both wounded and captured in Gard'ner's flank show. Sergts. Dickson and Care were also wounded. At a later date Sergt. Woolley was returned to the British lines by the Germans. He informed me that this counter-attack was most disastrous to the Germans, as their casualties were most heavy. Sergt. Woolley remained out in the bush half the night and saw wounded men being carried back in a continuous stream. The British fire had been most effective. When the British wounded prisoners had been collected by the enemy they were immediately carried back to Maba, as the Germans were in a deadly fear of being attacked again on the 25th. If they had been so attacked by fresh troops they would certainly have broken.

At this crisis of the campaign it is quite possible that if the British had got through to Mawa the whole campaign might have taken very different lines, and possibly been greatly curtailed. But *ifs* cannot be taken into account in war, and for some reason or other the battle was not continued on the 25th.

At 6.15 p.m. the enemy ceased firing. About this time Lieut. Hilton met Lieut.-Col. Sargent on the road; the Colonel came up himself in command of 15 Company and half 16 Company; this force was to form a new rearguard; Lieut. Hilton's retirement had left No. 10 Company by itself to hold the enemy's advance. It was Col. Sargent's intention to relieve this company which had borne the brunt of the fighting throughout the day. This company, under Capt. Robinson, had done extremely good work during this trying action ; their discipline had been maintained under the most trying conditions.

Capt. Robinson was later awarded a very well earned Military Cross. The M.C. was also awarded to Capt. Armstrong of the 3rd Nigeria Regiment and Lieut. Winter of the 4th Nigeria Regiment, whilst Lieut.-Col. Sargent was awarded the D.S.O. There is no doubt that it was through Col. Sargent's personal leadership in this action that the 3rd Nigeria Regiment and the Nigerian guns were saved.

Col. Sargent advanced with 15 Company and half 16 Company for a distance of half a mile, where a firing line was established, covering the retreat of No. 10 Company. After seeing that this company was safely withdrawn he handed over the command of this force to Major Roberts. When Col. Sargent left the firing line he was within two miles of the water holes of Ngwembe.

There is little doubt, in the light of after events, that if this firing line could have been considerably reinforced during the night that followed, and an attack had been delivered at daybreak, this action would have been turned into a decisive victory for the Nigerians, as the Germans were very disorganized. Oberleutnant Otto, who later became one of the German chief leaders, was wounded in this action.

> Capt. Robinson and Lieut. Hilton were now ordered to retire to Col. Archer's position at the stream three miles in rear. At the time neither Col. Sargent nor any of the troops that formed the front line had any idea that Col. Archer had retired right back to Kibongo, but all thoroughly believed that an entrenched position was being prepared at the stream for them to fall back upon. Thus it transpired that these companies, together with the Headquarters of the 4th Battalion, were forced to retire to Kibongo. 15 and 16 Companies held their position until dark, when they retired the best part of a mile, where they again established a firing line, No. 15 Company forming the advance picquet. The night was spent by them in collecting the 3rd and 4th Nigeria Regiments' loads that had been discarded by the carriers when they stampeded; a good many of these and a few wounded men were recovered. At 10.30 p.m. Col. Sargent arrived back at Kibongo. At 12.15 a.m. on the 25th January Major Badham left for Ngwembe in command of a relief force, with a large number of carriers to bring in all the recovered loads. Only two companies were available for this duty—one from the 4th Battalion and one from the 1st Nigerians.

> To describe this march so as to do it full justice would be impossible. It turned out to be the most uncomfortable march that troops could be called upon to perform. The night was pitch dark—a darkness that could almost be felt. A white handkerchief

hung upon the pack of the man in front could not be seen at the distance of one foot. The only possible way to keep touch, was for each man actually to hold on to the man in front of him in the column. At 2.30 a.m. it came on to rain in a manner that is only possible in the tropics—a deluge that is unknown in more temperate climates. The path at first became greasy, so that one slipped back half the distance that one went forward. Later the path became a stream several inches deep in water and mud. Great credit is due to Company Sergt.-Major Morakinyo Ibadan, the Acting Regimental Sergt.-Major of the 4th Battalion, for the way in which he guided this column. On looking back it seems almost a miracle how he managed to retrace the path to Major Roberts' position, 7 miles distant from Kibongo, through an almost trackless bush. For his services on this night he was awarded the D.C.M.

The head of Major Badham's column reached Capt. Hetley's company (16 Company) at 3.50 a.m. The return march was commenced at once, as it was absolutely necessary to get all loads away under cover of the darkness.

About 4.30 a.m. something or other frightened the carriers, and they commenced at once to stampede. As there were quite three hundred of them, matters began to look serious, but thanks to the large number of Europeans present the stampede was stopped in time. The last load that could be found left the 16 Company position at 6.30 a.m. 15 Company remained in position till all the loads were away in order to cover this withdrawal in the event of the enemy again becoming active Fortunately for all, the Germans had had enough the day before, and were only too glad to let the Nigerians withdraw uninterrupted. Not a shot was fired by the other side, though without doubt they knew what was going on. The whole of Major Badham's column got back safely to Kibongo. Though many loads were saved, both the 3rd and 4th Battalions lost a very large amount of private kit and supplies in this action; also a fair number of boxes of ammunition were never recovered.

It is estimated that the enemy's force that took part in this action numbered about six hundred rifles and many machine-guns. This was afterwards verified by Major Gard'ner and captured Huns. There were in addition two companies in support. The number of their casualties is unknown, but it must have been very large. Three Europeans were actually seen dead, and thirty Askaris were found lying on the ground apparently dead between the two captured machine-guns in Major Gard'ner's flank attack. The British casualties, in addition to those already mentioned, were forty-three native soldiers killed, forty wounded, and eight taken prisoners or missing. The failure of the flank attack was partially due to the large European casualties at the outbreak of the German counter-attack. Deprived of the majority of their officers, the men were unable to cope with the enemy's determined counter-attack, delivered as they always were in East Africa, with great strength and fierceness, and supported by well-directed machine-gun fire.

There is not a shadow of doubt that the enemy's native soldiers bayoneted or, in other ways, murdered many of the Nigerian wounded. It was subsequently ascertained that only eight men had been taken alive, six of whom were later sent into the British lines under a flag of truce, being too severely wounded to be able to take any further part in military operations. On the 25th January the Germans sent in, under a white flag, a letter from the German Commander stating that forty wounded men were in their hands, and requested medical stores for their use. Either they lied, in order to get from the British for their own use much needed medical necessities, or thirty-two Nigerian soldiers were subsequently murdered.

Though this action could not be called a success, it proved to the authorities that Nigerian troops could give a good account of themselves under the most unfavourable conditions. That this action was not a British victory was no fault of the native soldier as a fighting man. The fortune of war was not with the Nigerians in this action. On the 23rd and 24th January the enemy had been greatly reinforced at Ngwembe, unknown to the British Intelligence Department. I think that these reinforcements came from Kibambawe as much as anywhere, for at least two companies had withdrawn from before Sheppard and Pomeroy's patrols. The force sent to take the position was not nearly strong enough, and the available reinforcements were too far away to be of use when most needed. On the same day as this fight took place 40 German Europeans and 200 Askaris, with 1 field gun and 2 machine guns surrendered at Likuju to a detachment of Gen. Northey's force.

On the 27th January the Nigerian Brigade was concentrated at Mkindu, leaving only a post at Kibongo.

We now enter on a period of comparative inaction. The rain had started in real earnest, and the 120 miles of road from the railhead (Mikesse) to the front was already in so bad a condition that motors and all other wheel transport could no longer use it. The Nigerians now experienced what it was to be dependent on a single line of communication, in a country so badly infected by the tsetse fly and horse sickness, that every ounce of food had to be carried for 85 to 90 miles by carriers. I would here refer the reader to Lieut.-Gen. Hoskins' official dispatch, dated 30th May 1917, but not published till the 27th December 1917, an extract of which is given below:

> All seemed to be going well when on 25th January heavy rain began to fall, ushering in the wettest season known in East Africa for many years. By the 27th the lines of communication from Mikesse to Kibambawe were interrupted by the washing away of bridges and the flooding of roads; and operations in all areas were henceforward seriously hampered by the untimely rain.
> It is perhaps hard to realize the difficulties which the rainy season in East Africa entailed for a force acting from such widely separated bases, with several different lines of communication running through every variety of difficult country and necessitating in some cases as much as 130 miles of porter transport. In the Mgeta and Rufiji valleys, roads constructed with much skill and labour, over which motor transport ran continuously in January, were traversed with difficulty and much hardship a month later by porters wading for miles in water above their waists. The Dodoma-Iringa line of communication crossed the

great Ruaha in the dry weather by an easy ford; when the rain had really set in supplies had to be transported not only over a flooded river, but also a swamp on each side of it 6 feet deep and as many miles wide. Considerable anxiety was caused by this extensive flooding across the Dodoma-Iringa communication, and every effort was made to cope with this. The Iringa Column was kept as small as possible, and special flat-bottomed boats were prepared, but eventually it became necessary to switch on to a new line along the road which runs south from the railway at Kilossa. The valley of the Rufiji and its various tributaries became a vast lake, in which the true courses of the streams were often only discernible with difficulty, if at all. Patrol work had to be carried out for some time in canoes, and the men found themselves making fast to the roofs of houses which had lately formed their quarters.

The conditions of the Kilwa area were equally trying, as roads became impassable for motor transport, and animals died a few weeks after being landed. An even more serious factor, perhaps, was the sickness amongst the troops. The coastal belt and the valleys of the Mgeta and Rufiji even in dry weather are unhealthy for all but the indigenous African; and during the rains there is a great increase in malaria, while dysentery and pneumonia strike down even the African native.

In 1916 many of our troops in East Africa spent the rain season in high and comparatively healthy localities. It was impossible to do this in 1917 without withdrawing from ground which had been hardly won and out of which the enemy would have to be driven again with equal difficulty, should he be allowed to reoccupy it.

That the enemy had also to contend with sickness, and with sameness, if not with scarcity, of food, is certain; but in a minor degree, since his white men were more acclimatized to German East Africa, and his native soldiers indigenous to the country. He had the advantage of falling back on interior lines; of veteran troops from whose ranks nearly all waverers had by this time been eliminated; and of his power of living on the country as he retired. This last was accentuated by the fact that whereas we are accustomed to take and pay for only what the villagers can spare, the Germans have no scruples about taking all. And after using men, women, and children as porters so far as they require, they send them back in a starving condition, thus increasing the difficulties of our advancing troops.

Gen. Hoskins took over the forces in East Africa on the 20th January 1917. At this time the effective strength of the enemy's forces was put down at 1100 Europeans and 7300 Askaris, with 4 guns of 4-inch or 4·1 calibre, 16 smaller guns, and 73 machine-guns. In the light of what took place later, I think these numbers were under-estimated.

At one time it was hoped the supply question would be solved by using the Rufiji river for transport purposes, but this idea was very soon given up, for the river rose into a huge torrent with a speed of 20 miles an hour. At the end of January the situation of the Rufiji was most gloomy. The supply and transport situation was bad; there was no reserve of food in the advance depot; the number of carriers was not nearly sufficient; pack animals died after a single journey, if not before; mechanical transport drivers far back on the lines of communication were so rapidly falling sick that hundreds of light cars stood for days without doing one journey. Gen. Hoskins therefore withdrew from the river area all the troops he could.

Chapter 6
Operations During the Rains

This is no land for the white man; none can esteem her good,
But good, bad, indifferent, the warriors belong to the same brotherhood,
With this one exception only—that none but the strong shall thrive,
And all that are weak shall perish, as only the best can survive.

I do not know where the above quotation comes from, but it is a good description of the Rufiji area during the rains. Towards the end of January the question of supplies at Mkindu became most acute. On 30th January the Nigerian Brigade was put on half rations officially. On reading my diary I find that full rations had become a thing of the past some days earlier, though the belt was not felt to pinch too badly till 13th February, when the troops were placed on quarter rations. The total weight of all food issued this day was rather less than 13 ounces per man. The Europeans' food was very little better than the men's. Fresh meat for a long time past had not been seen at Mkindu. When we were lucky, its place was taken by bully beef, which appeared on the table in every form of *camouflage*. The men, driven by hunger, started to dig up roots, or picked herbs from the bush to eat, with disastrous results on many occasions. Crime became more common, as the men, seeing the supplies arrive by convoy from the river, used to try to take rice and biscuits out of the dump or the battalion quartermaster's supply stores. February, March, and April 1917 were all black months for the Nigerian Brigade. The hardships passed through during these three months must be unparalleled in military operations of our time. Our condition could not have been worse even if we had been in a siege. The men got terribly thin and wretched, till they became almost unfit to take the field in any active operations. The men went sick, and many died from eating poisoned roots and herbs, twelve men dying in the 2nd Battalion early in May from this cause. To give an instance or two of the state the men got into, will no doubt interest the reader, besides, if they were omitted, this record would be most incomplete.

A donkey died of horse sickness and was buried. Two days later the body was dug up and eaten by certain men. This happened several times with condemned cattle, till it was found necessary always to burn carcases.

A bridge was built over a stream between the main position at Mkindu and a detached position known as Stretton Hill. The spars forming the bridge were lashed together with strips of raw hide, dating back to the days of plenty, when a large herd of cattle supplied the meat for the troops at Mkindu. The bridge had been standing about two months, when one night all the hide was stolen, and the bridge left in a very tottering state. The hides were cooked down into soup, and so disposed of by the starving men.

Below is given a fair example of a day's rations for Europeans. The following was issued to the officers of the 4th Battalion on 4th April: Bacon, ½ oz.; jam, 1 oz.; condensed milk, ½ oz.; onions, ¾ oz.; fresh meat, 2½ oz., the total weight of each officer's ration being 1 lb. 2½ oz. On the same day to the men was issued half a pound of rice, with nothing in addition. Before leaving this doleful subject I quote a paragraph out of a brother-officer's diary of the 2nd Battalion, dated the 18th April:

> The men are getting thinner daily; Europeans are up against it now, and honestly have barely enough to keep body and soul together. Rations for Europeans for six days from 15th-20th April inclusive: flour, 3 lbs.; bacon, ¾ lb.; dried fruit, ¾ lb.; sugar, ¾ lb.; tea, 1½ oz.; salt, 1½ oz.; tinned meat, 2¼ lb.; onions, ¾ lb.; *ghee*,[1] 1 oz.

The troops during all this time of semi-starvation were called

---
1. A form of Indian butter.

upon to carry out many arduous duties, such as trench-digging, construction of dug-outs, house-building, patrols, and other military duties. That they performed their duties cheerfully and thoroughly speaks well for the credit of the black soldier. I am convinced that no other troops, whether they be Indian, East African, or White, could possibly have done better. Whilst on the subject of rations, when a full ration was issued it was ample, for it consisted of 1 lb. of meat, 1 lb. of bread or flour, abundance of vegetables, tea, coffee, cocoa, milk, sugar, salt, rice, condiments, lime juice, and, last but not least, *dop* (Cape brandy).

I have written at length upon this subject of rations, but so far have written nothing of how certain of us increased our food supply from local resources. I doubt if the reader has ever tasted monkey's brains on ration biscuits, bush rat pie, or stewed hippo's sweetbreads, but all three were consumed by the more daring Europeans of the Brigade, and thoroughly enjoyed. If any readers should doubt the truth of the above, I refer them to certain companies of the 3rd Battalion. Whenever food is scarce prices for all commodities rise out of all proportion. A good example of this is seen in the Klondyke gold rush. Thus on the Rufiji, at a sale of effects of Europeans killed in the action at Ngwembe on the 24th January, a bottle of brandy (Hennessy's three star) was knocked down at £10, and a tooth-brush for the remarkable price of £1, 13s. 4d. Everything else was sold at proportionately high prices.

Whilst the Nigerian Brigade was entrenched at Mkindu several small engagements took place, the first of these was at Luhembero Hill, a well-defined and isolated hill about 6 miles east of Mkindu. No. 13 Company, now under the command of Capt. Norton-Harper, went to this hill as escort to the Nigerian Brigade signalling officer, Capt. Williams. The escort consisted of 75 native rank and file, 1 machine-gun, and 2 officers, including Capt. Norton-Harper. The party arrived at their destination at 8.45 a.m. A strong position was taken up covering the signalling officer, who was at the highest point of the sugar-loafed hill. About 1 p.m. a sentry group north of the main position was rushed by a party of the enemy, but they managed to fall back on to their picquet. The enemy next attacked the picquet, but were driven off. Capt. Norton-Harper discovered that the enemy were attempting to work round his left flank, and delivered a bayonet charge against the oncoming Germans, who retired in disorder. As it was impossible to know the strength of the enemy, Capt. Norton-Harper could not press home his advantage and follow up the retiring enemy, for to do so meant leaving Capt. Williams unprotected. The whole action lasted about twenty minutes. The enemy's casualties and strength are unknown. 13 Company had one man killed and two wounded. The enemy in this attack disguised themselves with grass and branches of trees, and were thus indistinguishable from the bush. In this way they were able to get quite close to the sentry group before being discovered. On 25th February the Nigerian detached post at Kibongo was attacked during the night, but the enemy never pressed home his attack. On 2nd March Capt. Pring's company of the 1st Battalion was fired upon when on patrol duty south of Kibongo, with the result that he had a few casualties.

On 1st March the 2nd Battalion left Mkindu at 5.30 a.m. and marched *via* Kibambawe to Nyakisiku, 17 miles distant, where they joined the Cape Corps and Kashmiri battery. An attack on Tindwas had been planned for the 2nd March. The guide proved to know very little about the country, and in many places the water was waist-deep along the road. The position of the enemy was thought to be 4 miles distant, but the force advanced 8 miles before a shot was fired at them. A few rounds were exchanged before the enemy retired. One German Askari was killed and two were taken prisoners. Our casualties were nil. The force pushed on through swamp and elephant grass, and at last arrived at an evacuated enemy's trench. The British force returned the same day *via* Nyakisiku, at which place they arrived at 10 p.m., having to go through water neck deep on the return journey. On the 3rd March the 2nd Battalion returned to Mkindu, having marched 50 miles in 16 hours, through swamp, water, elephant grass, and mud. On arriving back at Mkindu the men received the magnificent ration of 1 lb. of rice only.

By the 5th March the supply question at Mkindu had temporarily improved. Gen. Cunliffe therefore issued orders for an attack on Ngwembe. The Nigerian Brigade was reinforced by the Cape Corps and the Kashmiri battery. The date of the attack was fixed for the 8th March—all troops having concentrated by the previous day. Later on during the 7th March, the Commander-in-Chief countermanded the attack on the grounds of supplies. On the 8th all troops returned to Mkindu or their own respective stations. A British aeroplane flew over Mkindu soon after the troops had arrived back, and dropped a message stating that Ngwembe was still occupied by a strong enemy force, and that they were waiting for us.

Before going further it is necessary to record in short what was taking place in the other part of the theatre. At the beginning of February Gen. Northey's force was distributed as follows : A small column at Likuju moving towards Kibinda was following up Wintgens' force that had been strongly reinforced. Col. Byron was at Songea; Col. Tomlinson at Kitande, opposing Wintgens. Col. Murray was between Ifinga and the Pitu river, opposing Kraut's force, that at about this time reinforced Wintgens. Col. Hawthorne with a column near Alt-Langenburg was marching towards Wiedhaven.

Gen. Northey, thinking it possible that Wingtens was preparing an attack on his line of communication, ordered Col. Murray to move to Tandala. A small mobile column under Capt. Anderson, 18th Hussars, was attacked by a much stronger force north of Milow on 16th February, and fought a most gallant action, but had to retire under cover of darkness. In this action Col. Fairweather of the South African Motor Cyclist Corps was killed. Another small force, consisting of a company of K.A.R., on 18th February, 6 miles from Tandala, was nearly cut off by the main body of Wintgens' force, but managed after a most desperate fight to cut a way through, and retired on Tandala. Luckily for that place Col. Murray's column arrived in the nick of time, and Wintgens, not wishing to fight a general action, moved north, abandoning a small calibre gun. Wintgens' force towards the end of February consisted of about 550 native rank and file and 60 Europeans. Col. Murray followed him at once.

On 25th February began a long chase in which the Nigerians were later destined to join. Wintgens was thus able to make his escape from Gen. Northey, chiefly on account of that general's force having to be so split up to deal with the numerous enemy detachments in this area.

A concentration by the enemy near Lindi was taking place all February. Brig.-Gen. O'Grady was reinforced in this area, and as soon as he was strong enough he immediately began to worry the enemy. The port of Lindi was prepared for the big offensive that was to be based on that place, and was to commence as soon as the rains came to an end.

At the end of February the 1st Division, under Gen. Hannyngton, held a line in the Rufiji area from Utete to Chemera, through Mamatews. Chemera was an important place on account of the light railway that was being constructed behind it from Kilwa towards Liwale. By the end of February the north bank of the Rufiji river was clear of all enemy.

In Gen. Hoskins' dispatch up to 30th May the following paragraph, which explains itself, appeared:

> Meanwhile the feeding of the various columns was a source of much anxiety to me and to all my column commanders. As the rains increased in the Kilwa area the animals died of fly, and light mechanical transport work became impossible; porter transport had gradually to be adopted inland, and a system of *dhows* and boats up to river-head on the Matandu river was instituted. Portions of the 1st Division located at Mohoro and subsequently at Utete were supplied by river transport up the Rufiji, under arrangements with the Navy, and the river became the main line of supplies for all troops in that area.
> The maintenance of the troops in the Iringa area by the Dodoma-Iringa line had become so precarious that in March the Kilossa-Iringa line had to be adopted, though it involved heavy casualties among porters and donkeys and much sickness among the white personnel. It was not until May that weather conditions again permitted of the Dodoma-Iringa line being used.

Difficulties of supply through the low-lying country between Kibambawe and the Uluguru uplands steadily increased, so that the troops were frequently on half rations. I therefore hastened the withdrawal of the remainder of Gen. Beves' force to recuperate and refit.

Sickness amongst Europeans and South African units had assumed such proportions as to necessitate their withdrawal to recuperate. I decided to send as many as possible to South Africa and to recall them in time for offensive operations after the rains.

The hardships of the campaign and the brunt of the fighting since 1914 had been borne by some Indian units and by the King's African Rifles. Those had also suffered severely from sickness, especially the Indians; but units were so weak as to make it impossible to withdraw any of the King's African Rifles, and only certain of the Indians were able to be sent to healthier ground to recuperate.

The 3rd Division, composed only of South African troops, had left the country early in January 1917. It was now decided to return the 2nd South African Division to South Africa. So by the time the offensive was recommenced there were very few combatant white troops left in East Africa. The strength of the King's African Rifles was raised to twenty battalions, which fact makes one regret the more the previous disbandments in this force. As this force at the outbreak of the war consisted of only three battalions, this effort speaks very well for British East Africa, and is an example to other African colonies. With the withdrawal of these two divisions the division organization was done away with, and columns were formed, varying in size according to the requirements of the operations to be allotted to each.

An organized Carrier Corps was now established, as it had been proved that it was essential that the white personnel who were to handle porters should understand the natives under their control, and be able to speak to them in their own language.

In March the Compulsory Service Act was put in force in British East Africa for both natives and Europeans. The Carrier Corps greatly improved the conditions under which the native served.

Up to this time the wretched carrier had to look after himself, and serve under conductors who did not know a word of his language. The carriers' conditions in the early part of this campaign were most unenviable, and they died by thousands monthly.

To return to Mkindu. On 13th March, shortly after midnight of the 12th-13th, the Kibongo post was attacked by a strong force. The enemy got within 150 yards of the trenches, but did not approach nearer. On the 13th the Brigade Headquarters moved to Mpangas on the Rufiji, orders having been given out that the 2nd and 4th Nigeria Regiments, under the command of Col. Sargent, would remain at Mkindu, and all other troops would be withdrawn to the river. The Commander-in-Chief had decided that the Nigerian Brigade should take over the whole of the upper Rufiji line. All South African and Indian troops, who for a long time past had been suffering severely from the climate and feeding, were withdrawn to a more healthy station. On the 14th March half the Nigerian battery, the signalling section, and a certain number of stretcher cases, together with 700 carriers, left Mkindu at 6 a.m. for Mpangas. This long convoy had for its escort three officers and forty-nine rank and file, with two machine-guns. The advance guard consisted of twelve rank and file, under the command of Lieut. Buchanan-Smith. This had to be divided again into the vanguard and main guard. Capt. Milne-Home, with two sections and two machine-guns, remained with the guns as escort; the remaining section of twelve rank and file formed the rearguard. There had been a fairly long halt at 6.45 a.m. to allow the long column to close up. At 7.30 a.m. two shots were heard in front, which Capt. Milne-Home took to be some one shooting game. This idea very soon proved to be wrong, as several German rifles were heard to answer. The convoy immediately halted, and the two available sections, numbering about twenty-four rifles and one machine-gun, formed up in a crescent formation round the guns. The German firing became very heavy, but the main body was unable to reply, owing to the advance guard being out in front. Shortly afterwards the main guard of the advance guard, numbering in all five rifles, fell back and joined the main body.

Lieut. Buchanan-Smith came back himself from the vanguard, and reported that he had seen five white men and a number of Askaris, and that every man in his vanguard had been knocked out. A number of Askaris were observed by Capt. Milne-Home breaking back through the bush on his right. They received the best part of a belt from the machine-gun with the main body. Many of them were seen to fall. During this period all the 3rd Nigerians who were wounded crawled back with their rifles and equipment complete, notwithstanding the fact that several of them were badly hit, and in fact one of them, Pte. Ahaji Maifoni, was shot through both thighs. Pte. Dodo Jalingo was shot through the lungs, and later died of his wounds, whilst a third soldier was wounded in eleven places.

Whilst the machine-gun was in action, one of the team, Pte. Suberu Ilorin, got a bullet through his arm, but he never ceased serving the gun, and only laughed when some one suggested he should go to the dressing station. The second machine-gun had been sent forward from the rear, but before it arrived Major Waller had been dangerously wounded, and Lieut. Vise had taken over the command of the guns.

Lieut. Buchanan-Smith, who was now in charge of the firing line, had been instructed that whatever happened this line must stand firm. Lieut. Vise, at about 8.20 a.m., discharged two rounds from his guns, with the fuses set at zero. After that there was only some desultory firing, the whole affair having lasted for one hour. The Nigerian casualties were Major Waller and his native battery-sergeant-major, both dangerously wounded, three rank and file killed, and nine others wounded; in all, fourteen casualties of all ranks.

Lance-Cpl. Awudu Kadunu in this action won the D.C.M. When with the advance guard early in the fight he captured an Askari, and while in the act of disarming him was attacked by another German soldier, whom he killed, afterwards shooting his original captive who was trying to run away. Later he killed a German European. Lieut. Buchanan-Smith accounted for two other Europeans, whom he shot with his revolver at point-blank range when the vanguard was first attacked. Thus ended what might have been a very unpleasant little show. The Nigerians were outnumbered, and were further hampered with a very long convoy and many carriers, who are always an anxiety to an escort commander. That the guns and loads were all saved was due to the personal valour and leadership of Lieuts. Vise and Buchanan-Smith, who were both awarded the Military Cross for the parts they took in this action. The Germans suffered many casualties. There were only three Europeans and three Askaris actually accounted for, but that they erected a dressing station and put up a Red Cross flag during the action is known, and further, when a careful examination of the ground was made later much blood and pieces of first field dressings were discovered around in the bush—from which facts it is believed that their casualties must have been quite heavy. The total loss of material to the Nigerians in this action was only one rifle and a hundred rounds of ammunition, both taken by the Germans from the body of a man who had been killed, and whose body could not be got back. There were several differences of opinion as to what the Germans were doing on the Mkindu-Mpangas road on this day. In the opinion of many people they could not be lying up for a food convoy, as they were facing towards Mkindu instead of Mpangas. If they had meant to ambush a supply convoy, it stands to reason they would have dug in facing the way that the convoy would come, instead of which all their firing pits were dug facing Mkindu. They were actually about sixty to eighty in strength, to judge by the volume of fire. It was later proved that they had taken up their position on the old road the night before the action, and had remained out all night watching the Mkindu road. It had been at first intended that Gen. Cunliffe and his staff should move back to the river on the 14th. At the last moment this was changed to the afternoon of the 13th. The last of the Headquarters to make the journey was Major Booth, who could only have passed the scene of the fighting an hour or so before the arrival of the Germans. If the Germans had intended to take the battery—that is, assuming that they knew the move was to be made on the 14th—they would have sent out a much stronger force than seventy rifles with no machine-guns. This fact proves that they never expected the battery with an escort to pass over this road on the morning of the 14th. It is equally certain that they were not lying up for a British supply convoy. It is therefore thought by many that they must have been *lying up* for the General and his staff, but by the greatest good luck, owing to the change of plans at the eleventh hour, their attempt to capture the whole of the Nigerian staff was frustrated. Information of their probable move from Mkindu must have got through to the Germans by a spy who probably was living in the British camp, disguised as a Swahili carrier. Capt. Milne-Home was handicapped by the feeling of over-confidence in the safety of the road, that had sprung up generally at Mkindu. Only a few days before this action I was watching a big convoy arriving from the river, under the escort of about twelve rifles. Turning to a certain officer, I remarked, "What a fine bag a convoy of this description would be for the enemy." The officer laughed and said that the road to Mpangas was as safe as any country road in England, and he would feel quite safe walking down it with his mother and aunts with umbrellas up to act as his escort. This well describes the opinion that every one had at the time of the Mpangas road. The reader can judge how great must have been the consternation of every one at Mkindu when this fight was heard to be going on not more than three miles from the Nigerian camp. On reading through a certain officer's diary who took part in this scrap, I was much amused to read an entry made on this date.

> Our company eventually went ahead and got to Mpangas about 4.30 p.m. Later in the evening a small mail arrived, which contained amongst other letters one from Mother and O—— congratulating themselves on my being out of France at a nice safe place where the show is over!!

Whilst the whole Brigade were at Mkindu there were several attacks on the Kibongo post, which gave rise to many false alarms. On a certain night the garrison of Mkindu were disturbed late in the evening and had *to stand to arms* for the remainder of the night, whilst silence reigned supreme at Kibongo. What had happened to the post no one knew. All was wrapped in the deepest mystery. Later it was discovered that the officer in charge of the post had been disturbed by a curious sound as of a great force moving between Kibongo and Mkindu. "My God," he thought, "I am cut off!" The silent foe could be seen moving from east to west in dark, shadowy batches, and as they moved they were seen to be driving in stakes. "They're putting up an obstacle between me and Mkindu," thought the officer; "surely I am undone." By making a big circular tour through the bush he managed to escape with his detachment from the *enemy*. Next day when the ground was examined the spur of many hartebeests was seen on the exact spot where the *enemy* had been seen the night before. The driving in of stakes turned out to be the hartebeests grazing, and as they moved forward they lifted up their heads, and as they halted so they put their heads down to graze. The *enemy* was a great herd of these antelopes, and the stakes were their horns! Owing to this false alarm four battalions stood to arms all night. It might have been a laughing matter if it had not been so sad!!

Talking about alarms, real and false, I wonder if my reader has ever encountered driver ants? They are more terrible than any German; they can make a reasonable being do the Marathon in record time; they will make a sane man jump into a stream or fling off his clothes and roll in the grass as naked as when he was born; they will take up residence in a house and no one will enter, whilst the rightful tenant of the house will gladly remain outside in the cold and rain rather than share his dwelling with the intruder. A whole company will take up their beds and walk on their arrival. Saintly men will rage like fiends when by chance a dozen or so of these *drivers* have the whim to wander up his trousers; whilst calm and self-possessed men will dance better than the average Dervish at the very thought of one or two down his neck. Their power to disturb is immense. They are invincible. I once thought that I, a mere human, could *straf* the driver ants that had honoured my house with a visitation during the night, but the *strafer was strafed*, and the house remained the sole property of the ants till at dawn they decided to go elsewhere.

On the 16th March a small patrol was sent out to the Kibongo neighbourhood by the 4th Battalion. The post had been withdrawn the day before. Company-Sergt.-Major Belo Akure was sent out in charge of this patrol, which included no Europeans.

This sergeant-major is a most remarkable native. He obtained the D.C.M. for extraordinary gallantry in a pagan expedition on the West Coast some years previous to the outbreak of the Great War. During the Cameroon campaign he obtained a bar to his D.C.M. He was most highly recommended by his captain and battalion commander for a second bar during the same campaign. He was awarded his bar for covering the retreat of a party of Nigerians by checking the enemy's advance by himself. He was ordered to conduct the retirement of an advance post that was being heavily attacked. The post was separated from the main position by an unfordable river 35 yards in width. He got his men into the only available canoe, and finding that it would founder if he got in himself, he lay on the bank and covered their retirement, being all the time subjected to heavy fire himself, one bullet actually cutting his sleeve. When his men landed he ordered them into the trenches on the other side of the stream, and then swam the river himself under heavy fire to join them. I have several times seen this sergeant-major in action, and can honestly state that I have never seen a braver man. It makes one feel quite ashamed of oneself when that nasty feeling of fear catches one deep down inside and has to be expelled, for one realizes that this native does not know what the feeling of fear is. His one idea is that his officers must on no account run into unnecessary danger ; on no account will he let an officer go in front of him on a road. Any cover that is handy must be reserved to conceal his officers, even if he himself must lie down in the open. I have seen him deliberately get in front of a European so that if anyone should be hit it would be himself.

To return to the doings of Belo's patrol. During the night the sergeant-major with three privates returned to the old perimeter at Kibongo. About 6.45 a.m. he saw a party of Germans approaching, which he estimated to be about fifty natives led by two Europeans. The enemy extended about 600 yards from the old Kibongo camp, and sent forward a few scouts. The two Europeans remained together in the centre of the extended line. They were marked down by the sergeant-major to be for his own private *bag*. He ordered the three privates on no account to fire till he had taken a deliberate and well-aimed shot at the fatter of the two Germans; the other he was not interested in, as he was only a thin man! From that moment poor *Mai Tombi* (the fat man) was as good as dead. The enemy's scouts had now approached the sergeant-major's position to within 100 yards. *Mai Tombi* was 50 yards in rear of the scouts. Belo Akure drew a careful bead on the poor fellow's *equator*. As he afterwards explained the case—"I shoot him 6 o'clock for belly." The German was seen to throw his arms up into the air and fall backwards. Immediately after the sergeant-major had fired his small party opened rapid fire into the crowd. A good deal of confusion took place, but when Belo saw that the enemy were fixing bayonets, he thought it about time that he and his friends got clear away, so he ordered the men to retire through the bush back into Mkindu, whilst he remained alone for another minute to cover their retreat, and to have one more shot at the Boche. Both he and his party got safely back to camp after a very pleasant morning's shooting!

On the 25th March Sergt.-Major Belo Akure had another little adventure, and for the part he took in both he was later awarded the Military Medal.

On this day Lieut. Travers of the 4th Battalion, with twenty-four rank and file, including the sergeant-major, went out on patrol duty in the Kibongo area. For some days past small parties of the enemy had been moving about in this district. Lieut. Travers intended laying up for one of these detachments. He therefore placed his patrol in small groups around in the bush near to the paths that had been lately used by the Germans. He, Sergt.-Major Belo Akure, and two other soldiers formed one group. At 1.30 p.m. a German patrol was heard coming through the bush. They actually passed within 15 yards of the sentry over the officer's group. The enemy's patrol, whose exact strength is unknown, was under a European. As soon as the European presented a good target the sergeant-major fired at him, wounding him in the leg.

The fire was immediately taken up by the rest of the group, but owing to the long grass it was difficult to see the Germans, but one German soldier was killed. He must have been a magnificent specimen of animal when alive, for he was at least 6 feet 4 inches in height. The trouble was now how to get the European away as a prisoner, as his friends were all round in the bush. Sounds of infuriated German Askaris, who frequently discharged their rifles at nothing, were to be heard in all directions. Once again Belo came to the rescue. He left his place of safety and went out to the German who was lying on the ground. History does not relate what he said to the wretched man, but badly wounded as he was, he got up and followed the sergeant-major to a place of safety. When he met Lieut. Travers he was about three shades paler in colour than a good-looking corpse. Sergt.-Major Belo Akure has a way with him! When he went out to the German he was liable at any moment to have been fired on by the enemy from any direction at a close range, as the bush was full of them. Having had their morning's fun, Lieut. Travers' party with their wounded prisoner got back safely to Mkindu through the bush. I have told these two anecdotes at full length in order to show the style of fighting indulged in during the rains in the Rufiji area. This sort of thing was the *daily round and common task*, and kept us all from dying of boredom.

The Nigerians were incessantly patrolling, doing convoy duty on supplies, or evacuating hospital cases. In these days the sickness both amongst black and white was very heavy. Every evening would find officers congregated at each others' huts, notwithstanding the fact that whisky was nearly an unknown luxury, and the ration of *dop* was, more often than not, conspicuous by its absence, though it was sometimes drawn together with a biscuit and a handful of rice and an occasional tin of meat between two or three Europeans. Life in these days was terribly monotonous and dull. I do not think we received more than one mail (certainly not more than two) during the whole time we were at Mkindu. We therefore suffered from a reading-matter famine as well as from hunger. The only thing to do when not actually working was to sleep. I spent more hours in a week in these days in the prone position than I have ever done before or since when not actually sick. On Good Friday 1917 an aeroplane came over Mkindu, and after dropping bombs on the enemy at Ngwembe it eventually returned to Tulo. All of us at Mkindu hoped that our friend the Boche enjoyed his Easter eggs!

From Easter onwards events need no detailed description. The supply question became weekly more and more acute. Shooting parties were organized to obtain meat for the troops, but game was scarce, whilst lions were plentiful. Between the lions and the shooting parties the little game that was in this area went up into the hills, too far away to be of any use to the hunter. Taking this part of the theatre as a whole, there was to all intents and purposes a complete lull in active operations. That the enemy were also suffering badly for want of food was the Nigerians' only consolation. As a proof of this, on 11th April two German Europeans and three native soldiers were brought into the Mkindu camp from the British post at Kipenio. The wire being damaged between that post and the British extreme right flank post on the river, a small wire party of one European and three native soldiers set out to repair the damage. This party had not long left Kipenio before they came upon a party of the enemy in the bush, consisting of two Europeans and seven Askaris. As soon as the Germans saw the small British party they surrendered. They were in a perilous condition. Their native soldiers, suffering from hunger, had all eaten a poisonous root that they had dug up in the bush. One of these wretched men had just died, and all the rest were in great pain, and no doubt dangerously ill. Three more died the same night at Kipenio. One of the three who were brought into Mkindu died the day after he arrived. This party were in a more or less semi-moribund state when found by the wire party, for they had been wandering in the bush for days.

On 16th April the question of supplies was getting even more serious. Orders were therefore issued for the Nigerian battery and the 4th Battalion to withdraw from the river and return to Morogoro on the Central Railway—the most cheerful news I think I have ever received in my life. On 30th April the 1st Nigeria Regiment was also evacuated to the railway.

The march back to the railway needs describing at length, for it would be quite impossible to find a worse road than that followed by the troops anywhere in Africa. The following account is taken from a diary written at the time the journey was made by the 4th Battalion:

> On the *18th April*, owing to the lack of sufficient accommodation on the lines of communication, only half the battalion could march together down them. Therefore the battalion was split up, and later, when Capt. Maxwell went sick, I myself was in command of the first party. Col. Sargent, with the Battalion Headquarters and the remainder of the battalion, followed two days later. The crossing of the Rufiji commenced at noon on the 18th. Capt. Maxwell's company completed the crossing without mishap. The ferry was able to accommodate ten men at one time, though the same boat had often taken as many as twenty armed men at once. At about 5.45 p.m. there were left of 14 Company only eleven men and three officers to cross. The Indian native officer in charge of the ferry ordered all the eleven men to get into the boat, and thus complete the crossing of all the native rank and file. All went well till the ferry was nearly across, when, to the horror of all who were standing on the banks, the ferry was seen to capsize. Out of the eleven soldiers and the three Indians only one soldier and two Indians were saved. This company lost on this day three non-commissioned officers, all of whom had the D.C.M. The Rufiji at the time was more like a millrace than a river, and was quite 300 yards broad. This was the very first accident of its kind that had ever occurred, though thousands of troops had crossed the ferry during the past few months. On the 21st April the detachment left Wiransi at 6.30 a.m., arriving at Dakawa at 5.30 p.m., a distance of twelve miles. The road was good to within a mile of the Mgeta river, when it became swampy. The bridge over the river was washed away a week before. The crossing was therefore made by means of a trolley on an overhead wire, which carried six men at a time. It

took four hours to cross the river by this means. From the Mgeta river to Dakawa is only two miles, but the road throughout was never less than two feet under water and thick black bog. At some places the water was waist deep. Near Dakawa crocodiles had been seen actually on the track itself, and had been known to have killed or mutilated carriers whilst they were walking along this road. Dead mules and donkeys and even dead carriers littered the road on each side in various degrees of putrefaction. The whole of the detachment was in a wet and exhausted condition ; it had rained very hard most of the day to add to all our other troubles.

On *22nd April* we left Dakawa at 9 a.m., arriving at Duthumi at 3 p.m., a distance of ten miles. The road was fair except at one place where there were about five hundred yards of quagmire.

23rd April we rested at Duthumi. The detachment was in a very bad condition, and there were very many sick.

24th April we left Duthumi at 6.30 a.m. for Tulo. It is doubtful if there could be a worse piece of road in the country or even in the whole of Africa. The distance is not more than twelve miles, but for nearly the whole way the road led through the worst sort of black stinking mud, it was throughout knee-deep in water, and sometimes the water was above the waist. To make matters worse large numbers of cattle and donkeys had died in the swamp, and having rotted, the stink was too bad for words. Two weeks before over eighty head of cattle had died in this swamp, together with several natives. The party arrived at Tulo at 3 p.m., after the worst trek up to date.

25th April the party left Tulo for Summit at 6.30 a.m. Much water was passed through during the first trek; in fact the road was frequently more like a rushing mountain stream than anything else. The party arrived at Mua river at 10.30 a.m. It took nearly five hours to cross this river by means of the overhead trolley. First the rope gave out that drew the trolley across the wire; then the trolley itself went out of order. The detachment did not arrive at Bottom camp until 3.30 p.m.; from Mua river to this camp was only two and a half miles. At this point of the journey the carriers were replaced by motor transport. It was impossible to get all the loads up to the Summit camp the same evening, therefore a guard was left to look after all the loads left behind. It was dark when the detachment arrived in camp. The whole distance traversed this day was only sixteen miles.

26th April: Lieut. Travers left Summit at 8 a.m. in charge of the detachment. He did not arrive at Ruvu top until after dark; the journey was about sixteen to seventeen miles over a fairly good road. The detachment was greatly troubled with heavy rain all day, and arrived in camp in the most exhausted condition. Nearly half the loads had been left behind at Summit owing to lack of transport, and these followed the next day.

27th April: A very large number of sick had to be admitted to the hospital at Ruvu; the detachment rested at Ruvu during the whole of this day.

28th April: The detachment left for Mikesse at 6 a.m. Its strength was now only 152; 74 rank and file had been left in hospitals along the line of communication. The party rested for the night at a half-way house nine miles from Ruvu.

29th April: The detachment continued the march to Mikesse at 6 a.m., and after a thirteen-mile trek arrived at that place at 2 p.m., without any further casualties.

30th April: Col. Sargent's party arrived at Mikesse; they were nominally half a battalion in strength, but when they had completed the march they were only 119 strong. The effective strength of the whole battalion on the evening of the 30th was only 212 present at Mikesse. All this sickness was due to the starved condition that the men were in when they left the river.

The state of the road, as seen by us during this march, explained for itself the shortage of rations on the Rufiji. There cannot possibly be any other theatre of war possessing so difficult a line of communication. In order to feed three thousand native troops, Europeans, and various departmental units, an army of at least twelve thousand men had to be employed. Mechanical transport drivers fell sick so frequently that in one month there was nearly a complete change of the personnel. These drivers had to work seven days a week without rest, and with insufficient time to even get their food. Their work was never finished till after dark, and it commenced almost before daylight.

Taking the road as a whole from Mpangas to Mikesse, words to describe it fail me. From Mikesse to Summit camp it was nominally passable for mechanical transport, but the only form of mechanical transport that could cope with this road was the Ford car. This fact is the most wonderful advertisement that any maker could wish to have. In many places the cars were up to their axles in mud, and in other places the cars literally bounded from rock to rock. Nowhere did a car get a clear run for more than a hundred yards at a time, yet these Ford cars managed to get through where no heavier make of car could possibly stand the road for even one journey. In East Africa the Ford car was nicknamed a *jigger*, after the jigger flea, for like the insect it can get anywhere! From Summit to Mpangas the transport generally used were porters, but donkeys were used in addition between Tulo and Dakawa. These wretched little beasts seemed to be a failure in those parts owing to the tsetse fly, from the effects of which they die at the rate of about a hundred a week. The porters obtainable in this part of Africa were not altogether satisfactory, as they were only able to carry a 50 lb. load at most. Taking into account all these difficulties it seemed little less than a miracle that the Brigade actually ever got the little rations that they did receive when at Mkindu.

On the 2nd May the whole of the 4th Battalion moved by train to Morogoro, where the Nigerian guns had moved a few days previously. Towards the middle of May the Rufiji began to go down, and the rain in this area came to an end in June, though it actually rained on every day in May except one in the Rufiji area. When the river had gone down a considerable amount of equipment of all kinds was found in the river bed, such as carts, harness, and even motors, all of which had been caught at the end of the last dry season when the river rose suddenly. At the end of the rains supplies at Rufiji greatly improved, till once again every one was on full rations; thus the end of May saw the end of the famine in this area. The troops during these months behaved in the most exemplary manner. One must remember that in the native's mind his daily food is the most important thing of all. For this he has been accustomed for centuries past to fight, and it has been the ruling factor in all the hundreds of tribal wars that have taken place throughout the length and breadth of Africa. If a native is denied his food, his chief pleasure in life is taken away from him, and he becomes morose and discontented. A happy nigger is he that has his belly full. The way these half-starved men carried out their duties would be a fine example to the best white battalions in any theatre. Though the last few months had been a very severe trial to both Europeans and natives, the Nigerian Brigade had fulfilled its allotted task of holding the line of the upper Rufiji. It is doubtful if any other available troops in this theatre could have kept going, let alone take the offensive again when called upon to do so at such short notice and with little or no time to recuperate. The result of the Nigerian Brigade holding this line throughout the rains was to force the enemy to retire still further to the south.

GERMANS AT HOME

A HOUSE AT TABORA BEFORE THE ARRIVAL OF THE ALLIES

A GUN CARRIER IN FULL 'MARCHING ORDER' CARRYING A GUN WHEEL OF THE Q. F. B. L., A VERY AWKWARD LOAD. WEIGHT 70LB.

On trek

The Germans in the act of damaging the central railway before retiring south

The Ngeri-Ngeri Bridge

The Grave of Captain Selous, D. S. O.

THE SWINGING BRIDGE OVER THE RUFIJI

GUN CAPTURED BY THE 2ND NIGERIA REGIMENT AT TSIMBE

A 'BAG AT' DUTHUMI

The Rufiji Valley near Kipenio

Company Sergt.-Major Belo Akure, D. C. M., M. M.

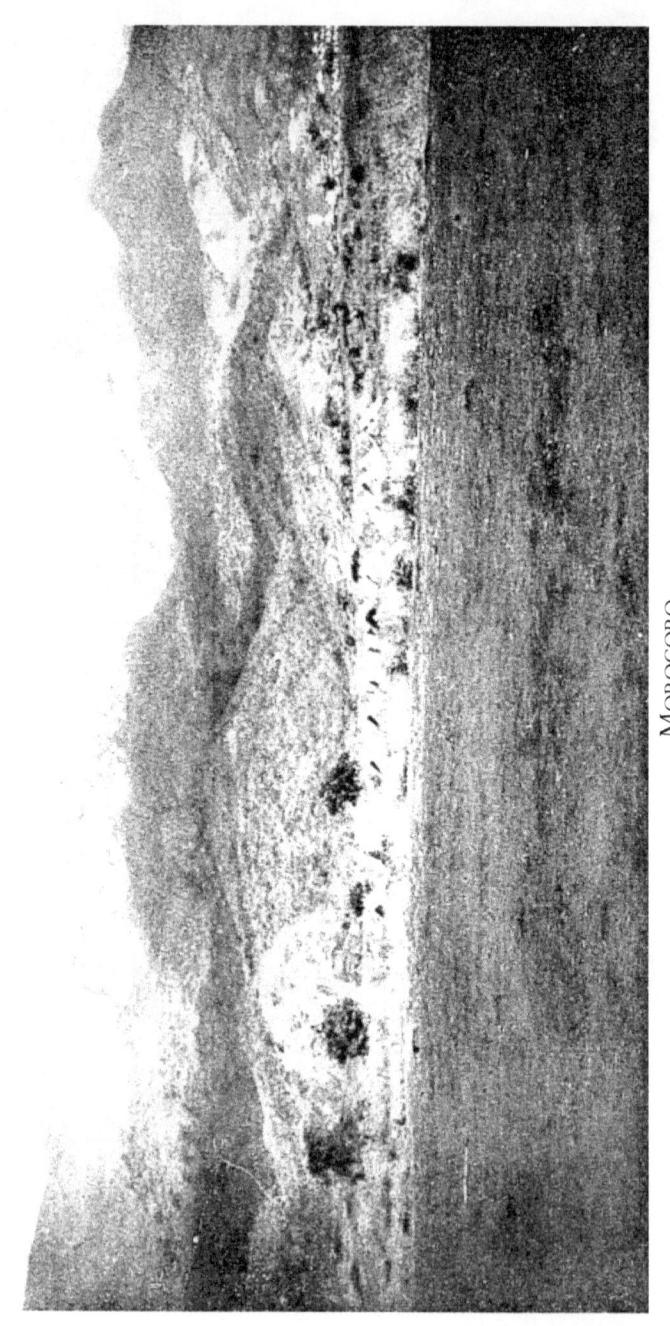

Morogoro

THE GERMAN WIRELESS AT MAHENGE

SPROCKHOF BLINFDFOLDED, WITH HIS WHITE FLAG BY HIS SIDE

CHAPTER 7

The Naumann Pursuit

We must now return to Gen. Northey's operations in the West. We left Col. Murray pursuing Wintgens, and on the 13th March Wintgens was at Alt Utengule. On the 18th he had reached St Moritz mission. Col. Murray, though continually attacking Wintgens, never could bring his main body to a decisive action, though many rearguard actions were fought. Wherever Wintgens went he stripped the country of food so that in rear of him the country appeared as if a plague of locusts had passed that way. In this way the pursuers were always dependent on their supply train, whilst Wintgens lived on the country. A British force was sent to Tabora to be prepared to move against Wintgens should he break north.

On the 21st March Col. Tomlinson with an advanced detachment was within three miles of St Moritz when he was heavily attacked and forced to retire after a sharp fight. Col. Murray tried to encircle Wintgens at the Mission, but once again the Germans were too sharp and slipped away to the east, where they got into a rich and fertile district. From here they next turned north-east, and by the 15th April were at Nkulu. Major Montgomery of the King's African Rifles, commanding the detachment which had been sent into Tabora, now marched to Kilundu, at which place he arrived on the 26th, but Montgomery's force was too weak to be able to do anything against the main body of the enemy He was therefore forced to fall back upon Sikonge. At Itigi, on the Central Railway, a mobile column had been formed. This force reached Koromo on the

30th April. Murray in the meantime was delayed in his advance by his ever-increasing line of communication. He only reached Sikonge by the end of April.

At this crisis of the pursuit Brigadier-Gen. Edwards was placed in command of all these columns so as to ensure their co-operation. Luck was, however, not with this General from the very first. A battalion of Indian troops had been despatched by train from Morogoro, soon after the 4th Battalion had arrived at this place, in order to reinforce Gen. Edwards. A railway bridge between Morogoro and Kilossa collapsed on the 7th May when this troop train was crossing it. The casualties amongst the troops were heavy, but what was almost as bad, the collapse of this bridge greatly delayed the whole of Gen. Edwards' operations.

Wintgens remained in the Kitundu district till the middle of May. The greater part of his troops were recruited from the Tabora and Muanza districts. This fact was of great importance in the campaign, for no doubt Wintgens should have gone south to reinforce the Germans in the Mahenge district, but his Askaris refused to go south, and to show their determination a few of them deserted. This is the only incident of its kind on record, where the Askaris did not blindly obey their German masters, but in spite of this their morale never suffered.

Again, it was a known fact that Wintgens was very jealous of von Lettow. It appears that when the two German blockade running ships successfully rushed the blockade with rifles, etc., on board, Wintgens was never given his fair share of modern rifles. Thus most of his force was still armed with old ·450 rifles of 1871 date.

Murray reached Kitundu on the 19th May only to find Wintgens had evacuated that place three days previously, and had marched north-west. It now looked as if Wintgens' objective was Tabora; and in fact, deserters amongst his Askaris and carriers corroborated this.

About this time Wintgens became seriously ill and surrendered himself to the Belgians after handing over his command to Naumann. Naumann now moved rapidly by night, and instead of marching on Tabora as expected, he turned slightly to the east and so eluded the Belgian commander and Gen. Edwards, who were now in close touch with each other and prepared to co-operate with each other.

From the 18th-22nd May the 4th Nigeria Regiment were resting at Morogoro. Most of the senior officers had gone on leave to Zanzibar. On the 23rd, about midday, Major Webb, now temporarily in command of the battalion, received orders to be in readiness to entrain at a few hours' notice for Tobora. Unfortunately, entraining orders were delayed for twenty-four hours, in spite of the fact that a train was at Morogoro ready to take the first half of the battalion to Tabora.

At 9 p.m. on the 24th May Major Webb entrained in command of half the battalion. Five hours later the remainder of the battalion entrained under myself. Thus began the long and trying pursuit of the most elusive Naumann by the 4th Nigeria Regiment.

We will now follow the adventures of the two troop trains separately. Major Webb commanding the first train received orders to detrain at Nyahua, a small station 30 miles east of Tabora. By this time Gen. Edwards had learned of the change of direction in Naumann's advance. Major Webb, on reaching Nyahua on the evening of the 26th May, detrained. No sooner had he done so than he received orders by wire to re-entrain and proceed back along the line for 26 miles to Malongwe.

Naumann was now known to be very close to the Central Railway. Major Webb expected to have this train attacked at any moment during the return journey. The train had only passed Kilometre Stone 744 by about two milometres when it came to a standstill. The engine-driver reported to Major Webb that he would be unable to reach Malongwe, then only a few kilometres distant, without taking on some wood at the wood stack close to kilometre 742. It was then just before dawn. All the information went to show that the advance guard of the Germans could at most be only a few kilometres distant; in fact the train had only stopped a short while before in order to pick up a wounded British native soldier who was lying by the side of the track, who stated that he had received his wound from a German patrol. A most uncomfortable half-hour was therefore spent beside the wood stack; as it afterwards came out that the very moment when the troop train was *wooding*, the enemy's advance guard was actually passing under the line by means of a big culvert at kilometre 744. There is little doubt that the Germans saw the troop train, and deliberately left it alone, as their chief object was speed ; thus they let go an opportunity of inflicting heavy damage upon British troops with little danger to themselves. Major Webb arrived at Malongwe at daybreak on the 27th and immediately detrained. A small patrol was sent back along the line towards Tabora with orders to make a careful reconnaissance as far as the next station. This patrol saw a large party of Germans at Kilometre Stone 744 at about 7 a.m. The party, under Lance-Corporal Moma Adija, fired on a group of Europeans that had crossed the line and were sitting down to eat an early breakfast a few yards north of the permanent way. Two white men were either killed or wounded by the fire of this patrol who shot at them at a range of only 30 yards. This incident put the Germans on the alert, and it was not long before they were able to repay the deed with interest.

As already stated, the second train left Malongwe about 2 a.m. on the 25th May. This journey was to turn out to be a chapter of misfortunes in itself, but it is typical of a railway journey on the Central Railway in those days. All went well as far as Dodoma, where several coaches of the first train were found waiting, owing to their train being too heavy to proceed further with all its coaches. All were crowded with troops. These trucks were attached on to the rear of our train. The engine was an old German locomotive that had avoided destruction with her sisters when the Germans retired from the Central Railway. She did her best to draw this long troop train, but during the night of the 25th-26th she came to a standstill. Early in the morning the driver came to see me to report that he could go no further without water. The men were turned out of their coaches, and with any vessels at their disposal, not even despising their canteens, they commenced to water the engine from a stream near by. This process of watering took about two hours A further delay was caused by something going wrong in the interior of the beast. By the time this was put right most of the water had boiled away, so that once again the men had to water the engine from the stream. It was nearly lunch time before a move was made, when with much puffing and blowing the engine came to rest at a small station, not more than four or five miles from where we had just watered.

Here the train waited for four hours till another engine came to the rescue. About 5 p.m. another long halt was made owing to there being another train on the next sector of the line. By 6 p.m. Ititi was reached. Here the first local news of Naumann was received by us. German troops were reported to be in the neighbourhood of Kitarara—a station about fifteen miles west of Ititi. Owing to this, orders had been issued that no trains were to go west of that place after dark. Kitarara was reached about 8 p.m. It was then dark, so all the troops were detrained, and picquets were put out round the station, where the troops bivouacked. The night was uneventful. The engine had been forced to proceed to the next station from Kitarara, as the water supply at this place had given out. Our engine was supplied with a truck heavily weighted with sand, which she pushed in front of her in case of bombs having been placed along the line by the enemy—the idea being that the truck would explode the bomb, and thus save the engine. The engine did not return till 7 a.m. the following day, and the journey was continued without further delay to Malongwe, which place was reached by 10.30 a.m Here the Headquarters of the battalion were waiting under the command of Major Webb. Half an hour before our arrival Lieut. Kellock, with a strong reconnoitring patrol, had left the station and patrolled down the line as far as the wood stack at kilometre 742. As soon as the second train had finished detraining half a company was sent to reinforce Lieut. Kellock's patrol, but before these reinforcements had left the station, heavy firing was heard from 1000 yards' distance down the line.

The Germans at kilometre 744, having been disturbed by Lance-Corporal Moma Adija's patrol, sent a strong right flank guard towards Malongwe. This force moved through the bush on each side the permanent way, and lay up a thousand yards away from the station in order to ambush any patrols passing across the guarded bridge, 600 yards up the line. The Indian guard on the bridge had seen nothing of the German party, and Lieut. Kellock's *point* walked right into this ambush, with the result that two rank and file were killed and five more wounded. It was quite impossible for this patrol to fire even one round with effect, as the Germans were so well concealed. After this the Germans fell back and Lieut. Kellock was able to proceed towards the wood stack. About 8 a.m. the Germans cut the wire between Tabora and Malongwe at kilometre 744, after having tapped into the wire so as to get all information possible of the British movements and position of troops. Thus Malongwe was isolated from Headquarters during most of the 27th. About midday a wire repairing party was sent on a motor tractor from Tabora to inspect and repair the line. This work was completed by 2 p.m., and the line once more reopened at about 3.30 p.m., the tractor being between kilometre 741 and 742, when it was seen by Company Sergt.-Major Belo Akura, who was on patrol duty near the railway, under orders from Lieut. Kellock to stop any engine or tractor proceeding from the direction of Tabora, and who held up his hand with this idea in view, and called upon the driver to halt. The linesmen inside the tractor were in a very jumpy condition, having been fired upon early in the day by a small party of Germans. Nigerian troops had not operated in this area before, with the result that Belo Akure was taken for a German. The driver of the tractor tried to reassure his passengers, but to no purpose, and Belo Akure was fired upon at a range of about only 50 yards. This immediately convinced the sergeant-major that the occupants of the tractor must be Germans, and he reported this to Lieut. Kellock, who was greatly puzzled by the whole incident. It seemed quite certain to him that in some way or other the Germans held the line to the west, and had captured some rolling stock. He therefore ordered his patrol to return immediately to Malongwe, as he wished to warn Major Webb of these facts, and he was also aware that Malongwe was held only by a small party, and therefore felt it his duty to return immediately so as to reinforce the garrison in case of a German attack. Thus through a chapter of accidents the whole German force had managed to cross the line to the north without opposition. On the night of the 27th-28th May this force camped near a stream 10 miles north of the railway. During the same night Major Webb received orders by wire from Gen. Edwards to pursue the German column. However, up to this time there was still some doubt as to whether the whole of Naumann's column had crossed the line or not. To this fact is due the delay in definite orders being issued by Gen. Edwards. During this night two companies of the 13th Belgians arrived at Malongwe from Tabora under the command of Major Larsen, the Belgian Commandant. The rest of this battalion arrived during the morning of the following day.

At 6 a.m. on the 28th the pursuit commenced in earnest. The pursuing column, on arriving at kilometre 744, turned north from the railway and followed the German tracks. Large patches of blood marked the spot where the German Europeans had had their breakfast the day before. Several carrier deserters were caught by the 4th Battalion *point*, and these were able to give useful information as to the Germans' movements. The Allied column, consisting of the 4th Nigeria Regiment and the 13th Belgians, camped for the night about two miles north of the German camp of the previous night.

Early on the morning of the 29th Lieut.-Col. Sargent arrived back from leave and took over the command of the Malongwe column, as it was afterwards officially known. On this day the march was continued, but the pursuing column failed to reach the second German camp north of the railway this day. From information received, Naumann was at this time very short of supplies, and was making extra long marches, partly to gain distance on any troops that might be sent to pursue him, and partly to reach a rich country as soon as possible, and there collect supplies for all his force.

On the 30th the Malongwe column reached the second German camp, after a comparatively short march. Here the Germans must have killed their last herd of cattle. To judge by the large number killed every man in Naumann's force must have received a big ration, and doubtlessly all ranks had been informed that no more rations would be available till the rich country was reached. At this camp Col. Sargent decided to halt with his main body, whilst I was sent forward with one and a half companies with orders to try to get in touch with the enemy's rearguard, and failing that I was to push on to a village named Ikungu Kawa Segela, for which place the enemy were known to be making. This advanced detachment marched from 2 p.m. to 8 p.m. without seeing a single German or arriving at the village. We therefore bivouacked in the bush and continued the march at daybreak on the 31st. At 8 a.m. one German soldier and two carriers fell into our hands. From these some very useful information was gleaned. The main German column, we learned, was still twenty-four hours ahead of us, having left Ikungu the day before, at which place they had spent one day in raiding the country for cattle and supplies. Having collected all they required for their immediate future, they had continued the march towards Sangenla, leaving behind them a small party who were unable to keep up on these forced marches. All this information was confirmed on reaching the outlying farms of Ikungu at 9 a.m.

From leaving the railway right up to Ikungu, the whole country passed through was dense elephant bush. In places the country had been pathless before the advance of Naumann except for innumerable tracks of hundreds of elephants. These great beasts had cut up the whole of the ground with the impression of their giant-like feet.

At 10 a.m. our point took prisoners two German Europeans, eight Askaris, and forty-two other natives. The wretched natives of the Ikungu had had everything looted from them by the Germans, including cattle, sheep, goats, and chickens; and after being roped together by their necks had been forced to carry these loads of loot for Naumann's force. The head man of the village was in despair when we arrived, and was only too glad to do anything in his power to help us, and furnished us with any information of the Germans' movements. On going through the prisoners' kit I found eleven pounds in silver, and was very pleased to be able to hand this sum over to the head man in the presence of the prisoners, as part-payment for the two hundred head of cattle that had been taken from him without one rupee having been paid towards their value. The Germans had descended upon the village without the least warning, had split up into small raiding parties, and in this way entered every farm for some miles round the Ikungu village. If only the Allied column had been a little quicker in starting from the railway, and been able to make march for march with the Germans, we should have arrived at Ikungu when the enemy were split up and engaged in looting the neighbourhood, in which case most of the Europeans would have fallen into our hands. As it was, the main German force had left the previous morning, and the rearguard about midday. On arriving at Ikungu I sent forward a strong patrol under a native sergeant with instructions to try to overtake the enemy's rearguard.

Evidently the Germans were not too well off in ·311 ammunition as they had abandoned two machine-guns at the village after having rendered them useless. Towards the evening the main body of the Malongwe column began to arrive at Ikungu, and continued to arrive till well after dark.

During the next two days the pursuit was continued. On the evening of the 2nd June the Malongwe column was only eight hours behind the German rearguard, whilst a patrol sent out by myself from Ikungu must have been within six hours of the Germans. During the 3rd and 4th June the forced march was continued. These two days were the most trying, as the country was now very undulating, and the weather had become very hot. Many of the Europeans of our column were by this time suffering from small attacks of fever.

By midday on the 4th the column overtook our advance patrol, which had halted at a small village on the 3rd, their reason for halting being that the Germans had been reported to have divided into two parties at this place. However, this information was not correct. No doubt our advance patrol had lost one more opportunity of taking the enemy's rearguard by surprise, for when they halted they must have been within two hours of the wily Hun. This failure of the advance patrol to gain touch with the enemy was a great set-back for the Malongwe column. By midday we arrived at Sangenla only to find that the enemy's rearguard had left that place the same morning. In these eight days the Malongwe column had marched over 120 miles, and both Europeans and natives were beginning to show signs of fatigue. Col. Sargent therefore decided to give his column a rest before continuing the advance. It was also necessary to collect supplies from the neighbourhood. Whilst at Sangenla news came in that a party of Germans, believed to be one company, had marched on to Singidda, whilst the main body had marched direct to Mkalama. At both places there were forts, but at the former there were not six rifles present to defend it against attack. The consequence was that Singidda surrendered without a shot being fired. The Germans treated the two British officials here most politely, and let them keep all their own property and money, but they took all the money away that was in the Government safe.

During 5th June the Allied column rested at Sangenla. In the course of this day many native reports came in of the enemy's doings in the neighbourhood. Pillage and rape seemed to be the order of the day with Naumann's troops, while several cases of murder were also reported. The Germans in East Africa were not far behind their brothers in Europe for frightfulness. Whilst on this subject, the few cases might be referred to that have already appeared in the English newspapers of the doings of these same troops in and about Tabora. Archdeacon Woodward, who was one of the civilian prisoners at Tabora in the German's hands, stated that prisoners of war, apart from all hardships, insults, and privations that they had suffered at the hands of the guard, had been subjected to such a course of treatment as was calculated to lower the prestige of the British race in the eyes of the native, and, further, when an appeal was made against such treatment the prisoners were informed that *they had no rights*. Service men on several occasions, under native guards, were compelled to drag a handcart from the prison court at Tabora for some considerable distance from the camp, and there collect, with their naked hands, cow dung, and place the same in sacks which were deposited on the cart, and then forced to drag back the handcart to the camp. This manure so collected was for the use of the garden belonging to their European guards, and was collected from places frequented by natives. This was done notwithstanding the fact that there were many native prisoners available for this purpose. Again, service men on numerous occasions under native guards were forced to carry raw ox hides from the prison at Tabora to a cattle *kraal* some distance away, and there forced to scrape and bury the skins in manure, and subsequently to draw water at a neighbouring well and wash these skins. After a certain lapse of time these skins were dug up and scraped when in a stinking condition, and the white men were compelled to carry these to Tabora and to pass on their way through the Askaris' barracks and Indian encampment. Again, service men, for a considerable period of their internment at Tabora, were forced to clean out the closets of native soldiers. These same European prisoners were continually being forced to drag a lorry through the town under a native guard, when in many instances their clothing, on account of its scarcity, was hardly decent, and, further, they were without boots or shoes. The worst case of all that I have in my possession is told by the Rev. A. B. Hellier, Inspector of Schools at Zanzibar, who was also an interned prisoner at Tabora. He states that on 22nd April 1916 forty-nine European prisoners, nearly all British, thirty-four of whom were ladies, twelve of whom had babies in arms, were taken by Dorrendorf, the German in charge, from Buigiri to Tabora. All these prisoners, after marching some considerable way, were placed in an iron goods-shed at the station, together with forty-one native prisoners, armed Askaris being posted all round the four sides of the shed. In this condition the European ladies and native prisoners were shut up all night. Dorrendorf gave orders that the ladies only were to be allowed to go to the lavatories, two at a time, under escort of Askaris. No one else was allowed to leave the shed all night. The Askaris at once assumed an insolent tone. After a time they actually refused to conduct any more ladies to the lavatory, but later relented. At about 2 a.m. the Askaris became very noisy, and some European in the party called out in Swahili, "Silence!" One Askari was very insulting, and brought

Dorrendorf and another German named Gerth—who incidentally was drunk, Dorrendorf himself being by no means sober. The former abused the English nation, and turning to one European prisoner said: "Wait till I get you to Tabora; but I don't suppose you will reach Tabora alive." He abused most violently a Catholic Sister of Mercy, and said all English women make more trouble than men, and finally instructed the guard to shoot at sight anyone who moved. As they left the shed they called the English occupants "swine." For twenty-two hours this party was left without food. It is hardly decent to go further with this narrative, but the insults these ladies had to put up with during the night were intolerable. I do not intend to go into details, but I have never seen natives treated in the same way as these white ladies were by these *Sons of Kultur*. If my readers can hold any brief for the Germans, I commend them to read the parliamentary papers on this subject, but what I have already written is sufficient to prove that German *Kultur* in East Africa was on much the same level as it has been in Europe.

Chapter 8
The Action of Mkalama

About 3 p.m. on the 5th June I was sent for by Col. Sargent, and received orders to take command of an advance detachment, and do all in my power to regain touch with the Germans. This party was to leave Sangenla the same night, and was to consist of two hundred picked men from both the Belgian and Nigerian Battalions, with four machine-guns. Native runners from Singidda had come into Sangenla during the day and reported that a small party of the enemy was still at the former place. It was to be the first objective of the advanced detachment to reach the junction of Singidda-Mkalama and Sangenla-Mkalama roads, before this German detachment arrived at this point, and there lie in ambush for them.

It was a very long and tiring night march. At the end of every hour a ten-minutes halt was made, during which time most of the detachment usually managed to fall asleep. Men nearly went to sleep whilst marching, and would wake up with a start as they stumbled on the track. At 8 a.m. the detachment had a rest for about three-quarters of an hour at an old German camp, which had been evacuated only a few hours before. Shortly before dawn the march was continued. If this account should ever be read by my companions on this march, I wonder if they will remember the dawn of the 6th June. At the time I well remember how struck we all were by the beauty of the scene, as we neared the village of Mbaba Iramba Kingangira—a long name for so small a village. Dawn in the Tropics is always wonderful, but I never remember being so impressed as I was on this particular morning after a long night march. From the thick belt of timber that follows the Mbaga stream we emerged on to the edge of a great plain, bounded on the north and east by mountains of the most peculiar rugged shapes; in fact, if I may be permitted to coin an adjective, almost *Heath Robinson* in contour. As we came out from the thick bush, already a pearly glimmer had caught the tops of these mountains. Hill after hill awoke from darkness to shadowy purple and grey, each standing out silhouetted against the ever-changing and brilliantly tinted sky. Away across the plain, where night still brooded, the jagged ridges, serrated and wonderful of contour, made a massive boundary of dark shadow to the great plain of the foreground. The tropical African dawn is as brief as it is beautiful. One after another pink-tipped hills passed from a shadowy pallor to the yellow glow of the young day, and then the full splendour of the day broke. Shafts of light pierced the purple shadows and engulfed the village-dotted plain, where gradually the last shadows were dispersed, and night had given birth to a new day. With the coming of day all tiredness and sleeplessness were gone, and all felt how good it was to be alive, exhilarated and hungry on such a morning.

At the village we halted for six hours, in which time we had killed and cooked some local chickens, and had rested in the shade of our ground sheets, rigged up on sticks. Unfortunately the village bees could not agree to us putting up our beds and resting under some big trees in which they had nested.

At midday Lieut. Fox with two sections of the 4th Battalion and one machine-gun proceeded to the road junction, seven miles distant. Here he prepared a position in which to ambush any party of Germans which should fall back along this road. However, a few hours after he had left I received news from the local natives that a German detachment from Singidda had passed the road junction at 5 p.m. on the 5th. About 4 p.m. the main body of the detachment continued the march, meeting Lieut. Fox on the main Singidda-Mkalama motor road at about 7 p.m. In the meantime Col. Sargent had sent on instructions for the advance detachment to push on with all speed, as he had just received information that the Mkalama fort was to be attacked by the whole German force on this day. The march was continued till midnight, when a five-hour halt was made. During the halt two messengers got through to me from Col. Sargent. From them we learnt that Mkalama fort was only held by six Europeans and thirty ex-German Askaris. There was therefore no room for any doubt as to what the advance detachment must do. The march was re-continued immediately to Mkalama; it was our own first intention to help, as far as we could, the besieged Europeans in the fort. By 5.30 a.m. on the 7th the detachment was once again on the road. Lieut. Fox was in command of the advance guard, and he had with him Sergt. Element and one machine-gun. At 6.30 a.m. it was confirmed that the Germans had effected a concentration at Mkalama, and were daily attacking the fort, and that they had given out to all the natives of the district that they intended to take the fort before continuing their march north. At 7.30 a.m. a local chief informed me that there was a German European in his village, marked on the map as Jumbe Showish. He pointed out to me a tree in the distance under which, he stated, the European and his Askaris had encamped the previous night. An attempt was made to capture this party, but to no purpose, for only a few shots were exchanged before the German made good his escape minus his donkey and loads, which fell into our hands. After firing some rounds the Germans were seen to be retiring towards Mkalama. From this time (8 a.m.) to 2.30 p.m. the *point* and vanguard were continually having to deploy, and flank guards had to be sent out to picquet the high ground commanding the line of advance. The general contour of the country greatly favoured a small rearguard action on the part of the enemy, as the country was very rugged and the road frequently passed through narrow denies. It is due to the most excellent work performed by the advance guard that the detachment was able to continue the advance at a speed of two and a half miles per hour without suffering a single casualty, notwithstanding the fact that the enemy's rearguard was continually sniping the detachment. One Belgian soldier received a bullet through his pack, which was the nearest any of our party were to being hit during the advance, though bullets kept on knocking up the dust along the road. At

2.30 p.m. the main body of the advance detachment was within two and a half miles of the fort, so that in thirty-six hours we had marched fifty miles, and fought an advance guard action for the last six hours of the march. The advance detachment had marched altogether 170 miles since leaving the railway ten days previously—that is to say, we had averaged seventeen miles a day. It must be remembered that this was done, as far as the 4th Nigeria Regiment was concerned, after a rest of only twenty-two days at Morogoro, to recuperate from the bad effects of the Rufiji area and weeks of semi-starvation.

By this time (3.15 p.m.) the detachment was about to debouch from a narrow valley on to a broad and open plain. Mkalama occupied a position on a low rise in the middle of this plain. At this point the whole detachment was deployed. Lieut. Fox was ordered to continue the advance of the point and vanguard towards the fort that was then clearly visible. The main body was to continue the advance a thousand yards in rear of Lieut. Fox. During the time necessary to carry out this deployment, I, with the senior Belgian officer, scrambled up a large rocky underfeature in order to get a better view of the plain and Mkalama fort. From here one tent could be seen about a thousand yards to the right of the fort. This, the guide said, marked the position of the German camp. It offered a wonderful range mark for guns, but alas! we had no guns with us. All was extremely quiet, which shortly proved itself to be the quiet before a storm. The Belgian officer was inclined to think that it was only a small rear party of the enemy at Mkalama, and that the rest had continued their march north. He had only just given this out as being his opinion, when without the least warning the enemy opened up a very heavy fire on to the rock upon which we were standing from a machine-gun on our right front, and by infantry fire along our front. We came down that rock, only obeying the law of gravity, which does not permit a body to exceed a velocity of thirty-two feet per second in the first second. Lieut. Fox was now very hotly engaged. Sergt. Shefu Katagum, who was in command of the point, did most excellent work. Holding his small party in the firmest control, he gradually withdrew his men from the advance position, and being amongst the last to retire himself, fell back on to the vanguard. The whole of the Belgian company went up to reinforce the vanguard, whilst the three remaining sections of the Nigeria Regiment were held back as reserve. I was at one time greatly tempted to reinforce the left flank, which was throughout this action the heaviest engaged, but to do so would leave me with no reserves in hand to resist a counter-attack. By 4 p.m. the enemy's fire greatly increased, and the Belgians' left was being seriously threatened. There was little doubt that the enemy were reinforcing their right flank, and were preparing a strong counter-attack against this flank. The Allied position was extremely good, but owing to the short front taken up by these sections (130 rifles and 3 machine-guns) it was very liable to be turned. At first we had it all our own way, and though the enemy's fire was extremely heavy, our firing fine only suffered from distant machine-gun fire on the right flank, where a concealed gun enfiladed part of our line. Most of the casualties that occurred were caused by this one gun. By 4 p.m. it was quite evident that the detachment was being opposed by the main body of the enemy and we were therefore hopelessly outnumbered. At 4.10 p.m. the Belgian machine-guns were doing very useful work, but it was only a matter of time before their left would be enveloped. At one place on the Belgian front a party of Germans and a party of Belgians were actually hunting each other round the same great boulder, so near were the opposing sides to each other on the left. At 4.15 p.m. I issued orders for the line to withdraw gradually to a prepared line in rear. In the meantime Lieut. Hilton had retired with the three reserve sections about four hundred yards.

At 4.30 p.m. Lieut. Fox greatly helped the retirement of the Belgians by inflicting heavy casualties upon the enemy with his machine-gun. A party of German soldier' under a European was seen by that officer to be grouped together about three hundred yards to his front, apparently quite unaware of the near presence of British troops, Sergt. Element, who was personally working the gun, was able to give them the best part of a belt, with the result that the European and many natives were seen to fall. This incident had the effect of stopping the enemy's advance on the left flank for a few minutes, which enabled the left Belgian section to disengage themselves and withdraw to the new position. Lieut. Riedemarkers, the Belgian officer in command of this section, was wounded about this time when trying to get back a wounded native soldier to the rear. By 5 p.m. the whole of the firing line had been withdrawn to the new position. Throughout this retirement the men were subjected to a very heavy rifle fire from the enemy. During the action the enemy from time to time treated us to a few rounds from a pom-pom, which greatly amused the men, being quite harmless, and apparently only able to make a great deal of noise. Soon after 5 p.m. all firing ceased except for a few shots from the direction of the fort. At 5.30 p.m. the scouts reported that the enemy were again trying to work round our flanks; and owing to the exhausted condition of the troops we decided to retire another thousand yards, and take up a safe position for the night, covering the main road by which we had advanced, and by which we expected reinforcements to arrive. A position was now taken up along a high and rugged ridge, which commanded all the country to the north for a thousand yards or more. The position was naturally a strong feature, with good water in the rear, and a safe place near to the water in which to put the wounded.

Both officers and men were too fatigued to take the offensive again that night; we were all too tired even to eat, and fell asleep just where we sat down after the final retirement had been completed. The detachment had been extremely lucky throughout the whole engagement, and had only suffered twenty casualties in all, of which only five were killed or afterwards died of wounds.

There is no doubt that the enemy's casualties were far in excess of our own. They certainly had more than one European casualty, according to local native reports.

At 1 a.m. on 8th June Col. Sargent arrived with the whole of his column, less three sections, which were still collecting food in the district. At 5.30 a.m. a Belgian patrol was sent forward to reconnoitre. At 12 noon the whole of the column advanced to the fort. To the great relief of all, when within a mile of the fort a small Union Jack, about the size of a large pocket handkerchief, could be discerned flying over the building. Thus we learnt that the enemy had not managed to take the fort. The garrison of six Europeans and thirty Askaris, under the command of Capt. Holland, had managed to last out the siege which had commenced on the 5th. Capt. Holland only arrived at Mkalama twenty-four hours before the siege had commenced, and had brought with him, to the otherwise unprepared people in the fort, the news of the German advance. The 4th June was spent in preparing for the arrival of the Germans. The water tank in the fort was filled, stores were laid in, and all windows made bullet-proof by the use of sandbags. When the Germans evacuated the fort in 1916 on account of van Deventer's mounted brigade's advance south, they had laid large amounts of dynamite at certain places in the fort walls. It is not known if this was done with the intention of blowing the fort up before they left, or if they had looked forward to the day when they would return, and, by firing a single shell into the walls, detonate all the charges of dynamite, and thus blow up the fort together with the British garrison. Luckily the dynamite had been discovered by Col. Kitchener, brother to the late Kitchener of Khartoum, soon after the German evacuation. The Colonel had had each place where there was a concealed charge of dynamite marked clearly with a black arrow. Owing to his foresight Capt. Holland was able to have all the dynamite removed within a few hours of the Germans' visit to Mkalama.

On the 5th June the German advance guard appeared on the plain. A white flag party under a German European was sent to the fort walls, and called upon Capt. Holland to surrender the fort to them. Capt. Holland, in the words of the *Classic*, informed the Germans that he would see them all damned first. Capt. Holland was informed that, as soon as the Germans got into the fort they would hang every Askari in it, as they were all German renegades. This threat failed to frighten Capt. Holland, who told the German they would have to get inside the fort first. He was able to give them the cheerful news that the Americans had declared war against them, of which fact up to this time they were not aware.

The attack on the fort was commenced at once by several 1-pounder shells being fired into the west end of the fort at the very place from where the dynamite had just been removed. The 1-pounder failed to make any impression on the walls of the fort, which were extremely well built, having only been completed in 1910. Capt. Holland reassured his Askaris by informing them that a relief column was well on the way. However, the three days and nights that followed without any signs or news of relief began to tell upon them. Matters began to look serious on the morning of the 7th, when the Askaris found themselves with only seventeen rounds left apiece. If relief had not arrived on the 7th, it is doubtful if the fort could have held out for another day, as the Askaris would have deserted during the night, knowing that they could expect no mercy from their late German masters if they should ever fall into their hands. The noise of the action of the 7th was therefore most welcome to the gallant holders of the fort.

The Germans had evidently had all they could wish for in this action, for they spent the night in packing up and clearing out of Mkalama. They had no wish to get themselves into a general action on the following day. Owing to the condition of the troops after this long march, a rest had to be made at Mkalama. This enforced rest was most unfortunate, for it gave the Boche the chance he wanted of getting away and showing us all a clean pair of heels.

On 10th June Capt. Norton-Harper, with a company of the 4th Battalion, moved to the Subiti river in order to try and harass the enemy in crossing this unfordable river, but he was too late, for the Germans had got across in boats, which they had afterwards destroyed. On this day the first aeroplane arrived over Mkalama fort, but thinking that we were Germans, dropped darts upon us. with the result that one cow was killed. Altogether it was a most unfortunate affair, for if the pilot had only known who we were, we could have told him that the Germans were at the very moment crossing the Subiti only nine miles away. If he had gone on to the river he could have bombed them and dropped darts to his heart's content and to the Boche's great annoyance, for most of the German carriers were local men and had never seen a plane before. If a few bombs had been dropped upon them they would have certainly stampeded and left the Germans in the lurch. On 15th January the pursuit was recommenced, but during the remainder of the time that Col. Sargent was in command of this column we never once again came up to the enemy.

The country north of Mkalama was most delightful. Here there was everything a man could wish for—open and healthy country, wonderful shooting, and an abundance of fresh food and milk. This country in times of peace would be a veritable Paradise for the hunter. Elephant, giraffe, antelope, buck and every kind of wildfowl were all waiting to be shot. We, for our sins and Naumann, were unable to take advantage of what the gods had put in our way. From the 15th-22nd June the column continued the advance, having arrived on the latter date as far north as Tirimo. This place was destined to be the end of our march north. Here Col. Sargent received orders by aeroplane to return to Tabora *via* Shinyanga.

The country north of the Sibiti was friendly to the Germans, thus they were kept well informed of all our movements. There is no doubt they had meant to march to Muanza on Lake Victoria, but on arriving at the Simiyu river they learned that the Allies were prepared to meet them in strength at that place, and they therefore turned off north-east and marched on to Mashachi. From here they went due east to Ikoma, where they rested and awaited developments.

After the 4th Nigeria Regiment left the column to return south the 13th Belgians marched with all speed to Ikoma, where they unfortunately met with a bad reverse.

From Ikoma, Naumann marched south, when the 1st Nigeria Regiment unsuccessfully took up the pursuit. Naumann was not eventually forced to surrender till mounted troops were used against him, in conjunction with the Cape Corps, some months later. The 4th Nigerians had a long but uneventful return march to Tabora, where they arrived on the 10th July, having covered five hundred miles on foot in thirty-six marching days. We arrived back at Morogoro on 14th July with a good deal better knowledge of German East Africa than we had when we left Morogoro seven weeks before. Up to that time our ideas of East Africa had been limited to a perfect knowledge of the Rufiji area and the railway from Dar-es-Salaam to Morogoro, but beyond that we had seen nothing. Gen. van Deventer referred to the Naumann episode as being a *remarkable German raid*. Naumann with his six hundred followers, wandering over the northern part of the country, had proved exceedingly troublesome, and they were not finally disposed of until 2nd October, when the last remnants, consisting of three Europeans and fifty-three Askaris, were captured. Naumann had from start to finish covered about two thousand miles. There is no doubt that the force which carried out this raid was composed of first-class Askaris, thoroughly well led. After heavily engaging the Belgians at Ikoma, Naumann moved westward towards the Magadi Lake, south of Kondoa Irangi, near which place he narrowly escaped capture. After threatening Handeni, he was next heard of as being near Moshi, but on finding Allied troops ready for him there he doubled back along his own tracks, re-crossing the Kondoa-Irangi-Handeni railway, where he was finally brought to bay. Such a raid could only have been carried out in bush country like German East Africa, where the bush is often so thick that two considerable forces might pass within a mile of each other, both being unaware of each other's presence. It must also be remembered that the Germans lived on the country, being quite indifferent to the feelings of the local inhabitants, as they have always been, whether in European, African, or any other theatre of war. The seal of the German must at all times be set upon the enemy's country! The grey wolves of war are ever willing to do their work of slaughter and destruction, be it in Europe or Africa. The peaceful villagers of East Africa have, like the villagers of the Ardennes, suffered murder and outrage, whilst frenzied ferocity has raged through both. Burnt and ravaged homesteads are the paw-mark of the grey wolf either in civilized Europe or in darkest Africa.

Chapter 9
The Rufiji Front

During April the Intelligence Department patrols had gradually worked down the river and had succeeded in getting into touch with similar patrols pushing up stream from the Delta. The work of the I.D. was done chiefly by canoes. On 8th May the combined patrols succeeded in occupying Mtarula, Loge-Loge, and Mpanganya. These were the last remaining enemy positions on the south bank of the Rufiji. A number of enemy Europeans and Askaris, comprising the enemy's rearguard, were captured at Mpanganya, while a large hospital full of sick and wounded enemy also fell into the hands of the I.D. The 2nd and 3rd Nigeria Regiments had been left at the Rufiji Front, when the remainder of the Brigade had returned to Morogoro. The general situation in German East Africa at the commencement of the dry weather in 1917 was as follows:—The enemy had been cleared from both banks of the Rufiji and were holding the Kitope line, approximately 35 miles south of the Rufiji delta to the junction of the Luwegu and Rufiji rivers. British troops held the coast-line from the Rufiji delta to the north mouth of the Rovuma river. The enemy held Mahenge and had posts along the upper Ruaha river at Kidode, Kidatu, and Ipakara, from which places it had been impossible to drive them owing to the early arrival of the previous rainy season. The Belgians held the western portion of the country, with Tabora as their centre. Gen. Northey's columns from Rhodesia had occupied Songea. Songea to Tabora was clear of the enemy, whose forces in this area had broken north across the Central Railway, as just described in the last two chapters.

German raiding parties had crossed the Rovuma river and penetrated into Portuguese East Africa. The German civil administration had moved to Liwale, on which place a large number of troops were based.

At the end of the rains in May active operations in the Rufiji area became more possible, but until the road to the Central Railway via Duthumi could be made fit for motor transport, the supply situation rendered a general advance impossible. Patrol work on both sides became increasingly active, and there were several minor engagements. In one instance a patrol of the 2nd Battalion, with a few I.D. scouts, succeeded in surprising and rushing an enemy's camp 35 miles south of the river. The attack was quite unexpected, and the camp was captured with all the food supplies and personal kit. The enemy fled to the bush, leaving behind them one European and several Askaris. Other patrols of the 2nd and 3rd Nigeria Regiments pushed down the Maba road and succeeded in reaching that place after several small engagements, but the Nigerians were unable to remain here owing to lack of supplies, and to the fact that the enemy were in strength at Kitope, 15 miles south of Maba.

The enemy were therefore encircled and confined to the southern part of the country. They were cut off from communication by sea, not only by the blockade, but by reason of our troops being in possession of the coast-line. The Germans, however, so it was reported, were still able to receive wireless messages at Mahenge from Germany via Damascus. They certainly had a wireless almost to the very end of the campaign in German East Africa, by which they received instructions from Europe.

On the south of the German forces lay Portuguese East Africa, with a Portuguese force close to the Rovuma river. On the north lay our columns operating from the Rufiji river and the Central Railway. On the west and south-west Gen. Northey's columns were operating from Rhodesia; on the north-west were the Belgians based on Tabora, whilst from the east strong British forces were operated from Kilwa and Lindi.

Many costly experiences have proved how impossible it is to make certain of enveloping an enemy's force in the African bush.

In German East Africa the difficulties are greatly accentuated by the vastness of the theatre in which the forces are operating. The enemy were well armed and were numerous. They were fighting in their own country with their backs to the wall, and they were led by a general who was a genius, in whose ability to hold out indefinitely against the Allies both Europeans and Askaris had unlimited belief. The conquest of German East Africa was far from being a completed fact, notwithstanding that the English newspapers had for months past stated, much to the disgust of the troops taking part in the campaign, that this, the last German colony, was conquered.

In conformity with the general plan of operations a composite column under Lieut.-Col. Uniacke, consisting of the 2nd and 3rd Nigeria Regiments, was to demonstrate strongly against the enemy's forces on the Kitope line. Lack of water made a direct advance impossible, and the columns were obliged to follow the Rufiji, which hereabouts makes a complete right-angled turn to the south. On the 5th July the 2nd and 3rd Nigeria Regiments left Kipenio and marched to Nyangandu. This march south was continued on the 8th to Mswega, on the Kitope river. Up to this time it is doubtful if the enemy knew of the Nigerian advance in this area. On the 10th July the 3rd Battalion and one company of the 2nd attacked the German camp near Mswega. The German occupants escaped through the thick bush, leaving the camp, supplies, and European kit in the hands of the Nigerians. The Nigerian casualties were light.

On the 13th July Col. Uniacke's column advanced to Mswega. Patrols reported that the enemy had evacuated Itete and Kitope. A sharp engagement took place on the 15th between an enemy patrol and a company of the 2nd Battalion. The Germans suffered several casualties before retiring. A company of the 3rd Battalion occupied Kitope on the 21st, after the enemy had put up a small rearguard action. The column then moved south on the 23rd, and after making a demonstration, returned to Mswega, drawing a certain number of the enemy after them. On the 25th July the enemy attempted to ambush a 3rd Battalion company, but were driven off. However, on the following day they attempted the same again, with some success. The enemy on this occasion were in strength, and included a large proportion of Europeans. On the other side two companies of the 3rd Battalion were engaged. It was necessary to drive the enemy out of their position on the road, so as to permit the remainder of the column to get through without being harassed. A sharp fight ensued, in which the Nigerians were successful and managed to dislodge the enemy from their position after a two-hours' fight. The 3rd Battalion companies suffered seventeen casualties in this engagement, of which five rank and file were killed. The Germans did not get away without their quota of casualties, and at least one European was killed and many Askaris were either killed or wounded. This little engagement was a most creditable piece of work on the part of the two 3rd Battalion companies. The thickness of the bush and the strong position taken up by the enemy made their success all the more creditable. The 3rd Battalion's comparatively small losses in this engagement were due entirely to the excellent leadership of the two company commanders engaged, and to the exemplary behaviour of the men. Pte. Joseph Williams got wounded in about half a dozen places during this action, of which the destruction of his lower jaw was not the worst, and yet three days later he was seen in hospital at Mpangas with a cigarette stuck in his remaining upper lip, and asking for food. At the time of writing this native is at Sidcup getting a new face. All that know him wish him luck, and hope that he will enjoy his *chop* as much with his new face as he did with his old.

On the 29th July this column, having accomplished the object for which it had been sent forward, fell back to the Rufiji, arriving at Kipenio on the 31st July. A small party of the 3rd Battalion were left out in the Kitope district in order to watch the enemy's movements. Active operations in this Rufiji area having now come to an end, the 2nd Battalion was ordered back to Morogoro *en route* for the Kilwa area. The 3rd Nigeria Regiment was left behind to watch the Kitope line and to prevent any attempt on the part of the enemy to break back north across the Rufiji river.

The rest of this chapter now deals only with the doings of the 3rd Battalion, from the time the 2nd Nigeria Regiment moved back to Morogoro until the 3rd Battalion rejoined the Brigade in the Lindi area at a most opportune moment during the battle of Mahiwa. Though this is a digression, it forms a most important link in the whole story.

The month of August on the Rufiji was quiet and comparatively peaceful. The British West India Regiment gradually took over various posts from the 3rd Battalion. At last, much to the joy of all ranks, that battalion moved back to Dar-es-Salaam, arriving there during the second week of September, and embarking on the *Hong Wan 1* on the 18th for Lindi. *Hong Wan 1* is more fully described in the following chapter. It is enough, therefore, to say that the 3rd Battalion did not suffer from being more comfortable or the reverse during their journey round the coast than the 4th Battalion.

Two days later Lindi was reached. Lindi is just a typical African coast town. All such towns really differ only in size from each other. If I were to write a description of Tripoli, I should also have described Kilwa or Lindi. The chief buildings are the *Boma* (fort), the barracks, prison, and various hospitals. Along the quay there stands an assortment of European houses of different shapes and sizes. The town itself stands on the south side of a creek that runs two or three miles up into the interior.

On the 21st the 3rd Battalion marched 14 miles to Mingoyo, a small European settlement at the top of the creek. The march to this place was very hot and trying, as the road led through acres of sisal[1] and deep sand. The Lindi force headquarters were at this time at Mingoyo, which place was very overcrowded and uncomfortable, so that all were pleased to move on the following day to Schaedels farm, 2 miles out of Mingoyo, where a comfortable camp in a plantation was awaiting the arrival of the battalion.

The fighting line was only 8 or 9 miles from Schaedels farm. Here the enemy had made a prolonged stand. On the 23rd the

---

1. Sisal has the same appearance as an aloe, but is of taller growth and much stiffer substance. Several blows with a sharp matchet are required to sever even one spike. Its commercial value is high, as it is used for the best rope fibre, etc.

battalion moved forward to a camp, which for want of another name is known as C 23, after the square on the map in which it happened to be. This camp was very congested, and to add to other inconveniences was under German shell-fire from a 4·1 naval gun off the *Königsberg*. Though forty to fifty shells fell into the camp there were scarcely any casualties, but the very fact that shells fell into the camp at all greatly increased the excitement of life generally, and kept all ranks alert both by day and night. Whilst at this camp the 3rd Battalion received the first news of the battle of Bweho Chini, which is described at length in the next chapter. Great was the joy and pride of all Nigerians at the great doings of their sister battalions of the Brigade, but the joy was not unmixed with envy of the opportunity of being able to deliver so great a blow at the Hun. So far the 3rd Nigeria Regiment had not had a fair chance of giving back all that they owed the Boche for the 24th January.

In the meantime an attack upon the German position at Nrunyu was being delivered by No. 4 Column, under the command of Col. Thomson; Col. Taylor was the Column commander, but he was at the time sick and did not return till the 26th September; whilst No. 3 Column, under Gen. O'Grady, made a flanking movement. The enemy's position was heavily shelled from near Camp C 23. An infantry attack was attempted through fields of sisal, which in itself forms a better obstacle than any abatis ever thought of. The attack could not be pressed home, but the enemy could not stand the accuracy of the British gun fire, and were forced to evacuate their position at Nrunyu on the night of the 25th-26th September.

The 3rd Battalion now formed part of Col. Taylor's column. Mtua was now the next immediate objective. The 3rd Battalion, with the rest of No. 4 Column, passed through the enemy's lately evacuated position at Nrunyu without any further opposition. The country in this neighbourhood was very thick bush. Mtua was entered at 7.30 p.m. on the 26th. The next day the battalion moved to the Nongo stream, where they encamped. The Germans had now taken up a strong position on the Nengedi stream.

At daybreak on the 28th No. 4 Column left camp, with the

3rd Battalion leading. After a short distance the Nigerian advanced guard gained touch with the patrols of Column 3. A little later the vanguard became engaged with some of the enemy's posts, and drove them in. This small action had only just occurred when Gen. O'Grady suddenly appeared on the scene, and stated, in language that unmistakably had its origin in "that most distressful country," that this was Column 3's battle, and had nothing to do with Column 4. Only those who have met Gen. O'Grady, or know him by reputation, will understand that when he says that it is his battle—well, it is his battle—"enough said." The 3rd Battalion were therefore withdrawn from the fight, and the advance guard was relieved by Column 3. The battalion remained on the road in reserve, while a big battle raged about two miles or less ahead. The Kashmiri Mountain Battery was in action just in front of the 3rd Nigeria Regiment; rifle and machine-gun fire ahead was very heavy and continuous till about 4.30 p.m., when a message came back for support. The 3rd Battalion immediately moved forward, but by this time the firing had considerably died down, though to make up for this it had come on to rain in torrents. Lieut.-Col. Badham, commanding the 3rd Battalion, was shown the position and the state of affairs, which was more or less as follows:—

The Germans had been holding a crescent-shaped hill covering the Nengedi water. Gen. O'Grady's column, consisting of 1st/2nd and 3rd/2nd K.A.R., and Bharatpur Imperial Service Infantry, after having had a hard fight and suffered pretty severe casualties, had gained the crest line, but could not push on along the level ground beyond. The object of the 3rd Battalion was to continue the line on O'Grady's right, search for the German left flank, and, after turning it, drive it back. The Nigerians now advanced through the densest undergrowth that they had experienced up to date in German East Africa. It was most difficult to keep direction, especially as the guides had run away in the dense bush. The enemy, by holding their fire, gave the 3rd Battalion no idea of the lie of their position. However, at last the point of deployment was reached, and the two leading companies of the 3rd Nigerians were ordered to go forward, Capt. Armstrong on the left and Lieut. Buchanan-Smith on the right, and get touch with the enemy. Owing to the dense nature of the country it was very hard to keep the line, with the result that the centre was well forward Col. Badham was actually informing the Brigadier of the position of his battalion when the action started afresh, and at very close quarters. To judge from the sound the enemy were round the Nigerians' right rear as well as on their right flank. On account of the dense bush and the fact that darkness was setting in, it was difficult at the time quite to appreciate the situation, but it transpired that most of the leading company had deployed, followed by half the second company, when they were not only fired upon from the front, but also from the extreme right and right rear. It was therefore necessary that Lieut. Buchanan-Smith's company should right-form, so as to conform to the enemy's movements, and be able to meet this unexpected development. Thus the two leading companies were more than at right angles to each other in formation. The movement was well carried out. The Germans were preparing a counter-attack upon O'Grady, and had no idea of the presence of the 3rd Battalion. Just before this counter-attack was launched the leading half company of Nigerians walked right into the surprised Germans. This wedge had been driven into the enemy's troops when they were awaiting the order to advance to the counter-attack. So taken aback were the Germans that the counter-attack was completely broken up, and the troops dispersed all over the bush. At 7.30 p.m. the enemy's bugles were heard from all quarters, sounding what was presumed to be the "assembly" or "rally," in order to collect all the scattered parties. Amongst other calls that sounded that evening was the regimental call of the Royal Dublin Fusiliers, but how the German native buglers had ever got hold of this call will remain a mystery to the Nigerians till the Day of Judgement. Both Capt. Armstrong and Lieut. Buchanan-Smith were wounded whilst leading their companies in this action, together with three other officers, whilst twenty-five rank and file of these two companies were either killed or wounded. These casualties were very light when taking into account the extraordinarily close range and the density of the enemy's fire, doubtlessly the failing light saved these two companies from many more casualties. It is also thought that the bursting in of these two companies, in this wedge formation, on a prepared counter-attack, greatly upset the morale of the enemy's troops, who were *rattled*, and consequently their fire was inclined to be wild, and was not carefully controlled.

The Nigerians " dug in " for the night of the 27th-28th on the same ground that they had gained.

The following day was spent in clearing up the battlefield and burying the dead. The only excitement that broke the monotony of the 28th was the return of the German, Sprockhoff, who had arrived in the British lines with a white flag of truce shortly before this action. A regular *Brock's benefit* was indulged in by all, commencing about a quarter of an hour before he was sent back to the German lines. Every gun, machine-gun, Lewis gun, and rifle was discharged with the greatest rapidity, to the utter astonishment of the Hun, who expected every moment to be attacked. Suddenly every gun and rifle ceased firing as Sprockhoff emerged from the British line with a cloth over his eyes, and commenced to walk the hundred yards that separated the opposing sides. Unluckily the practical joke was a little spoilt by some kill-joy Boche putting his face above the parapet when Sprockhoff was only a short distance from his own lines, or he might have walked right on to a friendly bayonet point that was awaiting the arrival of the supposed British attack, as he stepped over the German parapet. At 6.30 a.m. on the 30th September the 3rd Battalion marched off to a point that had been dictated to them on a map. Owing to a guide not materializing, two hours were lost in getting on to the right track. Two roads led to the objective; the 3rd Battalion were to advance by the right of the two tracks, whilst the 3/2 King's African Rifles proceeded along the left track, or the trolley line. The two battalions were to keep touch with each other throughout the operation. The delay of the 3rd Battalion was unfortunate, as the K.A.Rs. got ahead, and came into action before the Nigerians could co-operate on the right against the German's left. As so frequently occurred in the East African campaign, the map in no way showed the country of which it was reputed to be a picture. Except for the fact that some of the names occurred on the map that were known to exist in reality, there were no other points in common between the map and the country. A nice map of Switzerland with a few East African names upon it would have been just about as useful. The map in question was a *Missionary* map, and the absence of veracity on the part of the map was merely a reflection of a similar trait noticeable among those of German persuasion who gave the map its name! The order of the companies as they finally arrived upon the road was No. 10 Company, under Capt. Robinson, advance guard; Nos. 12 and 9 Companies, Capt. Ambrose and Lieut. Southby respectively, main body; half No. 2 Company climbed Chirumaka Hill in order to watch the right flank; one section of this company acted as connecting files between the Nigerians and the K.A.Rs., whilst the remaining section of this company stayed in camp in charge of the transport.

At 10 a.m. the advance guard got in touch with the enemy's patrols, which they drove in, and an hour later the advance guard was heavily engaged.

The enemy was strongly holding all the approaches to the Nyengedi stream. The country was chiefly composed of thick bush, with here and there a farm clearing. Thus all extended order movements were difficult and most irksome. About a mile and a half beyond, where the advance guard had first gained touch with the enemy, they were finally held up, and a line of hasty entrenchments were dug. Lieutenant Sutherland-Brown and Capt. Carson were sent forward with two sections of No. 12 Company in order to reinforce the advance guard line. In the meantime the main body in the rear dug in a strong defensive line. The firing now became very heavy in front, and the advance guard suffered heavy casualties. They fought with the greatest gallantry and held on to their position in spite of everything that the enemy did to drive them out of it. The Hausa and the pagan Afikpo district carriers did excellent work during this fight by keeping the advance guard supplied with ammunition and water, showing the greatest contempt for danger throughout the day. With the advance guard the ammunition began to run short owing to the necessity of keeping as big a reserve as possible in hand for the main position. Owing to this fact, and that the casualties incurred by the advance guard were very heavy, their position began to get very serious. Capt. Robinson now had to think of withdrawing his company, and this retirement was accelerated by the Germans commencing to shell their position with some accuracy, and at the same time attempting to turn their right flank. Capt. Robinson therefore stated his views to the CO., but whilst he was at the telephone at 1.30 p.m. he was hit. He immediately ordered the withdrawal to commence.

The retirement was carried out with the remnants of No. 10 Company in single file along the narrow bush path—the only fine that could be taken owing to the denseness of the bush. The last to retire was Capt. Robinson, sitting on the back of his orderly, Pte. Afolabi Ibadan, whilst the bugler carried the orderly's rifle and kit, Company Sergt.-Major Sumanu deliberately following in the rear of his wounded captain so as to shield him with his own body. He was hit on the way back, so the bugler had to stop behind to help the sergeant-major, with the result that he himself got hit in turn. For this action Capt. Robinson's orderly, Pte. Afolabi, was decorated with the Military Medal, and the company sergeant-major was mentioned in dispatches. Eye-witnesses of this retirement by No. 10 Company described it as being as fine a sight as any soldier could wish to see. The men, in single file, walked steadily back along the road that gradually rose all the way to the main position. Notwithstanding the fact that the enemy were sniping the road, and the men were getting knocked out all the time, there was not the least confusion. The men themselves were full of fight, and kept on turning round in order to shout *terms of endearment* at the Huns. On reaching the main body every European of the advance guard, except one, had been made a casualty. The remnants of No. 10 Company, and the two sections of No. 12 Company that had supported them, after having been given as much water and ammunition as could be spared, tool; their place in the firing line, which had already been dug for them. The Germans now made two determined efforts to turn the right of this position, but both were finally repulsed by No. 9 Company. Lieut. Southby, for his most excellent work and gallantry on this day, was later awarded a very well-earned Military Cross. The Germans, finding they could not turn the right, delivered a continuous frontal attack up the road, but were heavily repulsed. Owing to the fact that the 3rd Battalion had by this time a certain amount of cover, they suffered fewer casualties in the afternoon than they had in the morning when their advance guard had been fighting only in the open, but even so Capt. Collins, their adjutant, was badly wounded, whilst one other officer was killed and another wounded. This fight had been one of individual initiative, and several very conspicuous acts of gallantry occurred, two of which are here recorded. The first was the case of two recruits who had joined the 3rd Battalion at Morogoro on 17th September. They asked leave *to go over the top* and shoot some German Europeans who were believed to be collected round a machine-gun on the road. At the time all was quiet in front. Leave being granted, out they went through the bush till they came close to their objective, into which they emptied their magazines at point-blank range, eventually returning unscathed. They claimed to have shot several Europeans, but whether this was the case or not, their example had the best possible effect upon their comrades, more especially on the old soldiers, who could not think of being outdone by recruits.

The second case was that of an enlisted gun-carrier named Abudu Dinga, who had spent the whole morning passing backwards and forwards along the bullet-swept road, quite regardless of danger, to the advance guard line with water and ammunition. In the evening, when food and water had to be sent out to the top of Chirumaka Hill for the detachment four miles distant, Abudu Dinga volunteered for the job, in spite of the fact that he had been working hard all day in the extreme heat and constantly under fire.

The action was broken off about 6.45 p.m. On checking the ammunition, it was found that the men averaged only fifteen rounds each, whilst there were, only two belts left to each machine-gun, and four drums to each Lewis gun. But the Germans had had enough, and they retired across the Nyengedi, sadder but wiser men, after a pleasant day spent with the Nigerians. The Nigerians' method of fighting was not understood at all by the Hun. At a later date a German officer personally asked one of the Intelligence Department who were these new Askaris that had arrived, for they neither advanced nor retired, but just sat down tight and defied anyone to move them. This method of fighting was most particularly brought out at Bweho Chini, in this fight at the Nyengedi stream, and again later at Mahiwa. At 9 p.m. the 1/2 King's African Rifles arrived in support of the 3rd Battalion. The night was quiet except for an outburst of firing at a Nigerian bearer party that had gone out to bring in the wounded. The first meal of the day was partaken of at 10.30 p.m.; for the Europeans it was tea and various tinned foods provided by the C.O., whose cook box had arrived at the firing line; and for the men it was rice and bully beef.

Gen. O'Grady arrived early on the 1st October. When walking round the position he remarked that the men did not seem the least bit *rattled*, which, from a leader of his calibre, was more than just a complimentary remark. Once again I am forced to put upon record the un-chivalrous doings of the enemy on this day. Early on the 1st, bearer parties had been sent out to bring in the dead and wounded. It was found that both had been stripped of all their clothing, whilst one dead officer had been robbed of his ring and identity disc. Should this ever be read by the friends of any officers who were killed in this day's action, it will be some little recompense to them to know that the Nigerian Brigade, at a later date, took heavy toll in exchange for these acts of *Kultur*.

During the 1st October the 3rd Nigerian Regiment marched back to a camp on the Lukuledi river after six days spent in the bush.

In this action the enemy had employed six or seven companies, that is to say, about 750 men, against the advance guard of the 3rd Battalion, who numbered at most 180 men. The strength of the whole 3rd Nigeria Regiment was not more than 400 rank and file. The casualties in the 3rd Battalion in this action were regrettably high, consisting of three officers killed and nine other Europeans wounded, and ninety-eight rank and file killed and wounded.

In the actions of Nyengedi and Nengidi the enemy had been dislodged from two successive strong positions, and in both actions the 3rd Nigeria Regiment had played a most important part. On the 2nd October the 3rd Battalion rejoined Column 4 at a most congested camp near the scene of the Nengidi fight. On 6th October there was a good deal of shelling on both sides, but neither side seriously damaged the other. This was continued on the following day. On 8th October a German patrol managed to fire about a hundred rounds into the ammunition dump, having got round to three miles in rear of the whole of Column 3 and a certain portion of Column 4. One bullet actually was alleged to have entered the Column Commander, Col. Taylor's, hut. On this date the 3rd Nigeria Regiment left Column 4 and proceeded to Chirumaka, and there formed with the 61st Pioneers, the *Reserve Column*. This was rather a misnomer as the battalion was abreast of Column 3 and No. 2 Company held a ridge on the west of the Nyengedi, which was more advanced than any other post in the force.

On 10th October patrol encounters were numerous, and a section of No. 12 Company of the 3rd Nigeria Regiment had a small brush with the enemy during the morning. At 1 p.m. quite a number of shots were exchanged at the British watering-place, but little damage was done. On 12th and 13th October the British guns shelled the German position at Mtama. This bombardment was very pretty to watch, as shells were seen bursting all over the Mtama Hill. The Germans returned the fire with a few rounds from their 4·1 guns and 4-inch howitzers, but to no purpose, and they were finally forced to fall back from their Mtama position without a decisive fight—which position was occupied by the British on the 14th-15th October, the 3rd Nigeria Regiment moving into Mtama on the later date.

CHAPTER 10

The Nigerian Brigade in the Kilwa Area

On the return of the 4th Battalion to Morogoro they found a large draft of over 150 men awaiting them under the command of Major Gibb. Major Gibb arrived at Dar-es-Salaam from Nigeria on the 30th May 1917 with the European and native reinforcements for the Brigade. The men he had brought round were excellent material, and did very good work in the heavy fighting later in the Kilwa and Lindi areas. The Gambia Company, under the command of Capt. Law, M.C., arrived at the same time from the Gambia via Sierra Leone, together with a large number of carriers from Nigeria and Sierra Leone. The opportunity was taken, when at Morogoro, to put Europeans and natives through various courses of machine and Lewis gun, Stokes gun, and bombing. Many native soldiers were found to be very useful as bomb throwers.

On the 2nd August the 1st Nigeria Regiment was ordered to entrain for Dodoma, and from there take up the pursuit of Naumann, who at that time was reported to be moving south. However, after a short period this battalion was recalled, as orders were issued, during the second week in August, for the Nigerian Brigade, less the 3rd Battalion, to concentrate at Kilwa. On the 10th August the 2nd Nigeria Regiment left Mpangas for Morogoro, their posts being taken over by the 3rd Battalion. This battalion had just completed eight months in the Rufiji area. After six days at Morogoro, spent in refitting, they entrained for

Dar-es-Salaam. Here the men were all advanced a pound each, and the three days before embarking were spent in shopping and other forms of amusement. The men thoroughly enjoyed these few days of relaxation, but it was unfortunate that the 2nd Battalion could not have spent a few more days resting in this way before embarking. For a few days in August there was a great gathering of Nigerians in Dar-es-Salaam, and a few cheerful evenings were indulged in at the Burger Hotel and the Roumanian Café, where the Scottish element made itself heard in the shape of ultra-Scotch songs. A wonderful people, the Scots! If any nation has earned for itself the motto *Ubique*, the Scottish race should have it. In my many wanderings round the earth I have always found that where two or three white men are gathered together, there is a Scotsman in their midst!

The 4th Nigeria Regiment, the Nigerian Battery, the Gambia Company, the West African Field Ambulance, a section of the 300th Field Ambulance, and the Nigerian Brigade Headquarters embarked on the s.s. *Hong Wan 1* at Dar-es-Salaam. The *Hong Wan 1*—more commonly called *the One Lung*, was a Chinese-owned ship, and was therefore no ordinary vessel. *One Lung* she was to all who knew her and who wished to be polite to her, but I fear she suffered from every disease that a ship could suffer from. It is hardly fair to laugh at her, for she is, or was forty years ago, the pride of the City Line, when she was then known as the *City of Edinburgh*. She was then one of the fastest and finest ships afloat, but now—! Dar-es-Salaam to Kilwa by an ordinary ship is only a few hours' run down the coast; by the *One Lung* it developed into a three-day voyage. As she was only victualled for a short run, food and drink became a little short before the journey's end. To add to other discomforts of overcrowding, short rations, etc., she was inclined to be *lively*, so that all and sundry had something to do in their spare time for several days after disembarking. For some reason or other she used to carry in her bows two pigs. No doubt they were the pets of some Chinese member of the crew, as they were never killed and put to their best use on the table, for food was at all times scarce and uninteresting, consisting mostly of tinned beef. The *pets* were encouraged to sing the overcrowded passengers to sleep in the afternoon, when they were wont to quarrel over the rations served out to them by their Chinese master. This, added to the crowing of a cock that nearly met a violent death many times upon the voyage, rendered sleep often difficult. The *Hong Wan 1* was not all a bed of roses, as my reader has doubtlessly discovered by this time, but we must not laugh at her, for she is now an old lady of the sea, though by her behaviour she sometimes made one forget the fact. But in her old age she has done her bit on the East Coast of Africa to damn the Potsdam crowd.

From Kilwa-Kisiwani, the anchorage, to Kilwa town is an easy two-days' march. The troops from *Hong Wan 1* arrived at Redhill or Ssingino—a camp near to Kilwa—on the 26th August. The 1st Battalion arrived a few days later, and the 2nd Battalion arrived on 3rd September. This completed the concentration of the Nigerian Brigade, with the exception of the 3rd Battalion, whose doings have already been described in the previous chapter. The first week of September was employed by the Nigerian Brigade in field training. The country round Kilwa readily lends itself to practising infantry manoeuvres, being open and very undulating. On 8th September the Brigade commenced its march to the front, which was destined not to come to an end till some miles south of the Rovuma river, three months later. Little did any of us realize what was before us as we marched away from Redhill Camp. On the whole we had enjoyed our few days' rest at Kilwa. It was nice to be altogether once again, and we had all made the best of the opportunity of enjoying life. In the Kilwa area the Nigerian for the first time had a chance to become acquainted with his brother of the East, with the result that the Nigerians became fast friends with the *Hapana* soldier, as he was usually known to the Nigerian Brigade. When a patrol of Nigerians met a patrol of King's African Rifles they would always greet each other by the Nigerians saying "Jambo!" which in Swahili means *Cheerio*, or *Good morning*, and being answered by the term of endearment "Yumyum!" which being interpreted means *cannibal*! The Swahilis, to the very end, always thought the Nigerian soldiers were man-eaters, but this never gave offence, but was looked upon as a huge joke and rather after the nature of a compliment by the light-hearted sons of the West. To the Nigerians the Swahili race generally were either known as *Hapanas* or *Jambos*, the former word being the Swahili for *No*, which was about the first Swahili word picked up by the average Nigerian.

The Nigerian Battery, the 1st, 2nd, and 4th Nigeria Regiments, the Gambia Company, the Nigerian Pioneer section, the Nigerian Stokes gun section, the Nigerian Signal section, and the two field ambulances, together with a supply and ammunition column, had concentrated at Mssindyi, the temporary headquarters of Gen. Hannyngton, by the 17th September. Mssindyi itself was an uninviting spot set in the bush 80 miles from Kilwa, and reached after five hot and dusty days' marching along the newly-cut motor road. A few days before the arrival of the Nigerian Brigade the Commander-in-Chief, Gen. van Deventer, had arrived at Mssindyi, and had there established his headquarters.

On the 15th September two sections of the 4th Nigeria Regiment with two Lewis guns, under the command of Lieut. Griffiths, left for a few days' patrol duty to Luale, in search of water for a brigade camp. On the 12th September a big draft of 1800 recruits arrived at Dar-es-Salaam from Nigeria. A thousand of these were now ordered to join the Brigade immediately, as they were urgently required to act as carriers in the forthcoming offensive. On 16th September news reached the Brigade that Naumann had sustained a bad defeat at the hands of the Cape Corps, under the command of Col. Dyke, and that about half the German column had been forced to surrender. The Commander-in-Chief inspected the Brigade on the 17th. On the following day the advance was commenced. The enemy were strongly entrenched at Mihambia and Ndessa, barring our advance by the main road, and covering the only reliable water holes in that immediate neighbourhood. The object of the operations was to drive the enemy from their position, and at the same time cut off their line of retreat to the south and east by a wide flanking movement, which was to be undertaken by the Nigerian Brigade.

Scarcity of water was the great problem, but a small supply was reported by Lieut. Griffiths at Luale Kati, some 20 miles south of Mssindyi.

On 18th September the Brigade concentrated at Msuras. The following day was timed to be the first day of the offensive, which was destined to continue till the end of the campaign in German territory. It was now decided that a Nigerian Column, consisting of the Brigade Headquarters, the 1st and 2nd Nigeria Regiments, and the Signalling section, should advance to Luale Kati at dawn on the 19th. The 4th Nigeria Regiment with the remainder of the Brigade, with all the loads and baggage, was to follow as soon as the water supply was assured, and when the road had been cleared to enable the supply cars to get through.

The 4th Battalion moved into the Msuras Fort on the evening of the 18th, having taken over from a detachment of King's African Rifles. The 1st and 2nd Nigeria Regiments moved forward *en route* for Luale early on the 19th. Heavy gun fire was heard by the garrison of the Msuras fort during the morning of the 20th, which lasted for about five hours.

At 6.30 p.m. the 4th Battalion of the Nigerian Battery, with all supply and ammunition columns, proceeded to Luale. The 25th Indian Cavalry moved forward an hour earlier. Both Gen. Hannyngton's No. 1 and 2 Columns were in action during this day. The night was very dark and the column was extremely long. The night march that followed was therefore slow and tedious. About 1.30 a.m. a sharp engagement was heard to be in progress in the neighbourhood of the Lungo-Ldedda road. The head of the column reached Luale at 6 a.m., after having completed a very trying march.

Most of the 1st and 3rd Nigerians had moved forward from Luale before the arrival of the supply column; and the remainder of the 1st Nigeria Regiment followed, as soon as the 4th Nigeria Regiment had taken over the picquets and wireless station that had been established at Luale.

The 1st and 2nd Battalions camped for the night of the 21st-22nd at Luale Chini, in a wild and desolate cluster of hills, overlooking some miserable water holes filled with water that appeared to be a cross between pea-soup and ink. When at Luale Chini everything possible was done to avoid the detection of the enemy, who were now retiring before the pressure of Columns 1 and 2. The Nigerians were threatening their main line of retreat south.

The enemy had, as they always had, the great advantage of knowing the country, whereas the guides with the Nigerian Column were unreliable. Everything depended upon the Nigerians being in the right place, *i.e.* well across the German line of retreat, at the right time, so as to be able to offer battle before they could decide on another line of retreat—not an easy piece of tactics to bring off in a wilderness of unknown bush.

The Battle of Bweho-Chini

At dawn on the 22nd the column moved off from Luale Chini, the 1st Nigerians leading. To quote from the Intelligence Officer's report of the action: "It was a steamy, misty morning, and the start was greatly delayed by the difficulty of extracting the different units from the tangle of *kopjes*, bush, and elephant grass in which they had taken up position overnight." By 8.30 a.m. the leading company of the 1st Nigeria Regiment was about two miles from the village of Bweho-Chini, where it became engaged with what subsequently turned out to be a strong enemy's picquet. The enemy were driven out after a short engagement, and at 9.30 a.m. the advance guard entered Bweho-Chini. It was merely a farm hamlet with a few scattered huts, but through it ran a number of tracks, along which it was hoped some proportion at least of the enemy's forces would retreat, as it was on their most direct line of retreat south, and water existed farther along the road.

The Brigadier was left quite in the dark as to the enemy's movements, owing to the field telegraph line, back along his line of communication, having been cut during the night. Further, he had no idea of the whereabouts of other British Columns, or of their ability to co-operate with him, in the event of the Nigerian Column becoming engaged with the main body of the enemy.

At 10 a.m. the 1st Battalion was concentrated in the neighbourhood of Bweho-Chini, where breakfast was cooked. After an hour's halt this battalion received orders to move back along the road by which they had just arrived for a short distance. They moved out of the village as the 2nd Battalion moved in. The 1st Battalion then proceeded to dig in lying trenches facing north and north-east. The front taken up by this battalion was rather congested owing to the shortness of the front allotted to them. In the meantime, after the 2nd Battalion had had their breakfast, they commenced to dig in facing east and west, whilst No. 5 Company was kept in support. The 2nd Battalion front was very extended, so much so that the south face was not occupied except at the south-east corner, no trenches were dug to fill the gap between the east and west faces of the perimeter on the south.

Gen. Cunliffe gave out that it was his intention to attack the enemy at Mawerenye. Shortly before noon all companies were ordered to cease digging defences and to form up into close formation. By noon both battalions were drawn up awaiting orders to move out to the attack. In the meantime a party, under Lieut. Hobson, had moved out along the Bweho-Kati road with all the baggage of both battalions. His orders were to hand over this baggage to the 4th Battalion, that were thought to be at this village on this day. A picquet had been sent out along the Bweho Ju road early in the day.

Soon after midday Lieut. Hobson returned with a German European, three Askaris, and forty loads of ammunition, of which six were .303. These six boxes came in most useful before the end of the day; he reported that the 4th Battalion were not at Bweho-Kati, as that place was occupied by a big German hospital. Not long before this officer returned another European had been brought in by the picquet on the Bweho Ju road. The fact that both Europeans were making their way towards Mawerenye, when taken prisoners, was proof enough that the enemy was still at that place, while documents found on the white prisoners gave conclusive evidence that the proposed line of retreat to the south was through Bweho-Chini itself. When this fact was proved beyond doubt, the G.O.C. gave up the idea of making an attack upon the enemy's position at Mawerenye. All the troops were therefore instructed to return to their places in the perimeter and continue improving their defences.

In order to clear up the situation two companies of the 1st Battalion, under Capts. Pring and Stretton, were ordered to move out along the Mawerenye road in order to to make a reconnaissance. It was 12.30 p.m. when these two companies moved out. Soon after this the reconnoitring party had left the perimeter, an aeroplane flew over the British position and dropped a message at the Brigade Headquarters. No sooner had this happened than Capts. Pring and Stretton became heavily engaged about 700 yards from the main perimeter. Some people who were present think that the Germans opened fire upon the aeroplane, but this is doubtful. In any case the volume of fire was so great that everyone realized at once that they were being opposed by a very strong force. In fact it was afterwards learnt that the German strength at Bweho-Chini was 6 single and 2 double companies, in all about 1100 men, with 20 to 25 machine-guns, and over 100 Europeans.

The Germans were heard to sound the charge on their bugles. Immediately afterwards the two 1st Battalion companies were almost enveloped. There is little doubt that the Germans were not in the least aware of the fact, when they first commenced the attack, that two battalions were blocking their main line of retreat. They attacked under the impression that they were opposing a reconnaissance-in-force, consisting of one or two companies. They had been warned early on the 22nd that a force of this strength was in the neighbourhood by the small action of that morning, when their picquet had been driven in. The two 1st Battalion companies fixed bayonets and met the German charge with a heavy burst of fire. The German onslaught was in this way momentarily checked, but these two companies were practically surrounded. A most one-sided fight now ensued. The two Nigerian companies were attacked on all sides by a numerically much stronger force, but for all that they held their own most gallantly, and gradually fell back upon the main Nigerian position. This action of these two isolated companies was one of the finest pieces of fighting that ever occurred in the Brigade throughout the whole of the campaign. Every man fought like a Trojan, the most perfect discipline being maintained throughout the action. They eventually regained their original position in the line, but not before they had suffered very heavy casualties. The attack upon these companies commenced at 1 p.m. The first attack upon the main perimeter was delivered against the 1st Battalion from the east, and gradually worked round to No. 7 Company on the west.

No. 8 Company of the 2nd Battalion, under the command of Capt. Fowle, was very heavily engaged within half an hour of the commencement of the fight, and as their left was in the air, Capt. Gardner, commanding No. 5 Company, then in reserve, was asked to prolong No. 8 Company's line to the left with half a company. In the meantime the O.C. 2nd Battalion, realizing the danger of having the south face of the perimeter left open and unguarded by troops, had ordered half No. 5 Company, with one machine-gun and one Lewis gun, under Lieut. Studley, to move to position *B* on the diagram sketch, and there dig in facing south. No sooner was this completed than Lieut. Studley received orders to move up to Capt. Fowle's left, marked in the diagram (see maps) as *D,* so once again the south face was left with an ugly gap in it.

By 3 p.m. the Germans were attacking furiously from the north, north-west, and east, and had commenced to feel round the other sides of the perimeter for a weak place. At 3.30 p.m. Sergt. Maifundi Shua, the native sergeant commanding No. 3 section of No. 5 Company, seeing a small party of the enemy, under two German Europeans, actually in the act of feeling for a weak spot in the perimeter, ordered his section to charge with fixed bayonets. In this charge the gallant native was severely wounded, but not before he had buried his bayonet a foot deep in one of the Europeans. This sergeant had several times before showed the greatest devotion to duty. The Military Medal which he received after this battle was most deservedly won.

By 4 p.m. the enemy completely encircled the Nigerians and were attacking from the south with the greatest determination, having very rightly decided this to be the weak side of the perimeter. This attack was supported by three machine-guns, the firing of which was chiefly directed upon a big white tree at D.

Just before the attack had developed Lieut. Studley was once again moved. This time he was ordered to bring a machine-gun and one section to D, and there deploy in the open, no trenches having been dug in this part of the line. Capt. Gardner brought his remaining half company from A to the trenches lately dug by Lieut. Studley at B. Thus the whole of No. 5 Company, with the exception of one section still at C, now faced south. (See maps)

The Germans kept on reinforcing the troops attacking the south face of the perimeter, where without doubt they hoped to break through, but they were just too late to accomplish this, for No. 5 Company, having got into position in the nick of time, were prepared to resist the attack. The enemy, at last finding it impossible to break through, contented themselves with keeping up a terribly heavy fire against the troops lying in the open near tree D. This tree offered a splendid aiming mark for the enemy, who with *combined sights* searched to the right and left of this mark. The casualties to No. 5 Company were now thirty-three, of which one European was killed and another wounded. These casualties mostly occurred in one hour's fighting. Simultaneously with the attack on No. 5 Company, No. 6 was also heavily engaged near the big tree F by a German force operating from the south-east. This company also suffered heavily, receiving eighteen casualties in less than half an hour. (See maps)

The Germans pressed their attack with the greatest bravery, not seeming to trouble what casualties they incurred, but the Nigerian troops never moved from their position. It was by far the heaviest firing any Nigerians had ever been called upon to face up to date; further, it was their first experience of this kind of fighting.

At one time matters began to look pretty bad, as ammunition was rapidly running short. At the end of the fight about twenty-five rounds per man was all that was left, all reserves having been used up.

The enemy seemed to have unlimited ammunition, and a preponderance of machine-guns, which they worked with the greatest skill, moving up to within 60 yards of the Nigerians' perimeter in some places. However, their shooting was very high, or the Nigerian casualties would have been far heavier. One great lesson was driven home to the Nigerians in this action, and that was the great danger of depending on lying trenches; a very large proportion of casualties were caused by reverse fire. At Bweho-Chini everyone made up their mind that in future kneeling trenches would always be dug, with a high parados to stop reverse fire. The fighting continued with varying intensity up to 8 p.m. During this time the German bugles were constantly heard sounding the rally and charge. At 8 p.m. there was a lull in the fighting, lasting up till 9.15 p.m.

The defenders took the opportunity offered them by the lull to improve their defences. Many of the local carriers, as usual, had bolted during the day, preferring the chance of getting shot when leaving the perimeter to carrying ammunition from the quartermaster's dumps to the different parts of the firing line. Those carriers that remained in the perimeter were now collected and placed under cover. The dressing station, marked *E* on the sketch, had suffered badly during the day, being in a very exposed position, and so an attempt was made, under cover of darkness, to improve the cover around it.

At 9.15 p.m. the enemy recommenced their attack. This night attack continued till 11.50 p.m. At first they had the dim light of a young moon to guide them, though later the opposing sides fought in inky darkness, but the sting had gone out of the attack. The enemy's Askaris, primed with raw alcohol, and fighting with immense dash and determination, began to falter, though unceasingly urged to the attack by their European N.C.O.s, many of whom were seen flogging them unmercifully with *sjamboks* and rifle butts. By midnight the firing had died down, and the enemy withdrew the remnants of his force, and contented himself for the rest of the night with a certain amount of sniping, while the Nigerian listening posts could clearly hear the enemy busily engaged in removing their wounded and burying their dead. The dawn broke without any further attack being made; the enemy having failed in his attempt to break through, now found themselves threatened in the rear by Gen. Hannyngton's columns. They therefore split up into two small parties, abandoned considerable quantities of stores and ammunition, and made the best of their way south to Nahungu, which place lay on their previously-arranged line of retreat. On the night of the 22nd-23rd September, Lieut. Trengrouse of the 4th Battalion had tried to get through to the 1st and 2nd Battalions from Luale with medical stores and a detachment of the 300th Field Ambulance, but to his surprise, on approaching Bweho-Kati he found a German camp on the road, which put an end to his attempt to get there. A wire linesman was sent out the same evening to repair the telegraph line to Bweho-Chini. He found the place where the Germans had cut the wire, and repaired it, only to find it was cut at some other place as well. He attempted to find the second break when he came upon a German patrol. He was pursued half the night before he finally got clear away.

Unfortunately, as only too often happens in East Africa, the German troops had not behaved well. It is true that most of the Askaris were excited with drink, as water bottles picked up after the fight contained strong liquor. This might account for a certain amount of their barbarism, but the Europeans should have tried to hold the natives in check. The following quotation is from the *Cape Times* of 2nd March 1918:

> Reuter's agent learns that Gen. Sir Jacobus van Deventer, commanding in East Africa, has officially brought to the knowledge of the German Ex-Governor the following outrages committed by German troops: After the fight at Bweho-Chini on 22nd September, when the ground on which they had been fighting, and which had been occupied by German troops, was regained by our troops, the bodies of two officers who had been left on the ground wounded, and had so fallen into the hands of the German troops, were found stripped, and there could be no doubt that these two officers had been murdered. The original wounds which disabled these officers were in one case in the arm and in the other in the leg. When their bodies were found the head in one case had been smashed by a blow

with some blunt instrument, and in the other a rifle had been fired through the neck with the muzzle almost touching. There could be no doubt whatever that in these cases the officers had been foully murdered by German troops.

Both the officers referred to above belonged to the two companies of the 1st Battalion that had had to fight their way back to the perimeter early in the fight of Bweho-Chini. However, this most regrettable incident is only typical of the general behaviour meted out to British troops, if unfortunate enough to fall into German hands. In this action sixteen German Europeans and eighty-seven Askaris were actually buried by the British, whilst three Europeans and three Askaris were taken prisoners. After a fight with German troops, either in East Africa or the Cameroons, it was most unusual to find any dead German Askaris, still less was one likely to find any Europeans left behind on the battle ground, as it was a point of honour with them to always remove their own dead. The fact of finding so many dead at Bweho-Chini proves that their losses there must have been most severe. From later information it was estimated that the Germans lost about forty Europeans killed, wounded and prisoners, and at least three hundred native rank and file casualties.

The 1st and 2nd Nigeria Regiments' casualties were 10 Europeans, and 124 rank and file killed, wounded, and missing. The officers killed in this action were Capt. Higgins, Lieuts. Jose, Stephenson, and Oliver.

The Commander-in-Chief granted the following awards in the field for this action: Lieut.-Col. Uniacke, commanding the 2nd Nigeria Regiment, the D.S.O.; Capt. Gardner, 2nd Nigeria Regiment, a bar to his Military Cross; Capts. Waters and Burney and Lieut. Studley, the Military Cross; Sergts. Tanti and Badger, the D.C.M., and four native rank and file were awarded the Military Medal. This long list of awards will show the reader what great importance was put upon the action by the General Headquarters Staff.

This battle of Bweho-Chini finally established the name of the Nigeria Regiment in East Africa as being a first-class fighting unit. A wounded German officer in one of our hospitals once said to a British officer in the next bed: "We Germans don't mind —— Regiment in the least, but we respect the men who wear green caps, and we take no liberties with them." Both the Nigeria Regiment and the Gold Coast Regiment wear green caps. One's enemies should be the best judge of these matters. During the long battle of Bweho-Chini everyone from the General downwards took an active part with rifle and entrenching tool. The men had fought magnificently throughout this day with a coolness beyond praise. Scarcity of ammunition, and urgent need of food and water, rendered pursuit impossible. Further, there were insufficient porters remaining with these battalions even to carry away the wounded, let alone the supplies that would be required to continue the advance. A number of German stragglers were, however, rounded up by patrols, while the remainder of the force were engaged in burying the dead. All the British were buried at the spot marked *cemetery* in the sketch.

On the 24th September a King's African Rifle patrol from one of the main columns gained touch with a Nigerian patrol, and telegraphic communication was re-established. Later in the day it was found possible to evacuate the wounded via Mawerenye, which had by that time been occupied by the Gold Coast Regiment.

Having buried the dead, evacuated the wounded, and destroyed such captured enemy ammunition and stores as could not be removed, the column moved to Bweho Ju on the evening of the 24th. The remainder of the Brigade moved to this place direct from Luale on the same day, having cut a motor track through the bush as they advanced

The Battle of Nahungu

Early on the 25th September Lieut. Stobart, the Nigerians' Intelligence Officer, had gone out in order to investigate the water supply at Nakin river, eight miles south of Bweho Ju. He, however, was unable to carry out his personal reconnaissance, as the water holes were in the hands of the enemy. He was fired upon by a German patrol, but was fortunate to be able to get away with no more serious a loss than one of his Indian escorts having his horse shot down under him.

At 11 a.m. Lieut.-Col. Sargent left Bweho Ju in command of the 1st and 4th Nigeria Regiments, in order to clear up the situation and take the water holes. By the evening two companies of the 4th Battalion were within three miles of the objective. On the 26th the advance was continued to the water holes, the vanguard meeting with slight resistance. The enemy, who were, as far as could be judged, only three Europeans and twelve Askaris in number, retired after firing about twenty rounds at the *point*. There were no casualties.

The 1st and 4th Battalions camped at the Nakin stream for the night 26th-27th. The advance had been slow; at no time had it exceeded more than a mile an hour. This was due to the very dense nature of the bush and to the large number of *nullahs* which had to be crossed. Gen. Hannyngton's force was heard to be in action early on the 26th, away to the left of Col. Sargent's column. During this day half the Nigerian Battery reinforced Col. Sargent.

The 27th September was the day ordered for the attack on the enemy's position at Nahungu. The attack was carried out by three columns. Gen. Cunliffe with the 2nd Nigeria Regiment, Col. Freith's battalion of the King's African Rifles, the Nigerian Pioneers, and the Nigerian Brigade Headquarters formed the right column. One company of the 127th Baluchis later joined this column. The 1st and 4th Nigeria Regiments, and one section of the Nigerian Battery, under Col. Sargent, formed the centre column. The Gold Coast Regiment, a battalion of King's African Rifles, a section of Indian Mountain Battery, and a section of Stokes guns, commanded by Col. Orr, formed the left column.

All three columns were to attack simultaneously Nahungu Hill, where the enemy had taken up a strong position. The advance was carried out on three converging roads, commencing early on the morning of the the 27th.

Col. Orr met with the greatest resistance, whilst the right was allowed to advance without much opposition At 3 p.m.

Col. Orr met the enemy in strength, and a sharp engagement was fought, but Col. Freith's battalion, reinforced later by the 2nd Nigeria Regiment on the right, had by this time made themselves felt, with the result that the enemy on the left slowly fell back. By 2 p.m. all three columns were in touch with each other, and were approaching the objective. The action now became general all along the British front, the enemy slowly falling back on to their prepared entrenched position on Nahungu Hill, from which they brought into action two guns against Col. Orr's column. One of these guns the Indian Mountain Battery put out of action by obtaining a direct hit upon its emplacement. The Nigerian Battery was able to do some useful work against the enemy's position at a range of 2500 yards. Though the German position was strong, it was liable to suffer from artillery fire, as it was on a very defined hill.

At about 6.30 p.m. the enemy delivered a strong counter-attack against Col. Orr, but the Gold Coast Regiment after a stubborn fight drove them back. The action continued all along the front till 8 p.m., when the firing died down, but up to 2.30 a.m. on the 28th the Germans still kept up an intermittent fire.

The Germans, feeling that they were being opposed by a strong force, and fearing for the safety of their line of communication, retired from Nahungu during the night of the 27th-28th, leaving behind them a field ambulance containing a number of European and native wounded.

The British casualties in this engagement were inconsiderable. The enemy, who were evidently shaken by the rapidity of our advance, and the severe handling they had previously received at Bweho-Chini, fell back without putting up a determined fight.

British reinforcements came up on the 28th, consisting of four Indian regiments, three battalions of King's African Rifles, and the 25th Indian Cavalry. The whole of the Kilwa force was now assembled at Nahungu. The supply arrangements here were wonderfully carried out. Within six hours of the enemy retiring a great dump had commenced to grow, supplies being brought up via Luale by hundreds of motors. The feeding of such a large force so far from the base was only overcome by means of unlimited motor transport, for the use of which the 4th Battalion and the Nigerian Pioneers had cut a wide track through the bush almost as fast as the columns had advanced. The staff work generally was exceptionally good in the Kilwa area.

During the previous ten days the whole of the Kilwa area had been cleared of the enemy, whose forces, with the exceptions of those in the Mahenge district, were now all confined to the country south of Mbenkuru river, which comprised what was known as the Lindi area. The approach to Lindi itself was best by sea via Kilwa, owing to the mountainous district that separated the Kilwa and Lindi areas from each other.

From the 29th September to the 2nd October the Nigerian Brigade rested at Nahungu. Whilst here the Brigade received the good news that Naumann had given himself up with 14 Europeans and 150 Askaris. We were all glad to hear that Naumann was now at an end. His capture had been effected by Col. Breytenbach's South African Horse and the Cape Corps, under Lieut.-Col. Morris, D.S.O. There were still a few German patrols actively employed in the neighbourhood of Nahungu, for on the 1st October the main wire back to Kilwa was twice cut by raiding parties. On this day six hundred loads of food stuffs, abandoned by the enemy near Nahungu, were brought into camp by a party of Nigerians.

On the 2nd October a big draft of Europeans and native rank and file arrived for the Nigerian Brigade; also a large number of South African machine-gunners were posted to the various battalions of the Nigerians, having not long arrived from South Africa for that purpose. The rank and file that joined us were all recruits, and were to be used in the forthcoming advance to the Lindi area as additional carriers, and as such did some very useful work in the big and final offensive. The following general description of the situation was published by the General Headquarters on the 1st October:

Lindi Area: Linforce has pushed the enemy to within a few miles of the Mtama.

The Kilwa Area: Hanforce (Gen. Hannyngton's two columns) are now 10 miles west of Nahungu. They are expected at Nangano about the 10th October. A general reserve of about a thousand men and two guns are being kept at Nahungu for the present.

The Nigerian Brigade is to be sent to strengthen the Lindi force, as determined resistance is anticipated on the Lindi-Massassi fine. They should arrive at Nyangao about the 10th October, when the advance towards Massassi will be vigorously pressed. A Belgian battalion and the Faridhkot Sappers and Miners are *en route* to Mssindyi, their object being to open a motor road towards Liwale.

The Western Area: Shorthose is holding his own at Tunduru. Murray is expected shortly at Abdualla-Kwa-Nangwa, and in conjunction with the Nangano force, will block the enemy's retreat southwards from Mahenge and Liwale areas.

Mahenge: Faire is pushing on to Saidi to co-operate in the Mahenge operations and prevent the enemy breaking westwards. Hawthorne is operating against Otto, and will co-operate in the Mahenge operations. In the event of the enemy breaking southwards he will pursue him, keeping to the west of the Belgians. The mutual object of the Belgian and British forces is to break up the enemy's opposition in the western areas. Speed is of the utmost importance.

Chapter 11
The March to the Lindi Area

On the 3rd October the march south commenced. The Nigerian Brigade had been taken over by Lieut.-Col. Mann, D.S.O., owing to Gen. Cunliffe having been put upon the sick list. It consisted of the 1st, 2nd, and 4th Battalions of the Nigeria Regiment, the Gambia Company, Pioneer section, the Stokes gun section, a Wireless section, Signal section, 300th Field Ambulance, a section of the West African Field Ambulance, and supply and ammunition columns. Major Pretorius, who knew the country well, was attached to the column in the capacity of Chief Intelligence Officer and Guide.

The actual distance from Nahungu to the nearest point occupied by the Lindi force (always known by the abbreviation of Linforce), was about 80 miles in a direct line over the hills. The main difficulty was the scarcity of water along the road, and the fact that rations must be taken with the Brigade for eight days, the whole necessitating a very large number of carriers who would greatly add to the already unwieldy length of the column, which apart from the supply transport numbered several thousand men. This difficulty was partly overcome by the substitution of several thousand donkeys for a large number of carriers. These, though partly obviating the difficulty, greatly increased the water problem and decreased the pace of the march by nearly half.

On the 3rd October the 4th Nigeria Regiment and Pioneer section left Nahungu for Mhulu—a small village 9 miles distant, which was to be the motor road terminus. From here to the south everything would have to be carried on donkeys or carriers. On the 4th the 4th Nigeria Regiment moved forward, leaving behind them the Pioneer section to improve the water supply for the Brigade by digging extra water holes. Thus at the very first halting place troubles began. The 4th Battalion marched 7 miles to Lihero, where it was joined by the rest of the Brigade on the 5th. On the 6th October the march was continued to Nahanga, a distance of 14 miles through a waterless track of bush. The information received this day was that the enemy had a post at Mtshinyiri, which had lately been reinforced, and another post at Mtete, 12 miles southwards of Nahanga. It must be clearly understood that during this march all contact with the enemy was to be avoided if possible, for the double reason of speed and secrecy. It was therefore decided that the march south would be continued via Tschipwadwa to the Nyengedi stream, and thus escape all German posts. A wireless message received on the 6th stated that the Lindi offensive would recommence on the 8th inst., and that the turning move from the south would synchronize with the move from the north. On 7th October the Brigade marched to Narumbego. The advance guard left Nahanga at 5 a.m. The distance was only 8 miles, but owing to the local guide leading the Brigade wrong, the distance was greatly increased. The direct road was due south, but the advance guard moved out due east, and by a circular route arrived at its destination at 3.30 p.m. The rearguard did not arrive in till sunset. The country passed through was very undulating and hilly. The Tschipwadwa river rises in these hills and runs through a deep valley for the first few miles of its course. The path leading into Narumbego followed the stream from its source for about 4 miles. Owing to the undulating nature of the road, the march was most trying, and resulted in five Europeans and many natives becoming *hors de combat*.

The hills were densely covered with bush and long grass, which added greatly to the difficulties of the advance guard commander, who was forced to proceed with the greatest caution. From Narumbego an intelligence officer was sent out to Waholo and another to Mtete to watch the enemy's movements, and if possible, in the latter case, capture the post, which was reported to be quite small. Narumbego lay at the bottom of a deep valley, the sides of which were nearly precipitous. The main body of the column camped in the deep valley—a strong line of outposts holding the ground on each side. If the previous day had been hard, it had been a holiday compared with the 8th. On this day the advance guard left the valley of the Tschipwadwa river at 4 a.m. After an hour's hard climbing they reached the plateau to the south. The distance to the Mirola stream was only 13½ miles, yet the advance guard did not arrive in till late in the afternoon, whilst the ammunition column was still coming in at 1 a.m. on the 9th. Owing to the difficulty of getting the donkeys up the very steep hills, the donkey supply column did not reach their destination till well after daylight on the 9th, and even then five hundred carriers had to be sent back to help in the donkeys by carrying their loads for them. Numerous donkeys had died on the way, and a number of Europeans and natives fell out on the road owing to the heat and the length of the march.

In the early part of the day heavy gunfire was heard far away to the south-east; this being the first fighting heard by us in the Lindi area. The intelligence patrol that had been sent out from Nahanga succeeded this day in rushing and capturing three German Europeans at Mtete. They evidently had no idea that troops were in the neighbourhood, so great was their surprise when they were brought in as prisoners to see this huge column winding its way through the hills.

Not till 10 a.m. on the 9th did the rearguard eventually arrive from Mirola river, having been twenty-eight hours on the road. The road between Nahanga and the Mirola river is simply a native bush track, along which it was quite impossible to proceed in any other formation than single file. Although Intelligence patrols were out in front and on the right flank of the column, it was necessary to be continually on the alert, as the enemy were within easy striking distance. As this long unwieldy column of men, carriers, and donkeys slowly wended its way through this most difficult and hilly bush country, it offered a most vulnerable object for a German raiding party; hence every military precaution had to be taken at all times.

The length of the column was by this time greatly increased by the number of stretcher cases that had to be carried up and down this terrible country. Europeans and natives were beginning to go sick at an alarming pace, due to the heat and fatigue. Knowing the Germans as well as we did, it was quite out of the question to leave the sick behind to the tender mercies of a wandering party of the enemy's Askaris, as they often did with their own sick.

On the 9th, whilst the column was still at the Mirola river, a British aeroplane managed to locate us, and dropped a message to the effect that the Nigerians were now under orders of Brig.-Gen. Beves. At 10 a.m. a wireless message was received from Gen. Beves, ordering the column to proceed to Mahiwa via Mpembe and Mtshinyiri. The message stated that the column was to live on the country, and no longer be dependent upon a supply train. Col. Mann, in answering this message, pointed out the present condition of affairs in the Brigade, and added that the Intelligence Officer, Major Preforms, had pronounced this route quite impossible, owing to the scarcity of water along it.

The column halted by the Mirola river during the night, and very glad were all ranks for the rest. Sounds of heavy firing were heard from time to time during the day, which turned out to be Linforce approaching Mtama. Early on the morning of the 10th a wireless message was received from Gen. Beves, in which he stated that he quite realized the difficulties and he therefore cancelled his orders of the previous day. However, he directed that every possible effort was to be made to arrive at Mahiwa in rear of the main enemy's forces operating in the Lindi area. The ration situation was now becoming acute, and it had become more and more urgently necessary to gain early touch with the main Lindi forces. The whole country in front was reported to be as bare of food as that we had already passed through. There was, therefore, no chance of obtaining food locally for so large a force. The march was continued at 5.30 a.m. on the 10th. Tshitishiti stream was reached at 4 p.m. It had taken ten and a half hours to complete the 13-mile march. This march was nearly as trying as that of the 8th. The ammunition and supply donkeys did not arrive in before midnight, and the rearguard did not arrive in till the following morning. The length of the march in a direct line was not 5 miles, and at places the head and tail of this great column were almost doubled round into a circle, so that there was only a comparatively short distance of almost impassable hills separating them. The actual number of miles, however, marched could not have been less than 15 miles owing to the configuration of the country.

A wireless message received from Linforce stated that two days' rations would be sent out to the Nyengedi to arrive there by the evening of this day. From the Tshitishiti stream to the Nyengedi is 18 miles. It was, therefore, quite out of the question for the column, in its present state of fatigue, to reach there in time to meet the convoy, and a wireless message to this effect was sent back to Gen. Beves early on the morning of the 11th. Two companies of the 2nd Battalion were sent forward to the Nyengedi with instructions to meet the supply column. In the Intelligence Report issued this day it was given out that von Lettow with twenty-six companies had concentrated between Nyangao and Massassi. Gen. Hannyngton's force was slowly pushing south to the Lukuledi river by the main road via Ruponda, which place had been evacuated by the enemy.

At 12.30 p.m. the column continued the march—the advance guard arriving at Rupiagine on the Rondo plateau at 3.30 p.m. The distance was only 5 miles, but owing to the hard going and steep climbing the baggage did not get in till 7.30 p.m., whilst the ammunition column did not arrive till after n p.m. Before this climb to the top of the Rondo plateau was commenced, all the donkeys had been sent back to the coast at Lindi via Lake Lutimba; also 130 loads of ammunition, for which there were no carriers. The remaining boxes of ammunition had been handed over to the supply porters, as all supplies had by this time been issued. The country for some days past had been quite impracticable for donkeys, which had throughout the whole march greatly delayed the column. On arriving at Rupiagine, after a very hot march, there was found to be no water, and to obtain it the men had to descend to the valley about 1200 feet below.

However, the wonderful view across the Lutimba lake, to a small degree, made up for the discomfort of this hot climb. After a day spent in the hot bush, it was a great relief to look down upon so fine a panorama, and feel the cool fresh air of a higher altitude. The Brigade crossed the Rondo plateau on the 12th, arriving about midday at the Nyengedi, where two days' rations were awaiting us, in charge of the two companies of the 2nd Battalion; but the 300 carriers that had brought these rations had been sent back in error. Telephonic communication was established with Gen. Beves's headquarters, and orders were received to move on as soon as possible. By this time all Europeans and natives were utterly done up, and rest was badly needed, but owing to Gen. Beves's orders this was quite impossible. Accordingly, orders were issued for all sick and as much baggage as possible, to be sent from the Nyengedi to Mtua. No less than 283 sick were thus evacuated, of which 11 Europeans and 38 natives were stretcher cases. Personal loads were cut down to one per European. The column had now been on the road for nine days, and was already two days late in arriving at Nyengedi, but no troops could have made a greater effort to get through up to time. The road, however, had been quite heartbreaking, and the number of sick that had to be evacuated will testify to the hardships the Brigade had gone through in these nine days.

On the 13th October the Nigerians left the Nyengedi at 1 p.m. for Ngedi on the Rondo plateau, arriving at this place, after a steep climb over a bad road, at 4.30 p.m. Again the rearguard was delayed by the bad condition of the road, and did not even leave the Nyengedi till after dusk, owing to the slow pace the carriers were forced to go when descending into the Nyengedi valley. Though it was late at night, and bitterly cold by the time the rearguard arrived in, the column was under orders to continue the march at 4.30 a.m. the following morning. The strength of the Nigerian battalions by this time had been greatly reduced, and the three battalions together did not muster much more than a thousand odd rifles. The enemy's force was known to be at least two thousand Askaris, with three or four hundred Europeans, and several guns. In addition to this it was known that von Lettow had with him a mobile force of about six hundred picked men, which at any time he could throw into any part of his front or flanks as reinforcements, or be able to use them as a striking force on the offensive, while further reserves of about six hundred rifles were known to be at Mahiwa. Mahiwa was the key to von Lettow's position, as it was his central food depot. Reports received from G.H.Q. by wireless stated that Mahiwa was only lightly held, but this did not agree with local reports. Major Pretorius' information indicated that that place was very strongly held, and, further, that von Lettow himself with his mobile force was rapidly marching to Mahiwa from the north-west, but none of this information was credited by Gen. Beves, who was most insistent as to the necessity of rapidity of movement, in order that the Nigerian advance should synchronize with the frontal advance of Linforce, which was timed to commence on the 15th October.

Small patrol engagements on the 12th and 13th were in themselves sufficient information to the Nigerian Headquarters that the enemy were well aware of our flank move, yet orders were received at the Rondo Plateau camp to send one battalion across the Lindi-Massassi road at Nyangao, and to attack Mahiwa itself with the remainder of the force at dawn on the 15th October.

The Nyangao river was reached by 8.30 a.m. on the 14th. At 12.30 p.m. the column left the river, reaching Namupa Mission at 4.30 p.m. There was a small patrol action *en route* that led to the capture of one European and the death of one Askari. Later eight Europeans were taken at the Mission by the advance guard, of which two were Greeks and the rest German non-combatants. Two of the enemy food-stores were captured *en route,* containing in one case fifty and in another seventy loads of grain.

The advance was continued at 5.30 p.m., but the wrong road was taken, resulting in the column having to return to the Mission and there dig themselves in for the night, as it was impossible in the dark to pick up the correct road to Mahiwa from amongst the many roads that led out from the Mission, like spokes from the hub of a wheel. The column this day had marched from 3 a.m. till 10 p.m., whilst the rearguard was on the road from 5.30 a.m. till 1 a.m. on the 15th. The heat during the day had been intense, so that both Europeans and natives were absolutely exhausted by the end of the day. To add to all this, the G.O.C. Linforce instructed the Column Headquarters to press on immediately. However, this was impossible, for the bush all round was thick, and the guides were not only terrified in the dark but also wilfully stupid, and in the inky darkness of the night it would have been out of the question to wind this long column out again so as to get it into any military formation. When at the Mission I think we all realized that something big was going to take place shortly. One could not help thinking of those few lines from Henry V. between Westmoreland, Exeter, and Salisbury: "Of fighting men they have three score thousand." "There is five to one; besides they all are fresh." "God's arm strike with us! It is a fearful odds."

An uncomfortable few hours' rest was now snatched by the hungry and blanket-less troops on the damp ground. As no supplies had arrived before dark had set in there was no food to issue to the men, thus the long march from Kilwa area ended as it had begun—in utter discomfort.

On almost every day of this march the supplies and baggage had arrived in hours after the arrival of the advance guard, thus the troops, scorched by the heat during the day, were frequently forced to suffer cold by night. Rations were usually short, and when obtainable often not good. Cooking after dark was usually impossible owing to the necessity of secrecy and the close proximity of the enemy; therefore no fires could be lit. The men were in consequence frequently forced to eat uncooked rice and cereals, or, what happened many times during this march, they poisoned themselves by eating uncooked Cassava.

The route from the Kilwa to the Lindi area will never be forgotten by those that had the misfortune to take part in it. For general discomfort it was only eclipsed by the Rufiji, and the months of semi-starvation passed through in that area.

CHAPTER 12

The Battle of Mahiwa

I stated in the last chapter that orders had been received by the G.O.C. Nigerian Brigade, to detach one battalion from the column and send it to Nyangao in order to block the road lying to the east of Mahiwa, by which it was thought that the enemy might try to retreat. The 1st Nigerians, the Gambia Company, and two Nigerian guns were detailed for this duty. They left early on the morning of the 15th October. The 2nd and 4th Nigerians, with the remaining half of the Nigerian Battery, together with the Stokes gun section and Brigade Headquarters, left at 5.30 a.m. in order to make the attack on Mahiwa. The advance guard consisted of two companies of the 4th Battalion and the Stokes gun section, under the command of Major Gibb. Almost as soon as the head of the column was clear of the Mission station, Capt. Maxwell, who was commanding the leading company, became engaged, but he managed to press back the enemy who were only a strong rearguard left to watch the road. The main body followed the advance guard at 7.30 a.m., and were in their turn followed an hour or so later by the wireless section and rearguard.

One company of the 1st Battalion and the pioneer section remained behind at the Mission with the Brigade baggage, reserve ammunition column, and ambulances. The position of affairs at dawn on the 15th October was therefore as follows: A column of Nigerians was advancing south on to Mahiwa, which place was situated on the main Lindi-Massassi road, and about 10 miles south-west of Mtama; another Nigerian Column was marching on to Nyangao, also on the Lindi-Massassi road in order to block the Nyangao-Namupa road. Nyangao was about 3 miles north-east of Mahiwa. Linforce, consisting of Columns 3 and 4, were operating against the enemy at Mtama; another force, consisting of Columns 1 and 2, was moving down upon Massassi from the north; cavalry patrols were already operating south and west of Mahiwa. The object of the G.O.C. Linforce was for the Nigerian Column to occupy and hold Mahiwa, which he maintained was very lightly held by the enemy, and so cut off the retreat of the enemy's forces retiring south from Mtama; as he so aptly put it, "The Nigerians were to be the cork in the bottle!" The Germans' retreat north-east was denied by the presence of 1st Battalion at Nyangao. As stated in the last chapter, the Acting Brigadier of the Nigerian Brigade had very different information as to the strength of the enemy at Mahiwa than that given to him by the Linforce Headquarters. He therefore held very different views as to the possibility of success in the part allotted to him. At 8.20 a.m. Col. Mann received a telephonic message from Gen. Beves ordering him to press on in spite of all opposition. About this time the advance guard was again held up, but Major Gibb, on receiving these orders, instructed Capt. Maxwell that he was to press forward in spite of receiving casualties, and that he must be prepared to take greater risks. From this time forward 15 Company was continually in touch with the enemy, engaging them with varying success till 11 a.m., at which time the *point* was approaching the Mahiwa river. Here 15 Company was finally held up, and by the volume of fire that was delivered against them it became certain that the enemy were here in strength, and no longer consisted of only a strong rearguard. A sharp fight ensued in which 15 Company suffered several casualties, including Sergt. Spratt, who was killed. 14 Company, and later half 16 Company, reinforced 15 Company, and three sides of a perimeter were formed, which was later strengthened by the addition of a company of the 2nd Battalion, which had been sent up to reinforce the 4th Battalion at 12.30 p.m. Kneeling and standing trenches were prepared, and the Nigerians waited developments.

At 4.15 p.m. Col. Mann decided to try to locate and turn the enemy's right flank, as he had again received orders from Gen. Beves that the advance must be pushed on. It was quite impossible to continue the march straight ahead, as Capt. Maxwell was right up against a strong force of the enemy, who were well entrenched. No. 16 Company, under the command of Capt. Hetley, was detailed for this duty, and moved out due east at 4.45 p.m. One of his sections was deployed so as to form a screen of scouts. Later the two flanks of this screen were strengthened, whilst the rest of the company moved in single file through the bush, with flank guards and a rearguard out. After marching in this formation for about one mile a path was met with which led towards the south. The screen was wheeled to the right, and the advance continued in a southerly direction. After proceeding with great caution for about half a mile, Lieut. Fox, who was in charge of the screen, reported that the enemy were in front. The screen was halted and was reinforced, so that a firing line was built up, whilst the left half of the company was ordered to deploy to the left and right of the path in a semi-circular formation, so as to be prepared for an attack from the front or either flanks. Whilst this movement was being executed the enemy opened fire from the front, followed almost immediately by heavy fire from the right and left front. At this stage Corporal Abdulai was killed. He had throughout the advance shown the most marked ability in working the men under his command in the screen, and had been the first scout to spot the enemy. Two Lewis guns and a section were hastily pushed up to reinforce the scouts, and the enemy's fire was returned. Within five minutes the company was being fired into from the left flank, and within ten minutes from the left rear. The two machine-guns, under Sergts. Element and Hervey, came into action facing left, and Lieut. Kellock, with one section, formed a firing line facing in this direction. At this sudden burst of heavy fire practically every un-enlisted carrier bolted, taking with them most of the reserve ammunition and entrenching tools. The company was now up against an overwhelming force, and was nearly surrounded. From the rapidity with which the enemy's fire had opened and increased in volume, it would appeal that 16 Company had met a very strong enemy's force that was probably in the very act of moving up to attack the Nigerian Brigade.

The enemy were checked by the hot fire that was kepi up by 16 Company, but soon the lack of reserve ammunition began to make itself felt. First the machine-guns had to be put out of action for lack of ammunition followed soon afterwards by the Lewis guns. A retirement became absolutely necessary. This movement was carried out by alternate sections, and was only rendered possible by the gallant behaviour of the Nigerian troops that were outnumbered by three or four to one. Sergts. Element, Hervey, and Trollop greatly assisted this withdrawal by the bold manner in which they handled the machine-guns and Lewis guns. Lieut. Mulholland and Sergts. Riley and Eley were hit early in the fight. Special mention should be made of the devotion to duty and gallantry shown by Company-Sergt.-Major Tukeru Bouchi and Sergt. Awudu Katsena. Both these native N.C.O.s, by holding their men in the most perfect control and putting up a fight that will always be remembered as being amongst the most brilliant achievements ever taken part in by Nigerian troops. As the sections retired, so the wounded were carried back, whilst old Tukeru Bouchi, by his personal example of indifference to danger, kept up the men's fighting spirit. A retirement of this kind, by sections, is always very difficult for native troops to carry out, as one section does not like to see another retiring whilst they themselves are left to stand the brunt of the fighting; they prefer to sink or swim all together. On this occasion, however, as soon as the troops understood what was required of them, they carried out this difficult manoeuvre with the utmost steadiness, and supported each other by properly sustained and directed volley firing. Twice overwhelming numbers of the enemy attempted to charge, but twice they were driven back with heavy casualties. The company had nearly completed the retirement when Lieut. Kellock was hit, and the faithful Tukeru Bouchi fell mortally wounded. Both were got away to the rear, but the gallant old sergeant-major died cursing the Hun two days later. In his death the

4th Battalion lost a most gallant man, who was clean white right through, except for his skin. The ammunition in the men's pouches was exhausted before the retreat was completed, so the machine-guns and Lewis guns, except one, were all sent to the rear. The few rounds left in the belt boxes and magazines were collected and distributed amongst a dozen men. These twelve men with the one remaining Lewis gun now formed the rearguard. This small party kept up a most determined rearguard action, whilst the wounded were collected. Poor Sergt. Riley was never found, so had to be left to the mercy of the enemy. He has never been heard of since. One by one the wounded and the ammunition and tool boxes were found and carried back. Lieut. Fox, who was in charge of this small rearguard, was hit when actually working the Lewis gun. This officer had throughout borne the brunt of the fighting and had acted with the greatest gallantry. The command now fell upon native Corporal Sali Bagirmi, to whom must be given much of the credit for the magnificent way in which this small rearguard fought and held a force at least ten times their own strength, and prevented them from breaking through on to the defenceless wounded and men without a round of ammunition between them. The casualties in 16 Company in this action were very heavy, being quite 40 per cent, of the total strength. Three officers were wounded, one British N.C.O. was missing and believed to be killed, and another British N.C.O. was wounded, whilst no less than fifty-eight rank and file were either killed or wounded, the proportion of killed to wounded being very high.

This company had behaved magnificently under the most trying circumstances, and notwithstanding their very heavy casualties, and the fact that most of the carriers had run away, 16 Company saved every machine-gun and Lewis gun and brought in all the wounded that could be found. That this company had walked right into a prepared position, held by a strong German force, and had managed to escape still a fighting unit, speaks excellently for their fighting qualities and to the personal leadership of their commander, Capt. Hetley, who for this action was awarded the Military Cross.

Simultaneously with 16 Company's action a most determined attack was delivered against the front and right of the Nigerian main position. This attack lasted for about one hour, but was repulsed at 6 p.m. The firing on both sides was extremely heavy. Half a company of the 2nd Battalion was sent out to cover Capt. Hetley's retirement, and eventually returned, having suffered only a few casualties.

At dusk the enemy recommenced their attack upon the right front corner of the Nigerian position, and a most determined fight on both sides ensued, the bulk of the fighting falling to the lot of half 14 Company. By 7.30 p.m. the enemy withdrew. The 4th Battalion casualties on this day were heavy, numbering about eighty of all ranks. The enemy had done their utmost to break through this battalion, and must have suffered very heavily in their attempts. Owing to the fact that the reserve ammunition column was still back at the Mission there was now a danger of the firing line running short. Further, no rations existed except those that were actually carried on the men, and a small amount of cooked rice that had come up from the Mission shortly before dusk. Owing mainly to these two reasons, it was decided to withdraw the advance guard, and dig in for the night in the position already held by the main body.

The withdrawal was carried out without further fighting. The night was quiet except for a few snipers. Up to dusk the telephone wire back to the Mission was intact, as a message was received by the Brigade Headquarters from the 1st Battalion, stating that they were also held up at Nyangao by a strong force of the enemy. The party that had brought up the cooked rice from the Mission were fired upon on their return journey. Thus ended the first day of the battle of Mahiwa, which was to turn out to be one of the biggest battles that has taken place on African soil.

At dawn on the 16th patrols were sent out in all directions, and reported that the enemy were in strength on the south-east and west of our position. Before daybreak the troops were busily employed in improving their defences, and standing trenches were dug all round the perimeter. Col. Mann received a wireless message early in the morning from Linforce, stating that von Lettow, with four companies and two field guns, was on his way to reinforce the troops engaged in attacking the Nigerian position.

Water parties were fired on soon after it was light, and were thus unable to get down to the Mahiwa river to obtain water. At 10 a.m. a telegram was written out ordering the 1st Battalion immediately to proceed back to the Namupa Mission, and from there reinforce the Brigade, but this wire was never dispatched, as the line had been cut during the night. The enemy, during the morning, contented themselves with holding the water supply with machine-guns. Desultory firing continued all round the perimeter throughout the morning. The two guns of the Nigerian Battery, which had been in action most of the afternoon of the 15th, had, together with the Stokes mortar, greatly helped to drive back the enemy's forces, but both the guns and mortars had used up much ammunition in so doing. It was now found that the enemy were across the road in rear, and that all touch with the Mission had been lost. This was most serious, as it put both the guns and mortar out of action for want of ammunition. Further, the heavy infantry fight of the 15th had used up much of the first-line reserve ammunition, and it was impossible to get up any more from the reserve ammunition column back at the Mission owing to this unexpected action of the enemy.

At 2.30 p.m. our real period of trial commenced, for at this time the enemy commenced to shell the Nigerian position. At first only a 4·1 naval gun put over an occasional round, all of which failed to do any damage, but at 3.30 p.m. a 70 mm. gun came into action from the high ground on our right at a comparatively short range. At first there was no great cause for alarm, as the enemy had failed to get the range correctly. The 4·1 continued to lob its projectile over the perimeter, the gun itself being so far away that there was time to light a cigarette between the sound of the first report reaching us and the arrival of the projectile. The 70 mm., however, was a very different proposition, and by 4 p.m. it began to get the range of the 4th Battalion trenches, most particularly the left of 14 Company's line, with most disastrous results. The troops were helpless as the small mountain guns of the Nigerian Battery were useless against this modern 70 mm. quick-firer, and besides, our guns had very few rounds of ammunition left. Though standing trenches had been dug, no elaborate preparation had been made against modern shell fire. To those who are used to a bombardment as known in France, this kind of bombardment by two guns may seem ridiculous, but it is all a matter of preparation. One well-directed modem gun, firing high-explosive shells at the rate of one round a minute, against troops who are not prepared for shell fire, who cannot change their position, and cannot reply to that gun, is as bad as a heavy bombardment for troops thoroughly prepared for shell fire, and are either under cover or can drop back to another line of trenches out of shell fire. I maintain that the latter are, if anything, the better off, for nothing can be worse for the morale of troops who were situated as the 4th Nigeria Regiment was on the 16th October. Again and again the 70 mm. shelled these unfortunate companies. A sector of 14 Company trenches at one time received three direct hits upon it in succession. There were no alternative trenches to retire to, and no safe "dug outs" to shelter in. Every direct hit found its human target; the trees above this trench were dripping blood for two days afterwards from limbs and trunks of men that had been blown up and been wedged between the branches. It was a most ghastly quarter of an hour. Nigerian troops, before this, had never been exposed to heavy shell fire either in the Cameroons or in East Africa. The casualties in 14 Company became so heavy that the bombardment at last began to tell upon the morale of the men, and it became evident that it would be madness to attempt to keep this company in these trenches exposed, as they were, to certain death. Col. Sargent ordered the withdrawal of this company to a position 100 yards in rear of their trenches. Here the sections were reformed, and the men made to lie down whilst everyone awaited the orders to return to the firing line. Sergt. Evans was killed during this bombardment, together with a large number of the men of 14 Company, whilst the whole of this part of the line was littered with broken and wounded men trying to crawl back to the dressing station.

Fourteen Company had only retired a few minutes from the firing line when the bombardment suddenly stopped, and was followed immediately by a determined infantry attack. This was quite expected. The company commander of 14 Company half expected trouble, as he knew that his company had had more than enough to shake their morale, so he called upon all the Europeans to get back to the firing line, and carry forward with them the machine-guns and Lewis guns of the company. Capt. Norton-Harper, who was at the time battalion signalling officer, was amongst the first to respond, only to be killed by a fragment of shell a short while later. Lieut. Crowe, Sergts. Hunt and Stamp carried the guns back to the firing line themselves, and immediately opened fire upon the rapidly approaching enemy's infantry. When I personally arrived back at the trench, I found that the machine-gun carrier, Awudu Katsena, had already arrived back at the trench, and was sitting up cross-legged on top of the parapet, giving the advancing enemy rapid fire with my own private ·333 Jeffreys rifle. This machine-gun carrier, the reader will probably remember, has already been mentioned in this narrative in connection with the fighting on the 24th January, for which he earned the Military Medal. He is one of the most plucky men it has been my good fortune to meet; though he is little more than a boy in years, he does not know the meaning of the word *fear*. He promises to be another Belo Akure or Tukuru Bouchi. Always laughing and cheerful; always the first to be in a place of danger; loyal to the finger tips, Awudu Katsena is a man who sets an example to both black and white alike of what a soldier should be.

The men of 14 Company, seeing the Europeans running back to the firing line, immediately competed against each other to be back first at their respective posts in the trench. In five minutes from the time that the order had been given to return to the trench to repel the infantry attack, every mother's son that could walk was in his place. Many of the men had been wounded by the bombardment, but if they could walk and use their rifles they had, on their own account, returned to the trench, never knowing that the shell fire would not at any moment recommence. Many of these men had already been ordered to report themselves at the dressing station. The indomitable loyalty and pluck of the men of this company should be handed down to generations yet to be in Nigeria as an example of what the true Nigerian soldier is made of. It is too horrible to contemplate what would have been the fate of the 2nd and 4th Battalions, not to mention the wretched and defenceless wounded, if this company had not returned to its position in the line, but had left the gap open for the enemy to pour into the perimeter. The line was so formed that it would have been impossible for 15 and 16 Companies to have stopped the enemy by means of cross fire.

The Germans in this infantry attack, delivered at 4.30 p.m., must have suffered most heavily. Confident that their guns had so shaken the 4th Battalion, they came on in close formation against 14 and 15 Companies, and must have been mown down by machine-gun and rifle fire. The spirit of the men in these two companies was wonderful. They seemed to revel in the excitement. I have never before, or since, seen the men with their tails so up as they were immediately after the commencement of the German infantry attack. They sang and shouted war cries, whilst one or two men—foolishly I know—stood on the perimeter and danced, shaking their rifles above their heads at the already hesitating enemy. It was a sight for the gods, and one never to be forgotten by those who saw it. The Germans came to within 150 yards of the Nigerian trench at the double, then they began to hesitate, then to halt, and then turn round, and were last seen running like *long dogs*. By this I do not mean to infer that the enemy were wanting in courage, for they had already achieved wonders by getting up to within 100 yards of the Nigerians in the face of so deadly a fire. But they found themselves opposed to troops that were as good as themselves, and they had taken on the impossible. To advance further would have meant for them destruction and victory for the Nigerians. I take off my hat to one German European. He was foolhardy, but he was what the Americans would call *some man*. He, riding on a grey horse, personally led his men to the attack, and when they checked, he rode up and down their front encouraging them to continue the advance. In this way he got within 150 yards of 15 Company before he disappeared, never, I should think, to lead his troops on this earth again, for no less than two machine-guns and two score of rifles were aimed at him. In less than an hour the enemy retired in silence, and their great effort to break through was doomed to utter failure. During the attack the 70 mm. put two or three high explosive shells into the 4th Battalion's front, which had, before the end of the German attack, been reinforced by a section of the 2nd Battalion. One of these shells was responsible for Capt. Norton-Harper's end, whilst the 2nd Battalion's section and 14 and 15 Companies all suffered casualties from this gun during the attack. Many machine-guns and Lewis guns had been put out of action this day by shell fire, especially in 14 and 15 Companies.

At the same time, whilst this fierce fight had been going on, very heavy firing had been heard from the Mission side of the perimeter, which everyone correctly judged to be the 1st Battalion in action. I will therefore in another chapter give in detail all that occurred to this battalion after it parted company from the rest of the Brigade on the 15th October.

The 2nd and 4th Battalions had repulsed the enemy's onslaughts, but at a heavy price to themselves. Casualties had been most heavy, but, what was worse, the ammunition was rapidly giving out. Everyone was banking upon the timely arrival of Major Roberts' column, consisting of the 1st Battalion and the Gambia Company, and the night of the 16th still found us trusting in relief from this quarter, little knowing that Major Roberts had met with a reverse, and had been forced to retire. Just before dusk the enemy again made a half-hearted attempt to break through the Nigerian perimeter on the 14 and 15 Company face, but they met with no better results than in their first big attack. A curious thing happened in this action. It was passed round the 4th Battalion that the 1st Nigerians were approaching, and would come into the perimeter from the west. No one has ever learnt the origin of this message, but I strongly suspect the Germans themselves of having got this message passed round. The result was that 14 Company lost a golden opportunity of catching a large party of the enemy at close range out in the open, but in the bad light it was impossible to see whether they were friend or foe, and as the 1st Battalion were expected, orders had been given not to fire unless one was certain at whom one was firing. As this party of men did not come straight forward, but were seen dodging about in the bush, one's suspicions were aroused. At last it was certain that they were enemy, but by this time it was almost too late to do them any serious damage. Rapid fire was again opened, and a section of 14 Company charged the place where the enemy had last been seen, but with no good results, as they had already scattered. The night of the 16th-17th October was quiet, but great excitement was caused by the enemy fighting hundreds of small fires about 1000 yards away to the south, so that they resembled a long and well-lighted street in a civilized country. No one has ever learnt what the wily Boche was doing, but, as it seemed so self-evident that they wished us to fire at them, we restrained ourselves, and the peace of the night was not disturbed. Thus the weary soldiers lay down and rested as they were in the trenches. Everyone was hungry, as rations had long run out. Ammunition was very short. All the officers knew that if help was not forthcoming soon and the Germans gave us another day like the one just passed through, all would be up with us. No one knew what the next hour would bring forth, but luckily native soldiers do not look far ahead. "Sufficient unto the day is the evil thereof" is a very true motto for the Hausa soldier. The following few fines from *Punch* describe the feelings of all of us on the night of the 16th-17th October:

> Soldier, what of the night?
> Vainly you question me;
> I know not, I hear not, nor see.
> The voice of the prophet is dumb
> Here in the heart of the fight;
> I count not the hours on their way,
> I know not when morning shall come;
> Enough that I work for the day.

The 16th October was the most disastrous day to the Nigerians since the formation of the force, the 1st and 4th Nigeria

Regiments and the Gambia Company having suffered between them three hundred casualties in one day, not to mention the loss of a gun, described in the next chapter, and a number of machine-guns put out of action. The 2nd Battalion entirely escaped, and most curiously only suffered ten casualties during the whole of the two days' fighting. A patrol sent out early on the morning of the 17th reported that the Nigerians were surrounded except on the east, and that the enemy were entrenched. No news could be got from the 1st Battalion. The men had had no food, except half a pound of rice each, since the 14th October, and as already stated, ammunition was running very short. The G.O.C. Linforce asked by wireless if the column could retire on to Namupa Mission. He was informed that to do so would mean instant attack by a very strong enemy's force that was waiting for this on every side. Further, the column was handicapped by having a very large number of stretcher cases to evacuate, which in themselves would form a column nearly 1000 yards long. To quote from a diary written at the time: "The early part of the day was most depressing. We (the 2nd and 4th Nigeria Regiments) find ourselves literally besieged; ammunition is very scarce, and the men have eaten their emergency ration. To add to all these troubles, the enemy have got a machine-gun and snipers posted along the water, so that our men are continuously getting hit whilst trying to obtain water. As our trenches are dug in sand, more or less out in the open, the heat in them is terrific, and the men are willing to risk anything in order to quench their thirst. No news of the 1st Battalion, and as far as our Brigade Headquarters know, our convoy is entirely in the air; there is no news of any reinforcements or of a relieving column. At 10 a.m. we received news that the 1st Battalion and Gambia Company met with reverse yesterday in trying to break through to relieve us. In this attempt it is rumoured that they lost two hundred casualties and one of the battery guns. News is also received that our cavalry have suffered a severe reverse. These reports, on top of a lack of sleep and food, have not helped to raise our spirits. Matters are extremely critical, and if we are not relieved shortly we shall meet with disaster." This quotation will give my reader a very good idea of how matters stood on the morning of the 17th October. Everyone was asking, "Where can Beves's force be? Why have we not heard his guns at all during the past two days?" Our questions were answered at 10.30 a.m., when heavy firing could be heard away to the south-east. What a relief to all of us whose nerves had been stretched almost to breaking-point during the last forty-eight hours! By the volume of fire one could judge that there was a big battle in progress, which lasted throughout the whole day, getting nearer to us every hour. In spite of the approach of General O'Grady's Column, the enemy never left us alone, but kept up a steady machine-gun fire, continuously sniping our water parties. It was impossible to reply to this fire owing to the shortage of ammunition, and, for the same reason, out of the question for us to make a sortie from the perimeter and help O'Grady, by falling upon the rear of the troops opposing him. At 4 p.m. our wireless aerial was cut away by a bullet, so that we were entirely cut off from the rest of the world. At 4.30 p.m. the fighting on the south-east became much nearer, so that our hopes were raised as we saw a possibility of our getting out of the awkward position in which we had been landed. Patrols from the 2nd Battalion under officers were now sent out to try and get in touch with the 1st Nigerians and No. 3 Column.

On the 17th the 3rd Battalion arrived at the Mission from Nyangao, in order to reinforce Major Roberts. Early in the afternoon of that day the whole of this column left the Mission and marched back to Nyangao; thus the 3rd Battalion returned to the Brigade after many days, at a most opportune moment. Under cover of darkness Col. Mann's wireless was repaired, and at 10 p.m. a wireless message was received from Major Roberts stating that the 2nd Battalion's patrol had arrived safely, and was returning with twenty boxes of ammunition. By night time Gen. O'Grady was within one mile of the Nigerian position at point Y on the sketch. Though he was so near to us we were still besieged. When day broke on the 18th October the food situation was very serious indeed; the men would soon be falling sick and dying of starvation. Patrols reported that the enemy was entrenched on every side except the south-east, and were between Gen. O'Grady and our position. Orders were received from Gen. Beves to withdraw from the perimeter to the south-east. In spite of the previous discomforts endured and the heavy casualties sustained, many regrets were felt on the receipt of this order, for all we required was food and ammunition, for it seemed that we were giving up all that had been so dearly bought by us. Both Gen. O'Grady, in his magnificent effort to break down all obstacles in order to gain touch with us, and Col. Mann had suffered most heavily, and now we were called upon to retire and abandon our gains.

Col. Mann's Column was in the act of preparing to withdraw—in fact, the advance guard had already left—when a company of the 3rd Battalion suddenly appeared from the south-east, having been sent up to cover our retirement. Our column got clear only just in time, for as the rearguard was leaving, the enemy began to suspect the Nigerians' move, and again opened fire upon the old perimeter, which had now been taken over by the 3rd Battalion company. The 2nd and 4th Battalions, with all the wounded and the two guns, arrived back safely at Nyangao without any further fighting, though the battle was raging upon our right flank during the whole time that we were retiring, and in fact, one or two men were hit during our retreat by stray shots.

CHAPTER 13

The Battle of Mahiwa (2)

The 1st Nigeria Regiment, the Gambia Company, and a section of the Nigerian Battery, under the command of Major Roberts, moved out from the Namupa Mission at 7 a.m. on the 15th October, and commenced the advance towards Nyangao. They did not advance more than 600 yards before the advance guard was held up by a German patrol. A few shots were exchanged and the enemy fell back. The advance was continued for the next two hours with great caution, until the column was so heavily engaged that the advance was perforce brought to a halt half a mile from its objective. Major Roberts therefore ordered a position to be prepared on knoll Z, where a perimeter was dug. The 1st Battalion suffered several casualties in this advance, amongst them being Capt. Rickards, who was with the advance guard. No further attempt was made to advance to Nyangao this day, as the object of the advance had been secured already when the perimeter had been formed at Z,—that is to say, the Namupa-Nyangao road was blocked by a strong force capable of denying this line of retreat to the enemy, who were then falling back from Mtama. To advance further would have in no way improved the situation or helped in the general plan of action as laid down by Gen. Beves, whilst very heavy casualties would have resulted if a further advance had been attempted. Early in the morning of the 16th October orders were received by Major Roberts to return to the Namupa Mission, and from there reinforce Col. Mann's Column. No opposition was encountered on the return march, and the Mission was reached at about 11 a.m. After rations had been cooked, the advance was continued from the Mission down the Mahiwa road. No. 1 Company of the 1st Battalion, under the command of Capt. Stretton, left the Mission at 1 p.m., followed by two companies of the 1st Battalion and a section of Nigerian artillery, with the Gambia Company as escort to the guns; the supply and baggage column of the whole of the Brigade and the reserve ammunition column followed later with No. 4 Company of the 1st Battalion as rearguard. The advance guard met with no opposition during the first two miles of march, but they had no idea of what was lying in wait for them, nor did they know that Col. Mann's Column was, to all intents and purposes, besieged.

A German force of four companies, under the command of Gen von Lettow himself, had arrived on the morning of the 16th at Mremba Hill, where there was already a strong force opposing Col. Mann. From the top of Mremba, with a pair of good field glasses, the Germans could have almost counted the number of men in Major Roberts' Column as they left the Namupa Mission and descended the hill to the Nakadi river.

As Capt. Stretton advanced nearer to Col. Mann's position he could hear the heavy firing of that column as it was engaged with the enemy. He turned round to his subaltern and said, "We have got the Boche set this time, as he is already engaged with Mann, and we shall fall upon him in rear." He was so confident that he was right in this surmise, that he immediately increased the speed of his company, that had up to this time been proceeding with the utmost caution, and marched as quickly as possible to the sound of the firing in front. He never even sent back a report to Major Roberts of what he intended doing, and to this action was due the partial disaster that followed. Von Lettow, who had been waiting for the approaching company on the high ground to the west of the road, was able to fall upon Capt. Stretton shortly after he crossed the second of the two small streams, marked on the sketch, at a point only a mile from Col. Mann's Column. Capt. Stretton found himself surrounded, and narrowly escaped being annihilated. The remnants of his company managed to force their way back to the main body by rushing the enemy at the point of the bayonet. They suffered most heavy losses, leaving behind them their gallant commander, Capt. Stretton, and Lieut. Miller-Stirling, who were both killed. Thus the Brigade lost one of their very best company commanders—at all times a most gallant officer, a loyal friend, and a good sportsman—one who was beloved by his men, and endeared to every European in the Brigade that knew him. Capt. Stretton had been by no means fortunate whilst serving with the W.A.F.F.s., as he was also taken prisoner by the Germans in the Cameroon campaign, but in the Cameroons the Germans did not suffer from so much Kultur as their brethren in the east, and on the whole Capt. Stretton was treated with the utmost courtesy by his captors.

This most unfortunate affair greatly handicapped Major Roberts, who had received no information from the advance guard commander, and was therefore unable to appreciate the situation till most of the damage had been done. However, No. 3 Company was sent up in support to the right of the road, and No. 2 Company to the left of the road. Half the Gambia Company were sent to occupy a position in this line, across the road, in between these two companies. The other half of the Gambia Company was dispatched to the extreme right of No. 3 Company with the two Nigerian guns. No. 4 Company remained on the north bank of the second stream, on the left of the road.

By 3 p.m. all the companies except the rearguard were heavily engaged, chiefly from the front and right flank. By this time the entire rearguard had crossed the second stream. The baggage train was delayed on the right of the road, and the carriers were ordered to put their loads down and lie down themselves. There was a lull in the firing for a few minutes soon after 3 p.m., and the baggage column again commenced the advance up the road, but on the renewal of the heavy firing all baggage was again put down, and nothing further was done for about ten minutes, when a note addressed to the O.C. rearguard was received by the baggage officer. This note never reached its destination. It instructed the rearguard commander and the O.C. of the baggage to advance to a perimeter that was being constructed by the pioneers. On the carriers being ordered up they took fright, the bullets falling very thickly amongst them and hitting many of them, with the result that they stampeded to the rear, and were only checked at last by No. 4 Company, who had formed a line across the road, and with fixed bayonets were able to turn the carriers back to their loads. Until their return only four Europeans, a few orderlies, and a small baggage guard were left with the loads.

At 4 p.m. the firing was at its worst, and the two Nigerian guns came into action on the extreme right, firing with their fuses set at zero, so close were the enemy upon them. The remnants of No. 1 Company had fallen back on to the main firing line. The enemy were now attacking chiefly on the right front, and matters were becoming critical. The half company of the Gambia Company that were acting as escort to the guns were hopelessly outnumbered, and, after suffering terrible casualties, broke, and fell back in disorder. Both guns were put out of action through having their buffers perforated by the enemy's bullets, whilst the entire team of one gun were either killed or wounded, with the result that the gun had to be abandoned, and unfortunately fell into the enemy's hands. The second gun was also damaged, and as nearly as possible also fell into the Germans' hands, but was saved by the personal gallantry of Sergt. Tasker, who drove the rapidly approaching enemy off with a Lewis gun. The enemy, who had been attacking in the open, had some very heavy casualties, but they were the pick of the whole of the German force in East Africa, and were led in person by von Lettow.

The weight of numbers thrown in against Major Roberts' right flank was irresistible, and so orders were issued to No. 2 Company gradually to retire on the left to a distance of about 250 yards, and there dig in a fine of firing pits. In this position they remained till dusk. Half the Gambia Company were still with No. 2 Company, but they had lost touch with No. 3 Company.

The whole of the Brigade baggage and most of the ammunition were now on, or near, the road, in front of the line taken up by No. 2 Company. This was a very dangerous state of affairs as it was liable to be cut off at any moment from the new main position, and there were actually no troops out in front of No. 2 Company's line on the main road. Thus if the Germans had only known, they could have advanced along the road and taken the whole of the baggage without opposition. In fact, Lieut. Shaw of the Carrier Corps, who walked down this road with fifteen cases of ammunition, found himself before he knew where he was in amongst the Germans, and was forced to give himself up.

A number of carriers were sent up to the front and gradually most of these loads were withdrawn to No. 4 Company perimeter.

Major Roberts' second position became untenable, and orders had to be given for a general retirement to the Mission. Luckily for the Nigerians, the enemy had had all that they wished, and were not desirous for any more fighting this day. They therefore did not follow up Major Roberts, who was permitted to complete his retirement without further fighting. The Namupa Mission was reached at 7 p.m. Thus von Lettow had achieved his object, for Col. Mann was now left isolated without any immediate chance of assistance. No doubt the German Commander-in-Chief regarded Col. Mann and his troops as good as defeated, and looked upon it as only being a matter of time before he took the whole of them prisoners. The previous chapter shows how this catastrophe was avoided.

On the 15th October the 3rd Nigeria Regiment was ordered to be in readiness to move from Chirumaka towards Mtama as a reserve to Linforce. Further orders were to be issued later by the G.O.C. of that force. Column 4 had moved out two days before, and had made an outflanking march south of the Lukeledi, with orders to cut the Massassi road south-west of Mtama and to move to that place from the west, whilst Column 3 advanced from Nyengedi south-west on to Mtama. Orders were received by the 3rd Battalion to follow Column 3. The Nigerians on the 16th October had received considerable reinforcements, and this battalion now consisted of twenty-five Europeans and five hundred and twenty native rank and file. They arrived at Mtama at about 8 a.m., and there gained touch with Columns 3 and 4, who previously had met at Mtama, the enemy having retired towards Mahiwa. The march was resumed at about 9.30 a.m. and Nyangao was reached about 1 p.m., the distance being about six miles. Later in the day the G.O.C. Linforce placed the 3rd Battalion under the orders of Gen. O'Grady. Column 4 had moved out of Nyangao towards Mahiwa, and had almost immediately got into touch with the enemy—Column 3 remaining in support during that night. Native information was received to the effect that Nigerian troops (1st Battalion and Gambia Company) had been engaged with a party of the enemy just north of Nyangao early on the 16th, but had moved back again towards the north-west before the arrival of Columns 3 and 4.

The 3rd Nigerians moved at 7 a.m. on the 17th, in advance of Column 3, along a track running north-west from Nyangao, which was the same path that had been followed by the 1st Battalion on the 16th. Less than a mile from Nyangao the camp that had been occupied on the night of the 15th-16th October by the 1st Battalion was passed by the 3rd Battalion. This battalion proceeded on for about another mile till they came to some cross roads at which a halt had been previously ordered, and here information was received from Gen. O'Grady that Column 3 had turned off west from the late 1st Battalion camp, and so the 3rd Battalion was ordered to continue the march northwest, and to do their utmost to extricate the 1st Battalion and Gambia Company, who were reported to be at Namupa Mission. News had already been received that the Nigerians had suffered heavy casualties the previous day. The 1st Battalion had reported that their patrols were unable to get out of the Mission station towards Nyangao on the morning of the 17th, owing to the presence of the enemy. By this time Columns 3 and 4 were both heard to be heavily engaged with the enemy, and accordingly the 3rd Battalion moved on and reached the Mission station at about 1 p.m., without encountering any opposition. The 1st Battalion was found to be entrenched at the Mission and with them the whole of the second line transport of the Brigade. During the afternoon the move back to Nyangao was successfully carried out.

At about 5 p.m. the Staff Captain of Column 3 arrived with

orders from Gen. O'Grady, instructing the 3rd Battalion to follow on and join Column 3, who by this time had suffered extremely heavy casualties, as soon as the 1st Battalion with all their wounded had safely returned to Nyangao.

The 1st Battalion was clear soon after 5 p.m., and in consequence the 3rd Battalion moved back, and on reaching the cross roads at which the first halt had been made that morning, turned off south-west according to orders, and marched towards the sound of Column 3's firing. The track eventually got lost in bush, and, as it was now quite dark and the firing had died down, and the bush was very thick and thorny, it was decided to return to the spot from which Gen. O'Grady had turned off, and to follow his telephone wire. On reaching this spot the Intelligence Officer of Column 3 was found waiting to guide the 3rd Battalion to Column 3, but as it was now 11 p.m. and the men were tired, and as firing had completely ceased for some time, it was decided to bivouac there for the rest of the night, and to join Column 3 early the next morning. Gen. O'Grady was informed of this, and approved.

Early on the 18th food and water arrived, and a start was eventually made at about 7 a.m., and touch was gained with Column 3 by 7.30 a.m. Orders were now received to proceed west along a track and endeavour to gain touch with the 2nd and 4th Battalions, who were on the Mahiwa river without food and ammunition, and to escort them back to Nyangao. This was accordingly done, and one company of the battalion arrived at the camp and formed the rearguard to the 2nd and 4th Battalions, just leaving for their march to Nyangao—as stated in the last chapter. The battalion proceeded west along this track after having met the 2nd and 4th Battalions, as they were at the time under orders to attack some high ground west of the Mahiwa river; these orders, however, were cancelled, and one company of the battalion was now told to dig in across the track leading west to Mahiwa, and there to protect the right flank of Column 3, while the other three companies were given a compass bearing to march on so as to bring them to the Headquarters of Column 3, which was then about one mile distant. They were instructed to attack any enemy whom they met and who might be endeavouring to outflank Column 3, and in the event of not encountering any hostile forces, to report themselves to Gen. O'Grady at his Headquarters as soon as possible.

On arriving at Column 3's Headquarters without having met any opposition, the battalion, less one company, was ordered to continue the firing line of Column 3 to the left, towards Column 4, who were in action some 500 to 1000 yards further to the left.

Matters began to appear somewhat critical at this moment, so two companies advanced at the double, and took up a position on the left of Column 3, leaving only one company in support. Later this company was commanded to take up a position on the right of Column 3 with the right flank well thrown back. A gap between the left of Column 4 and the right of the two companies of the 3rd Battalion was first filled by a hundred Kashmiris, but these were eventually withdrawn and their place was taken up by the Gambia Company, who had arrived at about 1 p.m.

At 3 p.m. the O.C. of the 3rd Battalion was informed that it was the intention of the G.O.C. to withdraw Column 3 to some high ground just north of Nyangao, and that the 3rd Battalion was to cover the withdrawal, for it was his intention to get all other troops out of the firing line as soon as possible. The company that was still out on the track leading to the Mahiwa was to remain there till 2 a.m., and was then to send one section forward on patrol while the other sections withdrew. The 3rd Battalion, less this one company, was to remain in position till 11 p.m., by which time the new position would have been taken up.

At 5 p.m. the King's African Rifles and Gambia Company were withdrawn from the firing line and the 3rd Battalion's company on the right was extended out to the left, till they gained touch with the 3rd Battalion's companies on that flank. This company was digging in a new line when the enemy made a strong counter-attack at about 5.15 p.m., which lasted till 6.30 p.m., and during the whole time was most determined. It was, however, successfully driven off, and the enemy withdrew at 6.30. The 3rd Battalion remained in position according to orders, and did not retire till 11 p.m., when it fell back to its position in the new line at about 2 a.m., without any fresh disturbance from the enemy.

The casualties sustained on the 18th by the 3rd Battalion were Lieut. Ryan and Sergt. Tomlin killed, about six other Europeans wounded, fifteen rank and file killed, and a further fifty natives wounded.

The company which was left on the Mahiwa road, though they were in touch with enemy patrols all day, suffered no casualties.

On the morning of the 18th the 1st Nigeria Regiment and the Gambia Company were encamped at Nyangao when they received orders to move out at 9 a.m. in support of the King's African Rifles. They were to use the same path by which they had arrived from the Mission, passing through their old perimeter at *Z* (see sketch). From near *Z* they deployed and advanced east for about 300 yards, when further orders were received instructing them to move about 1000 yards south, and there support a K.A.R. battalion that was in difficulties. During the day the 1st Battalion remained in support, but No. 1 Company was later in the afternoon pushed up into the firing fine. The Gambia Company, however, did some very useful work, as already described, with the 3rd Battalion. It is most regrettable that Capt. Waters was mortally wounded in this action when in command of the 1st Battalion's advance companies. For his services in this action he was awarded a posthumous bar to his Military Cross.

In the fighting at Mahiwa, between the 15th and 18th October, the Nigerian Brigade suffered 528 casualties of all ranks, of which 38 were Europeans. The percentage of casualties was extremely high, for it must be remembered that the Brigade was by no means up to strength when it went into this action; but the Nigerians did not suffer such a heavy proportion of casualties as the Legion of Frontiersmen (Royal Fusiliers), who went into this action on the 17th October 120 strong, and came out only 50 strong. Their casualties occurred mostly when trying to cross the Nakadi river near point *Y* on the sketch. In this action

Lieut. Ryan of the 3rd Battalion lost his brother, who was killed when leading his platoon of Royal Fusiliers. Thus both brothers were killed within a very short distance of each other on the same day and in the same action.

This battle was one of the biggest engagements ever fought on African soil from the point of view of casualties on both sides—not excluding the great Boer War, the various campaigns in Egypt and the Sudan, and the Italian Abyssinian campaign. At Mahiwa the British lost 2700 casualties out of a total strength of 4900 infantry employed; thus the British losses were above 50 per cent, of the number of troops engaged.

Though the various columns were meant to be equivalent in strength to infantry brigades, their numbers were only—Column 3, 1500 strong; Column 4, 1700 strong; and the Nigerian Brigade, 1750 strong. The German casualties in this action were also extremely heavy, as they suffered especially in their attacks on Col. Mann's position and against the 1st Battalion and Gambia Company on the 16th October. In fact, their losses were so serious that they suffered later in morale, and with one exception never again made a determined stand against the British. I hope that some day a detailed account of the whole battle of Mahiwa will be written, as it is deserving a place in military history, for, besides being one of the greatest battles ever fought in Africa, it had far-reaching results on the rest of the campaign in German East Africa. In it whole companies of Germans were wiped out, and others so broken up that they were forced to amalgamate two or three companies into one. But from the point of view of this narrative, Mahiwa proved the indomitable courage of Nigerian native troops in action; though various units of the Brigade withdrew from the fight battered and bleeding, never was the spirit of the men better nor their morale so high as it was at the end of this battle. Those who had gone through this action unscathed were now seasoned soldiers, and, as such, fit to face anything they were likely to meet in East Africa. In these few days they had been through hunger, thirst and fatigue, had been exposed to high explosive shell fire and machine-gun and rifle fire from every side, and yet never once were they depressed in spirit—a fact that the Huns learnt to their cost, for the pick of the German forces had been used against the Nigerians, with the result that they had been denied the fruits of victory, and been forced to withdraw licking their sores.

The result of this battle, which lasted without intermission for four days, and was the most serious ever fought in the whole campaign, was indecisive. Though our casualties were heavy, we could better afford to suffer losses than the Germans at this stage of the campaign, and though the enemy had fought with the desperation and courage of despair, they were only able to check temporarily the British advance.

During all this fighting around Mahiwa, the Nigerian Brigade saw a good deal of Gen. O'Grady. His personal example in the firing line did much to inspire the men of his column, for wherever the fighting was heaviest, there the General would always be found, personally inspiring all ranks by his presence in the front line, and inciting all "to give the blighters brass, Begorra!" It was during the battle of Mahiwa, when matters were looking at their worst, that Gen. O'Grady was seen walking up and down the fine accompanied only by an orderly and inquiring of every one if they had seen O'Mara, his dog. Such coolness under fire does more to inspire native soldiers to do big things than anything else on earth. The gallant General is a most remarkable son of Erin, a born leader of men, who appears to revel in a real hot fight and to thrive on the smell of powder.

The 18th October was the last day of the Mahiwa battle, though a demonstration was made against the enemy's position during the 19th.

A SENTRY ON DUTY ON THE NYANGAO-NAMUPA ROAD

A Street in Lindi

A MACHINE-GUN IN ACTION AT MAHIWA

NIGERIANS IN THE TRENCHES

The Kashmir Mountain Battery in action during the Battle of Mahiwa

A Stokes gun in action in the Lindi area

The light railway in the Lindi area

A machine gun in action during the battle of Mkwera

Reserve ammunition carriers crossing a deep valley on the Makonde Plateau

Bringing up supplies at Ndanda

THE ADVANCE ON TO THE MAKONDE PLATEAU

THE NIGERIAN GUNS BEING BROUGHT INTO ACTION ON
THE MAKONDE PLATEAU

Indian Cavalry crossing the Rovuma into Portuguese Territory

Nigerian troops embarking at Lindi

CHAPTER 14

The Action of Mkwera

During the night of 18th-19th October the officer commanding the Nigerian Brigade received orders from Gen. Beves that the Nigerian Brigade was to attack the enemy's position at dawn on the 19th. Fortunately for the Brigade this order was cancelled by the G.O.C.-in-C, otherwise I doubt if this book would ever have been written, as it is quite possible that if the Brigade had attacked again they would have suffered extremely heavy casualties.

On the 19th October the command of the Lindi Force was taken over by Gen. Cunliffe, who had rejoined the Brigade earlier on this day at Nyangao. Col. Mann continued temporarily to command the Nigerian Brigade, whilst Lieut.-Col. Sargent relinquished the command of the 4th Battalion in order to accompany Gen. Cunliffe as his General Staff Officer. Later, Capt. Milne-Home of the 3rd Battalion was appointed Staff Captain to the Lindi Force. Gen. Cunliffe returned to Mtama, which was then the Linforce Headquarters. A big draft joined the Brigade on this day, consisting of 16 officers, 8 British N.C.Os, and 512 rank and file. Thus the battalions were once again brought up to their original strength.

During the 19th a demonstration was carried out against the German position by the British artillery and a battalion of King's African Rifles. The demonstration was extremely noisy, but I doubt if it achieved much. Except for patrol encounters the last ten days of October were uneventful. Advantage was taken by the lull to allot the new draft to the different battalions. A centre at Lindi was formed for the training of recruits who up to this time had not passed musketry. Reinforcements were hurried up from the base to the Mahiwa position, and all preparations were made for the final offensive.

On the 22nd the enemy returned three wounded Nigerian soldiers. These stated that after the battle of the 16th October they were picked up by the enemy and taken to a field hospital, in which there were quite a hundred German Askaris, amongst whom during the night of the 17th-18th October between fifteen to twenty deaths occurred. One of these returned soldiers was a Cameroon man, who had at one time been a German soldier, and knew a certain amount of the German language. All the Europeans, he stated, seemed to be deploring their very heavy casualties, and the impossibility of breaking through the British. The fact that these three men were decently treated by the enemy does not mean that the Germans were carrying out their usual role, but rather that these men were exceptions to the rule. After the battle of Mahiwa on the 20th, and on other dates, search parties went out all over the old scenes of fighting, and all brought back the most terrible reports of German brutality. Indian and Nigerian soldiers, who had obviously been wounded in the different actions, had been bayoneted later, in the most indecent manner, as they were crawling to places of safety. Any number of men were in this way obscenely murdered by the enemy. This kind of treatment of wounded would be expected in savage warfare, but it was hardly counted upon when fighting another so-called civilized nation. It is impossible to set down here the German brutality in detail, as much is not fit for print, but it is enough for me to say, that when some years ago I was in an action against a cannibal tribe in Nigeria, the cannibals' treatment of the wounded was not much worse than the Germans' treatment at Mahiwa. Capt. Stretton's small Nigerian *boy*, aged ten years, was found with his body a mass of bayonet wounds—a victim of foul murder. Close to the boy's corpse was found the 1st Battalion's pet monkey, which had been shot at close quarters and then had a bayonet driven through its body. These are only examples of the brutality of a nation that can sing *a Te*

Deum over the sinking *Lusitania*, and in cold blood shoot the master of the *Clan MacTavish* because he had tried to defend his ship. They are just hall-marks of the *Beast*.

The biggest patrol encounter that took place during the last few days of October occurred on the 24th, when a reconnaissance consisting of the 2nd Battalion and one gun of the Nigerian Battery proceeded out north-west from Nyangao, with the object of ascertaining the strength of the enemy in position west of the scene of the 1st Battalion's action of the 16th. The enemy were encountered near the Mahiwa river. They opened a heavy fire upon the reconnoitring force with guns, machine-guns, and rifle fire. Capt. Gardner of the 2nd Battalion, Lieut. Edwards of the Nigerian artillery, and six rank and file were wounded; the first-mentioned was wounded seriously. Similar patrols, but on a smaller scale, went out on the 22nd, 23rd, 25th, 28th and 29th. On the 28th a sharp engagement ensued between a 3rd Battalion company and a strong party of the enemy who were entrenched in their old position at Mahiwa. The enemy's machine-gun was silenced, but Capt. O'Connell was wounded, and four rank and file were also either killed or wounded. All the time that the 1st Battalion were in camp with Column IV they never had a dull moment, as the German had a *daily hate* consisting of the putting over of a few shells uncomfortably close to their camp. One morning I went to breakfast with Major Roberts, and during the meal our party went to ground twice like rabbits, whilst the Boche shells lobbed over the camp, bursting just outside the perimeter. Every one in the 1st Battalion seemed quite used to this pastime, for they informed me that it was good for the appetite to have a little exercise during the meals, and further, it encouraged the men to dig good trenches, and trained every one to take cover.

By the 6th November everything was ready for the renewal of the offensive. The enemy was still in strength at the Mahiwa position, but they were being threatened in their rear by a flying column of Gen. Hannyngton's force, and were in danger of having their communications to the south cut by the cavalry, who were working round in that direction from Ruponda towards

Massassi. The Linforce too had been considerably reinforced since the action of Mahiwa, the Cape Corps being amongst these reinforcements.

On the 5th November a startling rumour got about that a German airship had left Europe for German East Africa. At first it was thought to be merely somebody's joke, but later these rumours were confirmed, and there was no doubt that an airship did start from Europe, and actually managed to get some distance into the Sudan before it gave up the attempt. What has since happened to the Zeppelin no one knows, and if it ever got back to *The Happy Fatherland* or not is still a mystery. During the 5th November the Brigade, less the 1st Battalion and the Gambia Company, concentrated at Nyangao preparatory to commencing the offensive on the following day. The 1st Battalion, for the time being, remained attached to Column 4. The Gambia Company had by this time moved back to Mtama, and as from this date they ceased to form part of the Nigerian Brigade in the field they no longer figure in this narrative. This withdrawal was due to their weakness in numbers and the necessity of retaining a unit with the Linforce Headquarters for duty as *guards* to signal stations, dumps, etc., and to dig up abandoned German ammunition and stores, and to perform the thousand and one necessary and valuable, though unromantic, duties connected with an advance. The advance was commenced at 4 a.m. on 6th November. The 3rd Battalion was in front, and advanced via point Z (see maps) across the Nkadi river, from thence across the Namupa-Mahiwa road. On arriving here the direction was changed to south-west, and after crossing the Mahiwa river they arrived on the Mremba ridge by 11 a.m. During this advance the advance guard twice encountered some small enemy parties, but in both cases speedily drove them in. The country was difficult, and the bush near to the rivers particularly thick, so that progress was slow. On arriving at Mremba the 3rd Battalion proceeded south along the river in order to gain touch and co-operate with Column 4, but this they failed to do. During all this time Column 3, with the Cape Corps, had been heavily engaged at Mahiwa itself, but the Germans were at last forced to retire from this position owing to shell fire and the fear of the cutting of their line of communication by Nigerians operating on their left flank. The enemy now took up a position at Mkwera, to which place they were followed by Gen. O'Grady. At 2.50 p.m. orders were received by Brigadier-General Mann to proceed towards Mkwera and co-operate with Gen. O'Grady, who was then heavily engaged. There was some delay in carrying out these orders through the 3rd Battalion having to be withdrawn from a position they had taken up on the Mahiwa river south of the Mremba Hill, and also because the 4th Battalion had been instructed to water at the Mahiwa river. The Brigade, therefore, was not ready to move till 4 p.m., the 2nd Battalion remaining behind at Mremba, where they had to take up a position. The main road at Mahiwa was not reached till 6 p.m., whilst the rearguard did not arrive in till long after dark. The Nigerians were thus too late to be able to give assistance to Gen. O'Grady this day, during which time the Cape Corps had had a very sharp action, and had suffered heavy casualties. It was most unfortunate that the Nigerian Brigade had been forced to spend so barren a day, in spite of the fact that they had marched from 4 a.m. till 6 p.m., seemingly to little purpose.

Soon after our arrival at Mahiwa it came on to rain, and promised to be a poisonous night. The terrors of the night, as far as I was concerned, were greatly increased by the *buffalo bean*. It is quite possible that my reader has never heard of this vegetable. It grows on a low shrub, and as one walks through the bush one brushes off the short hairs which cover it with a velvet-like down. At first the presence of the bean is not even noticed, then slight irritation is felt round the bare knees and naked arms while the hairs of the bean work their way into the skin. The irritation gets rapidly worse as the hairs are blown by the breeze up the legs and all over the body, till the whole body is smothered in the dreadful thing. The more one scratches the worse the irritation becomes, and the more quickly it seems to spread. The only cure known by myself is to rub dry earth into the skin, but this, on a wet night, is impossible. The wet makes this dreadful complaint a hundred per cent, worse, till, maddened with irritation, one rolls on the ground and curses the bean, the bush on which it grows, and the country that has the audacity to produce such a bush. In my agony I remembered once laughing on a former occasion at a poor brother officer, who had been unwise enough to take an alfresco bath under a buffalo bean bush. The wretched man jumped about as naked as God had made him, yelling out all the time for mercy. The sight was so ridiculous that I, in my arrogance, laughed and mocked the one in pain. I was judged and punished for my sin that night at Mahiwa. This brings us to the end of *a perfect day* that had consisted of a fourteen hours' march without food, followed by a wet night and no sleep, all brought to a climax by *the bean*.

Early in the morning the Nigerian Brigade, less the 1st and 2nd Battalions, moved off towards Mkwera, the 4th Battalion leading. At 7.30 a.m. the advance guard reported meeting a post of the Cape Corps which was situated on the main road. From them we learnt that the Cape Corps were in a perimeter camp 400 yards to the left of the road, and that Column 3 were dug in about 500 yards to the left of the Cape Corps. Orders were given to halt, and the 4th Battalion *dug in* a line of trenches across the road, with one section on the left and the other three sections on the right of the road. The remainder of the Brigade entrenched themselves in the rear of the 4th Battalion. The 3rd Battalion patrol set out along the main road, but they had not passed the 4th Battalion picquet by more than 100 yards before they came under heavy fire from the enemy's post south-west of Hatia, losing four native rank and file wounded. A patrol sent out to the north-west met an enemy's patrol, and a few rounds were exchanged before the enemy retired, leaving behind them one dead Askari and one unwounded carrier. During the day the 1st Battalion rejoined the Brigade. An old German camp was found at Mkwera in which had been buried a considerable quantity of abandoned rifles and machine-guns.

The enemy evidently left Mkwera on the previous night in a great hurry, as the road in front of the 4th Battalion picquet was strewn with loads abandoned by German carriers.

One load contained the records and papers of the 25th and 15th Field Companies, which documents had only just lately been brought up to date. Another load contained a brand new Prussian officer's field-grey overcoat, which I still have in my possession, while several other loads contained chickens and preserved foods of all kinds. It was noticed that some of the canned food bore Portuguese marks, showing that they had been lately looted from our southern ally. Several papers found in these boxes had been signed by von Lettow, and by Muller, von Lettow's Chief of Staff.

On the 8th November Column 3 intended to advance to Nangoo, but the road was held at Hatia by what was reported to be a rearguard of one or two companies of the enemy. The 3rd Battalion was therefore ordered to clear up the position so as to allow Column 3 to advance without interruption. As there was no water at Mkwera, Column 3 and the Cape Corps, both of whom had not been watered for twenty-four hours, were unable to move till the afternoon, as it was necessary for them to obtain water from Mahiwa before advancing. In the meantime the 3rd Battalion, supported by the 4th Battalion, both under the command of Lieut.-Col. Badham, were ordered to clear up the situation. At the time most of us were very sceptical as to the truth of the I.D.'s report upon the enemy's strength.

At 11.15 a.m. the 3rd Nigerians moved out of the Nigerian perimeter, leaving the main road before they arrived at the 4th Battalion picquet, and following a path that led off half right into the bush towards the Lukeledi river, due north of Mkwera. Here the river flowed through a grass-covered *vlei* about 300 yards across, which was heavily timbered on both sides. No. 10 Company, under Lieuts. Hawkins and Catt, was advance guard. As this company reached the *vlei* they formed into extended order. A few rounds were fired at them from the south, and orders were issued to halt, since Lieut. Hawkins could clearly see the line of the enemy's position on the Mkwera Hill. This officer had not long given his order when the enemy delivered a powerful counter-attack against his right, which was repulsed by noon. The enemy immediately began to feel for his left flank with the idea of driving a wedge in between No. 10 Company and the main body. Hall No. 12 Company was sent up to prolong the line of No. 10 Company to the left. Shortly after the remaining half of No. 12 Company, under Capt. Luxford, was ordered to follow and to prolong still further the line to the left. This half company lost touch and direction, with the result that they emerged in the open to the left, and well in front of the remainder of the line. They were immediately received by a tremendous volley from the German main position, and suffered heavily before they could fall back and regain touch with the left of the 3rd Battalion firing line. This mistake cost this company 50 per cent, casualties. At about 1.30 p.m. Capt. Ford, who commanded No. 11 Company, moved up to the firing line to prolong the line to the left, No. 9 Company remaining with Col. Badham in support. Major Green was in command of the whole firing line.

The enemy now began to feel along the Nigerian front for a weak link in the defensive line. Owing to the temporary shortage of ammunition in the centre the volume of fire had died down here. This misled the Germans, who immediately delivered the most determined counter-attack against the centre, coming out into the open to a distance of fifty yards from the 3rd Battalion line. At this close range they managed to get a machine-gun into action and opened up a most deadly fire. The machine-gun was, however, an excellent mark for the 3rd Battalion, and the two Europeans working the gun were hit almost immediately. An attempt was then made to capture the gun, but the enemy had machine-guns on each flank of their position, which kept up a heavy cross fire in front of the derelict gun, making it impossible for anyone to come up to it.

An urgent message was sent to the officer commanding No. 14 Company, whose company was extended on both sides of the main road, to co-operate with the 3rd Battalion by demonstrating against the German position on the hill. This was carried out with three machine-guns, two Lewis guns, and all the available rifles of the company, and a most heavy fire was kept up for three-quarters of an hour. At 3 p.m. 14 Company advanced another 200 yards, and from this new position reopened a very heavy fire upon the enemy's position. They inflicted several casualties on the German post at the bottom of the Mkwera Hill on the main road. This demonstration greatly relieved the pressure on the 3rd Battalion; but by this time the 3rd Battalion were being hardly pressed, and Col. Badham, who had most of his battalion in the firing line, called upon Col. Gibb, the officer commanding the 4th Battalion, to support him with a company. 16 Company, that had up to this time divided the distance between 14 Company and the left of the 3rd Battalion, moved up to the 3rd Battalion Headquarters.

The Nigerian battery and Stokes guns were in action, but their F.O.O. had up to this time failed to pick up the target. By 3.30 p.m. the situation was by no means cleared up. One thing was certain, and that was the enemy were holding Mkwera in far greater strength than was ever supposed possible earlier in the day.

Capt. Hetley (16 Company) was ordered to send two sections forward to support Col. Badham's left. Lieuts. Balnave and Dean were in command of these sections, and had with them one machine-gun. No sooner had they moved forward than Capt. Hetley was ordered to reinforce the right with his two remaining sections.

At this time the Nigerian and German firing lines were within 100 yards of each other, and even closer than this in the centre. The 3rd Battalion had suffered so many casualties that they were unable to deliver a counter-attack. At 4 p.m. the enemy's bugles sounded and a determined counter-attack was delivered against Col. Badham's right. At first the enemy were partially successful and managed to gain a foothold on the extreme right flank of the Nigerian line, from which they poured in a heavy enfilade fire upon the whole Nigerian front, but after a fierce fight the enemy were driven back.

No. 10 Company had been in action on the right of the line all day, and had suffered most heavily, every European except Lieut. Catt having been hit. Great credit is due to this officer for his gallantry and leadership during this day, for which he was later awarded the Military Cross. Lieut. Catt had been promoted from the ranks only a few months before, and within six months of gaining his commission he was appointed an Acting Captain and awarded the Military Cross. It is most regrettable that this brilliant career should have been cut short so soon after this date, for within a few months of Mkwera Lieut. Catt died of enteric at Lindi. His death deprived the 3rd Battalion of one of their most useful officers.

At 4.30 p.m. Capt. Burney brought up a company from the 1st Battalion to reinforce the firing line, and was followed shortly afterwards by 14 Company, and later again by 15 Company—both of the 4th Battalion. Just before dark No. 2 Company of the 1st Battalion arrived. Evidently the enemy had been badly punished in this counter-attack, for shortly afterwards they withdrew, being threatened by the Cape Corps on the east of the main road. They retired in disorder, leaving behind them a number of rifles and much equipment. Their retreat was accelerated by a party of the Cape Corps suddenly falling upon their right, and capturing a machine-gun with very little opposition.

The German casualties in this action were very heavy, but the 3rd Battalion had also suffered badly, having lost 133 casualties, including Major Green, who died of wounds the same day. The 4th Battalion also suffered 17 casualties in this action.

The 4th Battalion, just before dusk, made good the ground between the Lukeledi and the main road. After meeting a patrol of the Cape Corps and another patrol from the King's African Rifles, this battalion, followed later by the remainder of the Nigerians, returned to their old camp at Mkwera. The rough sketch of the Mkwera fight may help the reader to follow this action more easily. Taking this action all round, it was one of the most determined that the Nigerians ever took part in during the East African campaign, and it was the last determined stand made by the Germans in German East Africa, for after it they usually contented themselves with strong rearguard actions only. Towards the close of the day our heavy batteries got into action against the Mkwera position, but it is doubtful if they served any useful purpose, as the fight was all but over by the time they started firing.

I am not superstitious, but it is a melancholy fact, that with the death of Major Green, 13 Company lost three officers who at one time or another had commanded them in East Africa; first Capt. Barclay, who was killed on the 24th January; then Capt. Norton-Harper, who was killed at Mahiwa; and lastly Major Green, who was their original commander when the contingent sailed from West Africa.

All the Nigerian dead after this action were brought and buried inside the Nigerian camp, between Mkwera and Mahiwa, on the north side of the road. I sincerely hope that the spot in which they are buried will someday be permanently marked in lasting memory of the Nigerian Brigade. General Cunliffe read the funeral service over the two Europeans, while the 13-pounders were thundering away about 200 yards in rear, and Gen. O'Grady's column was heard to be in action on the Nangoo road. The *mise en scene* was most impressive.

The Germans were in force at Mkwera, and very likely intended attacking the Nigerian camp, but were themselves attacked first. There were probably from ten to twelve German companies in this action—rather a different thing from the one or two companies that were reported to be present here by the Intelligence Department! The enemy, after the fight, fell back on to a prepared position at Hatia, where they intended holding the road again.

On the 9th November Gen. O'Grady attacked the enemy's position at Hatia, but after a sharp fight he failed to dislodge them. At 4 p.m. on the same day two 4-inch howitzers and two 13-pounders shelled the enemy's position from the Nigerian camp, the range being about 2½ miles. At the same time Column 3 opened a heavy machine-gun fire and Stokes mortar bombardment upon the Hatia position. For one hour the guns continued shelling this position as fast as they could be loaded. At 5.30 p.m. Gen. O'Grady developed an infantry attack upon the position, in which he suffered only six casualties and gained his objective almost without opposition. The enemy were completely demoralized by the gun-fire, and retired, leaving many dead behind them.

During the past few days the Germans had abandoned one 4·1 naval gun, over ten machine-guns, several hundred rifles, and much ammunition.

On the 8th November a force from Gen. Hannyngton's Division arrived at the Lukeledi, which had already been evacuated by the enemy. Gen. Northey had had further successes in his area, having captured 150 German Europeans and 180 Askaris. A 4th Battalion patrol brought in an enemy's Askari, who stated that he had run away from Hatia during the bombardment on the 9th. Evidently from his story the Germans must have suffered Hell in their entrenchments from our guns.

On the 11th November the Brigade marched early in the morning to Chikalala in order to support Column 3, which were attacking Nangoo that day, but Gen. O'Grady walked into that place without opposition. The march was continued on the following day: the Nigerian Brigade passed through Gen. O'Grady's column at Nangoo about 11 a.m. and arrived at Ndanda at 3.30 p.m. Ndanda had been occupied by Column 1 of Gen. Hannyngton's force on the 10th of the month. Here we found 21 sick and wounded Europeans, in natives, 17 German European women, and 24 white German children. These had been left behind by the chivalrous Boche. The Germans at least paid us the compliment of trusting us with their women and children, which is more than the British would do in the case of the Germans in the light of what had taken place at Tabora and other places in German East Africa, where women prisoners with children were subjected to every abominable insult. When the Germans found their women or sick and wounded a tie to them they never thought twice of abandoning them to the enemy and Fate. Thus again and again German women had to be taken over, fed, and cared for by the British. Many of these same women were frequently most lax in their morals, and were a constant source of annoyance to the Provost-Marshal at the base. At Nangoo the Germans had abandoned 3 other wounded Europeans and 63 Askaris.

The Nigerian casualties during the fighting of the past seven weeks had been 305 killed and 725 wounded of all ranks, of which casualties 77 were Europeans. These numbers do not include casualties in the Nigerian and Sierra Leone Carrier Corps, which were attached and accompanied the troops through all these actions.

At Ndanda direct touch was gained with Gen. Hannyngton's force. The arrival of Column 1 from the Kilwa area accounted for the fact that the Germans never made a stand between Hatia and the Makonde Plateau.

CHAPTER 15

The Operations of the Makonde Plateau

Early on the morning of the 14th November orders were received by the Nigerian Brigade Headquarters to send two battalions and a section of guns as early as possible towards Chiwata, in order to gain touch with Column 2. If necessary, the G.O.C. was to be prepared to reinforce this column. The 1st Nigerians left Ndanda soon after dawn, followed by the 4th Battalion, a section of artillery and the Stokes gun section. Progress after the first two miles was very slow because of the steep-sided dongas that had to be crossed and the mountainous nature of the country. It was only possible to advance in single file. Four miles out from Ndanda the road passed over a succession of steep hills, mostly commanded by greater hill features on the south and south-east. Owing to the close proximity of the enemy, every hill that commanded the road had to be picqueted, which entailed very hard work for the advance guard, and greatly delayed the advance. By 11.30 a.m. the 1st Battalion had reached a point on the road about 6 miles south of Ndanda, where the road, after descending a steep hill, turned west and led up a spur to the escarpment of the Makonde Plateau. The country to the east of this road was almost precipitous. Here the advance guard commander reported that the enemy were holding the high ground, over which the road passed, with two machine-guns. The Germans were in a position quite unapproachable from the front. To continue the advance this way would simply mean that whole companies would be mown down by machine-gun fire. It was therefore necessary to develop a wide turning movement, which was not complete until late in the afternoon. By this time it was too late to continue the advance, so the 1st Battalion bivouacked at the top of the plateau, and the 4th Battalion, together with the remainder of the main body, spent the night at the foot of this steep climb. The small party of the enemy, who had been holding the road with two machine-guns, retired as soon as they discovered that the 1st Battalion had turned their position. The patrols that had been sent out to the south-east reported that they had failed to gain touch with Column 2, under Col. Ridgeway. The reason was afterwards found to be a fault in the map, which showed the distance between Chiwata and Ndanda to be about three miles short of what it was in reality. All the patrols that followed the map must have gone north of this Column.

On 15th November the attack upon Chiwata was timed to commence. Column 3 blocked the eastern line of retreat. Column 2 had orders to advance along the high ground to the west, whilst Brig.-Gen. Mann with the Nigerians was to advance on Chiwata itself by the centre route. The advance continued at daybreak, the 4th Battalion leading. After a slight resistance the advance guard arrived at the outskirts of Chiwata at noon. Gen. O'Grady was heard on several occasions to be heavily engaged on our left. Some pretty artillery work was witnessed about this time, when Col. Ridgeway's guns on one ridge supported Gen. O'Grady on the opposite ridge, the two ridges being about three miles apart. The shells could be seen bursting along the edge of the precipice that faced this ridge, along which Gen. O'Grady was advancing. Chiwata was a mass of red crosses, and wherever one looked one could see them. They were painted on the roofs of houses, laid out in bricks upon the ground, fluttered from tree-tops and flag-staffs, and later, on entering Chiwata, a Red Cross armlet was seen on every Boche that one met. That the red cross was hopelessly prostituted, both here and at many other places in German East Africa, there is not a shadow of doubt. At Chiwata von Lettow's telegraph station was situated between two hospitals. Though the Cross was not displayed over this building, it was floating over the building on each side, so near that it really made no difference. Hence Col. Ridgeway, who had been in position within artillery range for over twenty-four hours, had been unable to shell the place, which at the very time was sheltering the German Commander-in-Chief and his staff. One must give credit to whom credit is due, and it is a known fact that the German Principal Medical Officer had violently quarrelled with von Lettow at Chiwata for his misuse of this hospital. The Germans had only evacuated Chiwata that same morning, leaving behind them all the British non-commissioned prisoners of war and both Indian and African natives. The officers they had taken with them, with the exception of one R.A.M.C. officer, who had been left behind to look after the sick. There were 67 prisoners of war liberated here, of which 33 were Europeans. Three of these Europeans had been in German hands for three years. There were also found in the different hospitals of the neighbourhood 96 German Europeans and 510 Askaris. A very large proportion of these were not sick; though left behind in hospital, they were only suffering from tiredness. The German Hospital staff, which also fell into our hands, consisted of two medical officers, seven European dressers, two European nurses, and one priest.

I had the opportunity of personally talking to many of these released prisoners. They all agreed that until comparatively recently their treatment had been by no means good, but when compared to that meted out to the native prisoners of war, they agreed that they had little to complain of. These wretched men had been systematically bullied, and had been at all times forced to work in chains, on the very poorest of rations—their taskmaster being one Tsetse (I have spelt the name the same as the insect, this being the way it was pronounced). Tsetse he was by name and also in character. This creature, reputed to be made in the image of his Maker, was a brute of the worst kind. The following story is told about his brutality to a Hausa prisoner of war. One of the prisoner's ankles was damaged by the leg-iron, and a sore developed that at first only lamed him. Instead of being handed over to the medical authorities he was forced by

Tsetse to continue working till the ankle became so bad that he became a drag upon the other prisoners on the same chain. He was therefore taken out of the chain and forced to go on working by himself. When, owing to the bad state of his leg, he was forced to sit down and rest, he was beaten and kicked by this gentle son of the Fatherland. The sore became worse, so that frequently the Hausa fell down exhausted, only to be driven on again with blows. At last death, in the shape of gangrene, released the wretched man from further suffering. Tsetse's treatment of natives was too bad even for the Boche, for he was later relieved, being put in charge of the British European non-commissioned prisoners. These he also bullied ; but Fate had a surprise in store for friend Tsetse. When he was in turn made a prisoner of war, his escort to Lindi consisted of a few of his own ex-prisoners. I hope that during this long march he was taught to repent of his evil. Another beast that was taken prisoner at Chiwata was an under-officer named Schutz. His sphere of activity was chiefly Tabora, where he had been in charge of the European prisoners of war, whose treatment has been described in another place. Schutz and Tsetse alike were on our black list, both being wanted for acts of cruelty. I believe they were both tried by a court-martial at Dar-es-Salaam. I only hope that the punishment they received was adequate for all the crimes they had committed against civilization. It is a pity that when one has to deal with wretched brutes of this kind one cannot put them through the identical treatment that they have meted out to others. I always think Tsetse would have been a most beautiful sight with a nice gangrene leg!

The advance of the three columns was continued on the 16th November, the Nigerian Brigade less the 2nd Battalion continuing to be in the centre, with the 1st Battalion leading.

The advance guard became engaged at 6.40 a.m., two miles south-east of Chiwata. The enemy had a strong rearguard on the far side of a steep *donga*, and when the screen of scouts arrived at the near side of this the enemy disclosed two machine-guns. The Stokes guns came into action immediately, and the enemy retired. The advance was continued for another three miles, and the advance guard arrived at the dry beds of the Mpangula and Mwiti rivers at 8 a.m. Here there is a wide and deep ravine, the far side of which had been reached before the enemy opened a very hot fire on the advance guard, who now became heavily engaged. The column was held up, which led to the 1st Battalion being deployed, and the section of the Nigerian artillery and Stokes guns came into action. The enemy, fearing they would be outflanked, retired eastwards at 11 a.m.

The Nigerian Column continued advancing at 11.30 a.m. The advance guard from this time onwards was always in touch with the enemy's rearguard, and shots were continuously being exchanged. The advance was necessarily slow, as the enemy disputed every yard. At 2 p.m. the advance was checked by the enemy, who were entrenched in a position west of Ngororo, and covering the water supply—their left resting on the high ground on the west of the road.

A company of the 1st Battalion was sent out to clear this ridge at 2.30 p.m., but met with considerable resistance, necessitating the G.O.C. reinforcing this flank with another company at 3.30 p.m. The remaining two companies of the 1st Battalion became more closely engaged as they came in touch with the enemy's main position on the road. At 5 p.m., as the enemy counter-attacked the Nigerian left, 14 Company of the 4th Battalion was sent as a reinforcement. The enemy were repulsed and driven off at 5.45 p.m. The Stokes guns did most useful work this day, and greatly assisted in repelling the German counter-attack.

Von Lettow ordered up two fresh companies, with instructions that the Nigerians must be driven back at all costs, but his troops were tired of the uneven contest. It was reported that the German Commander-in-Chief had a violent quarrel that evening with some of his subordinate leaders, who as good as declined to continue the attack against the Nigerians. It is said that these same leaders, with their following, composed the force that surrendered to the Nigerians two days later. The Nigerian Brigade gained touch during the evening with the 55th (Coke's) Rifles, which battalion formed part of Column 1, and had themselves lost touch with their own column commander, Col. Orr. In this entirely successful day the Nigerians lost only two killed and thirteen wounded, whilst the German casualties are known to have been far heavier—five of their Askaris being buried by us.

We had only one white casualty in this day's fight— Lieut. Winter, who was Adjutant of the 4th Battalion, and received what is commonly called a *Blighty* in the leg. He was sitting down resting in the shelter of a native hut whilst the 1st Nigerians were in action over a mile in front, the only parts of his anatomy that were exposed being his legs. I personally was strolling up to him in order "to pass the time of day," when to my amusement Lieut. Winter jumped up, and, after running round in a circle like one possessed of an unclean spirit, said, "Who did that? Something has stung my leg." On careful examination is was found that a kindly bullet had lodged in his calf, and had not had the indecency even to draw blood. This meant for the lucky receiver no more marching, work, or incessant fear of being plugged by people who evidently did not wish one well. It was reported that others sat down in the place vacated by this officer, with their legs out waiting for another *Blighty* to arrive, but all in vain. Thus this officer was for the second time in this campaign carried off in triumph to the hospital and to the flesh-pots of the base.

This reminds me of a few verses of a Rubayat that I came across in East Africa, written by a tired and weary officer in the lean days of the Rufiji:

> *Awake! A German in the hour of night*
> *Has fired a shot that puts all sleep to flight,*
> *And lo! the leaders of the W.A.F.Fs. have caught*
> *Fright of attack, thus all await the light.*
>
> *Dreaming of peace, of plates with food piled high,*
> *I heard a voice outside my hut to cry,*
> *Awake, my little one, and man your trench,*
> *'Tis raining, yet I leave my hut that's dry!*
>
> *Here with a loaf of bread beneath the bough,*
> *A flask of dop, a tin of jam, and thou*
> *O Boche, far banished in the wilderness,*
> *East Africa is Paradise enow.*

How often in this force The Black Brigade,
Whose officers are working night and day,
Has leader after leader with his pomp
Abode his hour or two, then went his way?

Lo! some who fought and loved the fighting best,
After a while back to the base were pressed,
And there have drunk their cup, with bellies full,
Have one by one crept silently to rest.

And we, that now are working in the room
They left, to double hours and extra duties' doom,
Ourselves will go to D.-S.-M. some day,
And when away ourselves make room—for whom?

Oh, eat your rations, and your dop defend,
Lest pinched is that on which your joys depend,
Then rest, and lay yourselves on Hunger's bed,
Sans dop, sans bacon, flour and milk—sans end.

It is a pathetic little poem, and, though a parody, well describes the feelings of all in those trying times. But this is a digression, and we must return to the story. The scouts sent out at dawn on 17th November found that the enemy had evacuated their position on the evening before. The 4th Nigerians were the leading battalion, of which 16 Company, under Capt. Hetley, formed the vanguard. The country passed through was still very broken, and this necessitated a slow advance.

After proceeding for about three miles the vanguard had arrived at a narrow spur that ran down towards the east from the high ground forming the plateau. This spur was commanded both on the north and east by far higher ground, and was situated a little to the west of the Luchemi. At 11.30 a.m. Capt. Hetley's *point*, which had descended nearly half-way down the valley, was fired upon from the high ground on the east and north-east, but by this time they had nearly managed to gain the Luchemi valley, before they were finally forced to halt. The road was commanded to the north-east, east, and south-east by under features of the Makonde escarpment. The enemy held the path with several machine-guns and rendered the road impassable. This country leading down to the Luchemi was far more difficult for an advancing force than anything yet experienced in German East Africa, and the fighting had now developed into regular mountain warfare.

As the 2nd Company in the advance (No. 14) arrived at the top of the spur, down which 16 Company had already descended, a party of the enemy could be seen retiring up the hills on the opposite side of the Luchemi valley, at a range of about 1500 yards. Two machine-guns were immediately brought into action, and opened up covering fire upon the hillside, on which the enemy could be seen moving. Capt. Hetley had in the meantime been reinforced by half No. 14 Company. This half company was sent out to the left flank at about 1 p.m. with the idea of dislodging some snipers who had taken up a position on the high ground north-east of Capt. Hetley. They had a very bad experience owing to the appalling nature of the country, and instead of dislodging the snipers they were nearly dislodged off the earth themselves! They came under very heavy fire, and were extremely fortunate not to suffer any casualties. A section of the 2nd Battalion who were sent out to support this half company had one man killed and another wounded.

By 4.30 p.m. it was evident that it would be quite impossible to advance any more troops into the valley without incurring very heavy casualties. Orders were therefore given to two companies to work out on to the high ground to the north-east and establish themselves there before dark, with the idea in view of working round the enemy's right at dawn on the 18th. The Kashmiri and Nigerian batteries meantime came into action and tried to silence the enemy's machine-guns, but without success. At 5 p.m. heavy firing was heard from the south-east, which was apparently Column I in action. The firing lasted till 5.45 p.m. The Nigerian Brigade co-operated as far as possible with gun and machine-gun fire. At dusk the Nigerians gained touch with a patrol of the 1/3rd King's African Rifles from Column 1. The enemy, now finding that they were threatened from the south-east, retired from the water in the Luchemi valley. Shortly before dusk Gen. O'Grady was heard to be in action far away to our left.

Throughout the day the Nigerian advanced troops had been in a very exposed position on the spur, and suffered in all three officers wounded and thirty-five other casualties, but luckily none of the Europeans were serious cases. These were the very last casualties to be received in action in the Nigerian Brigade during this campaign.

On the 18th November the advance was continued by the 1st Battalion. The enemy had retired during the night. The two companies that had gone out to the flank on the previous evening had to work over very difficult country, but they met with no opposition. Scouts that had crossed the stream at the south-east end of the Luchemi valley were in close touch with the 1/3rd King's African Rifles on their right. This battalion had taken up a position covering the water after their action of the previous night.

The two remaining companies of the 1st Battalion were ordered to advance down the spur on which all the fighting had occurred the day before, and take up a position covering the water. From there they were to send out patrols north-east and east, so as to gain touch with Column 3, and locate the enemy's hospital, which was known to be in the Luchemi district.

At 9 a.m. one of the 1st Nigerian companies was ordered to advance along the north-east side of the escarpment above the Luchemi, whilst a strong patrol was dispatched east along the Kitangari track.

The patrol that had been sent out to gain touch with Column 3 met with some slight opposition, but after a few shots had been exchanged the enemy retired. By 11 a.m. this patrol had gained touch with the Cape Corps from Column 3 and the Beluchis from Column 1. Lieut. Hart of this patrol now went forward north-east along the plateau. At 1.30 p.m. his advanced scouts reported that they had met a white flag party consisting of a British officer prisoner of war and a German officer. These officers informed Lieut. Hart that there were 259 German Europeans and 700 German natives wishing to give themselves up to the British, and also that there were 25 British, 2 Belgian, and 5 Portuguese officers, all prisoners of war, waiting at the hospital to be released. The Germans were taken over as prisoners of war, whilst the officers of the Allies were liberated. The following Nigerian officers on this day were set free: Major Gardner and Lieut. Jeffreys of the 3rd Nigeria Regiment and Lieut. Shaw of the Nigerian Carrier Corps.

A scouting party in the valley collected 299 rifles, of which 159 were British, all in good condition, but the enemy had managed to burn a considerable number of other rifles. There was every sign that the enemy had retired in great haste on the previous evening from the Luchemi valley, for they had left behind them a complete armourer's shop, a distilling plant, and much ammunition and supplies.

This was the very last time that any Nigerian troops were destined to cross swords with the enemy in the German East African Campaign, though still much remained for the Brigade to do before their active part in the campaign was to come to an end.

Chapter 16
A Digression

On reading through this account the reader will be struck with the serious style in which it is written, which will be misleading, because West-Coasters generally are not inclined to be too serious.

Whatever one can say for or against Nigeria, it is a country where laughter, rather than the reverse, is the order of things. One seldom meets a down-hearted Nigerian, be he either black or white. For instance, when a master receives a letter like the following from his late servant, he is not likely to be moved to tears if he still has any sense of humour left in him. This letter was written by a *boy* in Nigeria to his master, who was an officer in East Africa:

My dear Master,—I hasten to write to you chiefly to ask after your normal health. It is my greatest pleasure to write you this letter in order to bring to your understanding that I am still alive thinking of you day after day. Excuse me it will not be out of the way if I relate to you various circumstances that happened to me soon after you were sent away from Calabar. It was about two weeks after you left me in the hands of Colour-Sergeant X., then to the war in the service of the Crown, that Sergt. X. terminated my appointment a fortnight after without any reason being given. I left here in Feb. 1917, and so to Lagos in search of work. I am now a passenger in this colony, a stranger in a strange land. I shall be very glad if you will let me hear from you because of the kindness which you have bestowed upon me, since my life is still in existence in this life of battle. Remember that the post that you are now holding is a patriotic and prominent one, and I am proud of you, that I have a lawful master, who is now pushing forward in this world, and also in this terrible war. Remember, again, that you are now fighting for the right and for the Crown, as well as to keep your people from being fugitives.

I was too pleased to hear that you are now entitled to the title of Distinguished Service Order. May we pray that you may one day be entitled to a higher title such as General, etc.,—I remain, Your old steward,

John ——

The above letter may slightly amuse the reader, but it must be remembered that it was written by a son of Ham in all sincerity to his master in German East Africa, and is therefore an insight to the native mind, and shows his attitude towards the war.

No reference in this account has yet been made to the pleasant days spent by most of the officers of the contingent in Zanzibar, where ten days' leave was from time to time granted. Pages might be written on the curious old town, which is half Arab and half European, with its spike-studded doors, said to be relics of the days when elephants were used as battering rams, the spikes being so placed in the doors to give the poor beasts a headache should they attempt to charge them. The pomp and circumstance of the old days are gone, but the old-world atmosphere is still there.

Of the kindness of the people of the island to the Nigerian officers on leave one cannot write too much. Many a happy hour was whiled away on the *Stoep* of the club in gazing over the blue Indian ocean, and drinking cold drinks at pre-war prices. But let the poet of the W.A.F.Fs. speak to us upon this subject. The poor pen of the author gladly gives place to the real genius of the bard:

An Episode in the Campaign in German East Africa May-June 1917

1. The Lament
Squatting (not by our choice) on the Rufiji,
Foodless at times, and very melancholy,
Rolled flat as cyclostyles beneath a squee-jee,
Sufferers most frequent from the wobbles-colly,
We of the Nig.-Brig. felt not over skittish
When we went forth to hunt the elusive Boches,
Neck deep in swamps, with words robustly British
We cursed the Ordnance who issued no goloshes.

2. The Hope
To us repining thus Brigade Headquarters
Spake, "Ye who'd have ease awhile from Hun Askaris
May now up-stick and leave this waste of waters,
And revel ten days with the Zanzibaris."

3. The Journey
So up-sticked those to whom the word "Ndio"[1]
Had been vouchsafed by powers that be, God bless 'em,
And padded cheerful hooves past Behobeho [2]
Until they reached that beauty spot, D.S.M.[3]

From thence the brave in dhows propelled by breezes,
The timorous in steamers made the crossing,
And all planned pleasures with wild wondrous wheezes—
All that at least were not sea-sick from tossing.

4. The Hope Fulfilled
(a) The Town
Nor are we disappointed in our fond hopes,
Walk the bazaar and watch the vendors selling,
See how the ancient beggar with his wand gropes,
Blind in the eyes, he finds his way by smelling!

---

1. Ndio in Swahili=Yes.
2. Behobeho—Scene of the action of the 2nd Battalion early in January, and capture of the gun.
3. D.S.M.—Dar-es-Salaam, local abbreviation.

All picturesque in whites, blues, reds, and yellows,
Indians and Africans with clove and mango
Mingle their scents, and then the cheap-jack fellows
Show to what lengths experts' extortion can go!
Leave the bazaar—and mind you're wary at
Guides importuning—past the mart of shrill hens,
You will debouch before the Secretariat,
With jewels once resplendent—now with quill pens,
Still it retains some relic of its glory,
Spacious its halls and stout its doors brass studded,
We can well picture round it battles gory,[4]
And the great heads of elephants being blooded.
Pass to the Fort where guns of every nation
Show how the Dutch and Portuguese and Spanish,
Seeking in turn Colonial inflation,
Come, leave their marks behind, and simply vanish!

(b) The Life
Are you fond of your sport or a glass of old port,
Or is it merely the spending of pennies
Which will make you forget the bullets and wet,
Would you sooner have cricket or tennis?
You can get all these things, live richly like kings,
Play your bridge, sing in quartet or solo,
Kick a Rugby football, dance in the Club Hall,
Or show off your prowess at polo.
Disguised as a toff, you can sample the golf,
To your hand you'll find ready each plaything;
Quite peeled of your bark you may swim about stark,
Or when draped take a turn at mixed bathing;
And when those are over, return to your clover,
In which at the Club you're residing;
Gossip on the verandah or go and philander,
The war and its worries deriding.
After which my advice is—at still pre-war prices—
To sample gin, cocktails, or sherry,

---

4. It is alleged that all the doors were so studded to combat the use of elephants as battering rams.

And you won't have to try and enjoy every viand
From the soup to the crystallized cherry,
For perfection and plenty's purveyed to the twenty
Who sit in a state of hysteria
At the yarns they are told by the gallant and bold
F. G. C.,[5] *the Old Man of Nigeria.*

5. Envoi
Now Nigerians all, pray list to my call,
And I don't think our feelings will vary,
Drink a bumper of gratitude for all the beatitude
Conferred on us all in club, field, and hall.
By lesser and greater, from the lowest club waiter
To the Hon'rable Chief Secretary.

Those days spent in the Island were the greatest gift the gods could give a poor weary soul in the Rufiji area

Whilst the Brigade was still in the Rufiji area great alarm and despondency was caused amongst the Brass Hats by the frequent use of the Nigerian code by officers of the Brigade when writing to each other. It was noticed that certain groups of letters were always recurring. Experts were called in to decipher these mystic letters; India, South Africa, and the United Kingdom sent their astrologers to make plain these hieroglyphics. At last one mighty man of letters read the hidden meaning to be: "Send more whisky." High officials of the lines of communication and telegraphs nearly died of shock, the war was all but lost, and great was the *hate* that followed. Then an edict was published in which any future user of this wicked code was cursed by bell, book, and candle to eternal grief, and East Africa knew the code no more; however, the officer in Zanzibar who informed a brother-officer on the Rufiji, by means of this code, that he had at last taught his little dog to swim, was excused the extreme penalty of the law on account of possessing so merry a wit.

When the 1st and 4th Battalions, the Battery and Gambia Company were all together at Morogoro that station was anything but dull. In those days the 4th Battalion and Gambia Com-

---

5. F. G. C. = Brig.-Gen. Cunliffe, Commanding the Nigerian Brigade.

pany were out at Grut's Farm, three miles from the township itself. The *Powers that be* were under the firm impression that the enemy were signalling to each other from near the farm by means of lights, so two companies of the 1st Battalion were sent out to camp for a week near to the Gambia Company, their orders being to hunt the countryside for the unauthorized lights. Those were very cheerful times. The officers of these two companies were out to enjoy themselves, and there was never a dull half-hour. Their camp was on the main road, frequented every evening by *joy riders*. The occupants of these cars were sisters from the Morogoro hospital, who for the benefit of their health were sent out motor rides every evening. Great was their astonishment one evening when they found facing them notice-boards and danger signal of the A. A. pattern, which had been set up on the roadside, asking chauffeurs to drive slowly, and to beware of the school, etc. The travellers were also informed that teas were provided. The ultimate result of these notices was to hold up all the cars on the road, whilst the occupants were taken to a spot in the wood where there was a big camp fire burning, and round the fire had been arranged a circle of chairs, where all comers were served with cocktails à *la Gambia* and other forms of light refreshment. A most cheery evening was spent, and the sisters were not among the least to enjoy themselves. The bush resounded with the laughter of the fair sex, whilst the elves and gnomes nodded their heads at each other in horror at the invasion of their ancient home.

Talking about gnomes and other weird creatures of the bush, I shall never forget my fright when I was first introduced to the local Eve of the Rovuma area. My first impression of her was a creature that resembled a cross between a snouted pig and a good-looking Dachshund. The upper lips of these Rovuma maids have been pushed forward, in some cases over two inches, by inserting a small black saucer-like object into the lip itself, just where the male beast grows a moustache. It gives a snoutish appearance to the local belle, that is regarded by the Rovuma beau as most fascinating, but is rather terrifying to the stranger. If the lady is keen on her personal appearance, she still further adds to her beauty by slitting the lobes of the ears, and by means of attaching weights to the lower portions, greatly increases them in length, till they fall gracefully upon her shoulders. She has reached her zenith of beauty when her lips are pressed out two or three inches in front of her face, so that her face is distorted out of all recognition, and her ears reach down below her shoulders. It is wonderful what the daughters of Eve, irrespective of colour, will do to be in the fashion.

Another cheery period was spent at Kilwa when all the Brigade, less the 3rd Battalion, were assembled there. This was the last time that the happy family were together in a place where enjoyment was possible. We were to lose many of our best in the near future, but at the time the sky was cloudless, and no one was depressed by evil forebodings of what was in store for us. An attack on the gunner officers' lines was planned one night, the chief idea being to procure the wine of Scotland which was badly needed by the Gambia Company and their guests, who at the time were suffering from thirst. I regret to report that the gunners did not wait for the attack to be developed, but prematurely retired into the bush, abandoning their camp. The Gambia Company won a bloodless battle, and returned to their own camp in triumph, bearing with them the fruits of victory in the shape of one bottle of port and another of *dop*—their only casualty being one officer damaged by falling into a bath full of water. Those were happy days, and we thoroughly appreciated them. The relaxation was good for all after the lean and dull days of the Rufiji. It was good to find out that we had not forgotten how to laugh. The chief pastimes at the Redhill Camp at Kilwa were bathing and eating, whilst liquid refreshments and childish games of chance, such as *chase the ace* and *whisky poker*, were sometimes indulged in. The geography book of one's youth would describe Kilwa as standing on the shores on an inlet of the Indian ocean, its chief products being smells and tropical diseases; its exports Sisal and Germans; its imports guns, ammunition, supplies, and British. The town is not financially sound, as the value of its imports is far in excess of the value of its exports. Looking down upon Kilwa from the camp, the contrast of the white buildings from the vivid blue of the water, the bright green of the vegetation from the deep red of the rocks and cliffs, all went to form a beautiful picture; but, like all tropical seaports of Africa, it is more beautiful from a distance than at close quarters. The local Town Council do not seem to trouble themselves too much about sanitary matters and the congested areas problem. Many of the chief buildings of the town have suffered badly from shell fire, and general signs of decay are to be seen everywhere.

Many references have been made in this narrative to *dop* or Cape brandy. It must be explained that this was a ration in East Africa, though its issue was somewhat of a mysterious nature, only understood by members of the supply corps and the more brilliant of our quartermasters. *Dop* was said to be issued on three days a week, but try as hard as one could, one could never arrive at a station on a *dop* day. The old saying that "to-morrow never comes" was equally true of the *dop* issue. "*Dop* yesterday and *dop* to-morrow, but never *dop* today" is a quotation from that extremely clever work *Jambo*, by Capt. Lloyd of the Legion of Frontiersmen (25th Royal Fusiliers) and of *Punch* fame. We hope that his wound received on the 17th October, during the action at the Nakadi river, in the battle of Mahiwa, has in no way taken from his cunning! Again, the quantity of *dop* that constituted a ration could be well described by Euclid's definition of a point—"It had position, but no magnitude." Its colour was also curious, for one day it was pale brandy in tint, and the next was a cross between ink and gum in appearance. When the supply people wanted to give the troops a real treat *dop* was issued in old kerosine tins, which greatly improved its bouquet. It varied so in quantity, colour, taste, and smell that one could almost write a thesis on this one subject alone. However, *dop* when obtainable, regardless of its various attributes, was always welcomed.

A certain regiment, who were all brave men and true, had a most wonderful liking for *dop* in any form. Now a few men in this battalion were fellows of the baser sort and they were not satisfied with the ration that they were receiving, so they put their heads together in order to devise a plan by which to increase the supply. They noticed a cask of the precious nectar standing outside a certain supply *dump* not a thousand miles from the Rufiji. Now the keeper of the *dump* was a man that liked flattery and a friendly talk in the evening with anyone who came along. On this particular evening he was especially flattered by a visit from several men of this distinguished regiment, who engaged him in conversation, whilst one bold spirit attached a long rope to the cask, taking the other end of the rope away into the bush near by. After dusk that evening, should anyone have been near, he must have wondered at the strange noise of something rolling over the hard ground in the neighbourhood of the *dump* when no wheeled vehicle was visible. Next day the cask was conspicuous by its absence.

On looking back through all that I have written, it is an interesting fact to remember that when we were fighting hardest in East Africa the English papers were maintaining that the campaign in this theatre was at an end. On turning over a few *cuttings* I came across one dated 16th March 1917 from *The Times*. It is an abbreviated report of a speech delivered by Gen. Smuts in England soon after he gave up the command in German East Africa. It is so remarkable in the light of after events that I give it *in toto:*

> Regarding East Africa, the campaign in German East Africa may be said to be over. What is delaying the absolute end is the fact that March and April are the heavy rainy season. After April the Germans will have to surrender or go into Portuguese territory. They cannot hold out in German East Africa, and the Portuguese are quite prepared to deal with them. The German Governor and his Staff, the Commander-in-Chief and other officers are still doing their best to keep things going, but it is merely the remnant of an army that is left, and not a formidable fighting force.
> All South African white troops have, with a few exceptions, left the country, and the campaign will be brought to an end by the native battalions that I have trained. I soon saw that white troops could not long stand the climate. The native troops, who make splendid infantry, have proved very good fighters ; they have done magnificent work, and when the campaign is over will be available elsewhere. In May they can move, and the thing will be finished. . . .

It is hardly necessary for me to say that when we in German East Africa read this speech we were a little taken aback. It only helps to prove how our best statesmen and soldiers can sometimes be misinformed, and are thus guided to be overbold in their statements.

Another remarkable misstatement that appeared in the newspapers about the time of the battle of Mahiwa requires contradiction. The statement was to the effect that a greater proportion of European troops were taking part in the campaign than either Indian or African natives. In Appendix B will be found a complete summary of all units that were in German East Africa at the time of the Mahiwa action in October 1917. The proportion in the infantry in the field during this month works out to be as follows:

European	4.0%
Indian Infantry	29.8%
African Native Battalions	63.4%
West Indian Troops	2.8%

The proportion in the mounted troops were:

European	34.0%
African Natives	16.0%
Indian	50.0%

The Appendix shows which troops were actually at the front, and which were on the lines of communication at about this period.

Whilst upon this subject, I will call attention to Appendix A, which gives the names of every unit in German East Africa at the time of the arrival of the Nigerian Brigade in this theatre. It is interesting as it shows how white troops were replaced by natives in the field. However, on the lines of communication and at the base there were a very large number of Europeans employed even up to the time that the Nigerian Brigade left East Africa, as the following two facts will show. At Ndanda on Christmas Day 1917, 1000 Europeans attended a concert. They consisted of motor drivers, signallers, supply units, medical detachments, and the divisional headquarters. Early in September 1917, 2000 Europeans attended a boxing contest at Dar-es-Salaam.

It is grossly unfair to both Indian and African troops for English newspapers to make statements of this kind, which are calculated to diminish in the public eye the great efforts and sacrifice made by the coloured races of the British Empire in this last and greatest of all crusades.

Whilst on the Rovuma a tragedy occurred to a sentry belonging to a 15 Company picquet. At 4 a.m. on the 22nd December the sentry was heard to call out. At daybreak Sergt. Whittingham went out with two or three soldiers in order to find out what had occurred. To his horror he saw at about 500 yards in front of the sentry's post the man's corpse, and near to it was a lion, lioness, and cubs. When the brutes were disturbed they quickly left their *kill* and the body was brought into camp. On inspection it was found that the body had been badly mauled and the back had been broken. This was the third case in the Brigade of men losing their lives in this way since the Brigade disembarked in East Africa. Another case occurred in No. 11 Company, 3rd Battalion, when they were quartered in the Rufiji area. On that occasion a private on the extreme left of a line of scouts was killed by a leopard. When his body was found it had one paw mark on the face, and the skull had been badly fractured internally. From the above it will be seen that besides having to be constantly on the look-out for the enemy, the men were frequently in danger from wild beasts. In German East Africa everything possible that a man could be up against, except cold, existed: Germans, wild beasts, sickness, heat, hunger, flood.

In no other campaign could sickness have played so important a part. Out of curiosity, on Christmas Day 1917, I compared those Europeans present in the 4th Battalion with those that had been present on Christmas Day 1916. There were only nine out of forty-two Europeans present on both dates, and of these nine three had constantly been on the sick list. That is to say, that the personnel had almost been completely changed in twelve months. The 4th Battalion was far better off in this respect than any other battalion in the Brigade.

From time to time mention has been made of the Intelligence Department, the agents of which at all times were called upon to do most difficult and dangerous work. Many of these officers were Dutchmen from South Africa who had worked in German East Africa before the war. Major Pretorius had hunted elephant all over this colony, and knew as much of it as a man would know of his own back garden. Many of these I.D. agents were exceptionally brave men. I believe I am right in stating that both the Victoria Crosses given during this campaign were earned by I.D. officials.

Lieut. Harman, who was with the Nigerian Brigade for most of the time that we were on the Rufiji, was constantly patrolling round the flanks of the enemy's position, gleaning information first-hand of their doings. He was a fine type of an old-fashioned Dutchman, brave and as tough as a *trek* ox. He would go out for three or four days at a time in order to make a personal reconnaissance, with just enough food to last him and a ground sheet to lie on, his only escort being half a dozen I.D. scouts, usually ex-German Askaris. This little party would get right round to the rear of the German position and there lie up in the bush and watch the doings of the enemy. But the Intelligence Department had its black sheep like all departments, though most of their officers were really brave men. I have heard of one who, to put it in the language of the Coast, "feared too much." Many amusing tales were told about this unfortunate man by some of these hard-headed old Dutchmen. The following anecdote I have tried to set down on paper as near as possible as it was told me by an old South African belonging to the Intelligence Department. He tells the story about a senior officer, but one who was many years his junior in the knowledge of bushcraft and war. The two were out together on a patrol. "When we start the Captain is all the way asking—Where is the escort? Where is the escort? and I reply always that if I see the escort it is no good, and if I do not see them it means they do their work in the bush and it is good. When we come to some water the Captain asks—Is it safe to cross over? I answer that he is my Captain and it is for him to say, but always he ask the same question of the escort and if it is safe to go on. At last I get tired, and when again he ask at a water crossing, I say: 'Look the German foot;

he come, he go, he will come again.' He ask again if it is safe to go on. I just say: 'He come, he go, he will come again.' Then the Captain stop—'We will go back.' So we go, and I tell you that on the way out his ass is eating the tail off my ass, and on the way back my ass cannot catch up with the shadow of his ass!!!"

History does not relate the tenor of the report on the above reconnaissance.

At times like those spent by us on the Rufiji when mails were very few and far between, a few of the letters that were received from home were a little trying to us hungry people. Try to picture a scene, kind reader, like the following: An emaciated soldier dressed in rags of khaki, dully eyeing the ration issue for the day, namely, a little mealie meal and very little else, on which he has eked out a meagre existence for weeks. The locality, needless to say, was the Rufiji. To the wretched creature—a scarecrow of rags and bones—is delivered a mail. He reads his letters. For a short moment he forgets his troubles; his whole being quivers with emotion only to become listless again. One sentence in his letter from the kind-hearted old aunt far away has had this effect. My reader and I will glance over his shoulder and read his letter (by the way I am not in the habit of doing this sort of thing). We read: "We have found all sorts of substitutes for ordinary food, which is now difficult to procure; for instance, instead of oatmeal at breakfast in the morning we eat mealie meal porridge; when you come home you must try it!"

In this book little has yet been recorded of the doings of the personal boys of Europeans. These young Nigerians are worthy of special mention, for without them the lot of the European would frequently have been made doubly hard. As a class they were hard-working and faithful to their masters. At the end of a long day's march or fierce fight their work began. Dinner had to be cooked and a bed had to be made. When everyone in camp had a day's rest, the boys had to wash their masters' clothes and do a hundred small things for their personal comfort. Nor did they escape the dangers of the fight. Two were killed at Bweho Chini and another was murdered at Mahiwa. I have seen boys cooking food for their masters during the heat of a fight, only a few yards from the firing line itself. For fifteen months many of these youngsters never had a day's rest, and without grumbling served their masters as only a black man knows how to serve, with almost a dog-like devotion, through hunger and wet, long days and heat, hard fighting and long marches. At the end of the day's work they were always ready to laugh over the misfortunes of the past twenty-four hours. Theirs was faithfulness personified. Some people in their ignorance maintain that black men have no real affection. This I hold to be untrue, and only proves that he who makes such a statement does not really know the black man. I have known boys sit up night after night within call of a sick master, ready to do anything in their power to lighten his suffering. One boy I know of who of his own free will carried a machine-gun into action after the team had all been shot down. By this action he greatly helped to check the enemy's advance. A few masters, I fear, do not sufficiently appreciate all that their boys did for them during the fifteen months spent in East Africa, and because a few boys were thieves or scoundrels, they suspect every boy of being the same, and forget that they would be in a very awkward position if they had had no boy to work for them. Seeing all that I have seen I take off my hat to the boy that faithfully served his master through all these long months. His life was no bed of roses; he had much to contend with; he was often hungry, sick, and tired, but his day was never over till his master was comfortably in bed. He had always to rise in the morning an hour before his master, in order to make the early morning tea or cocoa before the real work of the day began. Truly he has earned the motto: "*Semper fidelis et impiger.*"

Chapter 17

The Last Phase of the Campaign

Von Lettow's movements after his action of the Luchemi were shrouded in mystery. His strength was thought to be 300 Europeans and about 1200 Askaris. That he intended to cross the border into Portuguese territory was a foregone conclusion, but before he finally went south it was equally certain that he would attempt a junction with Tafel's force, which was then known to be in the act of breaking south from the Mahenge district. To prevent this junction of the two main German forces was the first consideration of the Higher Command, after which to prevent von Lettow's escape south would be Gen. van Deventer's objective.

On the 19th November the Nigerian Brigade commenced a concentration at Mwiti, whilst the 4th Battalion was sent forward to Kitangeri. It is interesting to note that this place was reported to be the site chosen by the Germans as a landing place for the Zeppelin which was due to arrive at about this date.

Column 1 was on the 19th November *en route* for Newala.

For the first time in the East African campaign the German forces were known to be in full retreat. They had been forced to give battle day after day for more than two months, in which time they had been given no chance to rest. The result was that their morale and strength was beginning to fail, but it would be unfair if they were not given all the credit due to them for their dogged resistance, faced as they were by invariably superior numbers, except in the early part of the battle of Mahiwa, continually being compelled to give ground even after fighting a successful action, and always losing heavily in casualties, especially in their European ranks. In spite of all this, to the very end they kept their tails up, and fought a one-sided contest with indomitable courage and exemplary dash, and they never failed to leave their marks on their opponents.

In the seven weeks ending 17th November the Nigerian Brigade alone out of an effective strength of 170 Europeans, 2246 native rank and file, suffered 78 Europeans and 842 rank and file casualties; that is to say, over 45 per cent. Europeans and nearly 38 per cent, of other ranks of the Brigade were put out of action during this period. Added to this a very large percentage of the Brigade were already out of action through sickness and casualties received in action during the previous eight months. Other columns had fared no better than the Nigerian Brigade, and in fact Column 3 had suffered even more heavily.

On the 22nd November, owing to Tafel's movements, the Brigade was ordered to concentrate at Massassi. This was completed on the 23rd November, and at about the same time the enemy had made a further surrender at Newala, consisting of 160 Europeans and 75 Askaris.

A part of the 4th Battalion had marched over 50 miles in three days. The heat during this long march had been terrific, and the whole Brigade was suffering greatly from fatigue.

An abandoned 4·1 German naval gun was passed by the Brigade on the road near to Massassi.

Up north, Tafel had had some minor successes recently against Gen. Northey's troops, which had included the capture of two British food and ammunition convoys.

On the 24th the Nigerian Brigade and the Kashmiri Battery continued to march south from Massassi, and arrived on the 26th at a point on the main southern road, 13 miles south of Gongonuchi on the Bangalla river. The disposition of other British troops on this date were as follows: the 129th Baluchis were 6 miles west of Luatala, having just completed a 40-mile march. They had received orders to continue the march to Luatala. The mounted column, consisting of the 25th Indian Cavalry and a regiment of South African Horse, both under the command of Lieut.-Col. Breytenbach, were a few miles west of the Baluchis; a patrol under Capt. Nethersole and the 25th Cavalry at the Mwiti river were in touch with the 129th Baluchis. Column 1 was at the confluence of the Bangalla and Rovuma rivers; Column 2 at Naurus; Column 3 at Gongonuchi; and Column 4 was in reserve and split up on the lines of communication with their headquarters at Nangoo. On this day parties of the enemy were reported to be in the Nawbingo, a hilly district north of the Bangalla river.

At the time the 129th Baluchis were only 120 strong, under the command of two officers in addition to their commanding officer. The battalion was also considerably hampered by a large convoy, the carriers of which were appreciably fatigued after a very long march.

The patrol of the 25th Cavalry under Capt. Nethersole had been sent to investigate what had been reported as being an action between Tafel's force and a small British Intelligence post at Tshrimba Hill. The cavalry reported that on the 25th November several companies of the Germans attacked this post, but owing to the impregnable position taken up by the I.D. the enemy gave up this attempt to take the position, but unfortunately Capt. M'Gregor, the I.D. agent, who was in command of the post, was killed by a chance shot. The cavalry patrol was on its way back to Breytenbach's Column on the 26th, when they met the rearguard of the 129th Baluchis *en route* for Luatala. They accompanied the infantry for some little distance, Capt. Nethersole's intention being to leave them at the Mwiti stream after he had watered his horses, but they had not followed the Baluchis for more than a few minutes when the Indians' vanguard was heard to be in action. The vanguard had been ambushed, and came under very heavy fire from the front and both flanks, and almost immediately afterwards the whole column was in action. The Germans delivered a bayonet charge against the Baluchis' left flank, in which they inflicted heavy casualties upon them, and partially broke their flank. The enemy attempted to do the same against the right flank, but their attempt was frustrated by the cavalry. On this flank the Germans were caught by mounted troops in close order, in the open, at a short range. Heavy casualties were sustained by the Germans in this quarter, whilst they were in the act of assembling to deliver a bayonet charge. The commanding officer of the Baluchis was wounded about this critical time; the Indians being hopelessly outnumbered by the enemy were forced to retire, which they did in good order under the cavalry's patrol covering fire. They managed to take up successfully a new position, which they were determined to hold till the last, but for some unknown reason, at the very moment when matters looked most desperate for the Indians, who had suffered over 40 per cent, casualties in a few minutes' fighting, the Germans retired south and commenced to cross the Rovuma river on the same day.

To everyone's utter amazement a large party of Tafel's force, consisting of 30 Europeans, 180 Askaris, 640 carriers, and 220 native women, came into the British camp the same afternoon in order to surrender. Early in the morning of the 27th a flag of truce was sent into the Baluchis by Tafel, who offered to surrender with 62 Europeans and 1000 Askaris. Tafel, Lincke, and Schenfeld were amongst the Europeans wishing to give themselves up. The surrender was accepted and carried out on the 28th. Otto had been with Tafel up to the time of his surrender, but during the night of 26th-27th, he, with 5 other Europeans and 20 Askaris, broke away south in order to join von Lettow; thus 95 Europeans and about 1200 Askaris surrendered, after fighting a successful engagement, to about 100 Indian soldiers. No one was more surprised at this turn of events than the Baluchis and the 25th Cavalry patrol.

Tafel's surrender must be put down to the fact that on his arrival at Newala, where he expected to find von Lettow waiting for him, he found that he had been abandoned to his fate, von Lettow having evacuated that place some days previously. He was thus isolated and out of touch with any other German column, and without supplies. Had he crossed the Rovuma he would have found himself in no better a position, as he could never know when he would be attacked by overwhelming numbers. So far as he knew von Lettow might have already been forced to surrender, or in order to avoid that had bolted south into Portuguese territory.

Otto's action shows the style of man that he was. When he left Tafel he cut himself adrift with only a handful of faithful followers in order to go into the unknown, not even being aware from where he would get his next supplies. Otto, it will be remembered, was an *old friend* of the Nigerians, having taken a leading part in the action of the 24th January, when he had been wounded in the arm. News of this big surrender reached the Nigerian Brigade on the same day on which it had occurred.

On the 20th November Major Pinto, in command of about 900 Portuguese native troops, arrived at Ngomano from the south in order to prevent von Lettow breaking across the Rovuma at this place. Instead of preparing a position for defensive purposes, this column busied themselves in laying out an elaborate camp near to, and south-west of, the old Portuguese fort that stands on the south bank of the Rovuma commanding the confluents of that river with the Lugenda. The Portuguese appeared to have had a picquet at the fort and another a few hundred yards up the Rovuma river. On the 25th November von Lettow appeared on the Rovuma river a short distance upstream from the confluence. The Portuguese do not seem to have tried to prevent him crossing the river. In any case the enemy worked round to the west and attacked Major Pinto's force from the south, south-east, and west. A few rounds of high explosive were fired into the Portuguese perimeter from the north bank of the Rovuma. The Portuguese hastily entrenched themselves in rifle pits, which were, for the most part, not even bullet-proof. What the actual strength of the Germans was in this action it is hard to say, but it could not have been more than 1500 rifles, and probably a good deal less. The Germans appeared to have brought only four machine-guns into action, and these were used at a very close range. Our Allies fired at least 30,000 to 40,000 rounds from about 350 rifle pits. Major Pinto was killed early in the fight, together with eight other Europeans. Judging by the graves, the Germans only seemed to have lost one European killed in the action—a Sergt. Bachmann. The Portuguese native casualties were very heavy, and they were at last forced to surrender with 700 Askaris, 6 machine-guns, a quantity of ammunition, and six days' rations for 150 Europeans and 1000 natives.

The Portuguese were immediately relieved of all their clothing, and the Germans, who were at this time in rags, replenished their wardrobes. Von Lettow did not dare to remain at Ngomano one hour longer than absolutely necessary for fear of the arrival of British troops. He therefore left Hauptmann Klinkhardt, with one company as rearguard, at Ngomano, and he himself marched south, using the Portuguese soldiers as carriers for all the arms, ammunition, and supplies that had fallen into his hands. Before leaving Ngomano von Lettow smashed up all his own machine-guns and rifles for which he had no longer any ammunition, and took into use Portuguese rifles and British machine-guns, with which Major Pinto had been armed. Every box and package that the Portuguese had possessed the Germans looted. The Boches' treatment of their Portuguese prisoners was very different from that meted out to the captured Germans at the Lushimi by the Nigerians. At the Lushimi not a single German's load was looted. Carriers were supplied for their baggage, and their property was respected as much as their persons. As long as a German was not on the *black list* he was at all times treated with the utmost courtesy, and given every latitude possible with due regard to his safe custody.

Thus von Lettow escaped, together with the Ex-Governor of the Colony and a force of about 1500 of all ranks. A Berlin semi-official wireless reported that 1700 German Europeans and 9500 native troops had escaped into Portuguese territory; this, it is needless to say, was a gross misstatement of facts.

News of this disaster to the Portuguese reached the Nigerian Brigade on the 29th November, when they were at Naurus. It is useless to comment further on these facts. The reader must be left to draw his own conclusions on the whole affair. On the 30th November the Brigade moved to the Makanya river, cutting a motor road for themselves as they advanced. This brings us to the end of the campaign on German soil. By this date there was not a German soldier at liberty in the whole colony, and German East Africa was, a few days later, declared a British and Allied Protectorate. During the month of November no less than 1115 German Europeans and 3382 Askaris were either killed or captured, together with two 4·1 naval guns, one 4·1 howitzer, one 70 mm. gun, forty-three machine-guns, and a large number of rifles and much ammunition. Tafel's forces, before surrendering, destroyed one 60 mm. gun, one 37 mm. gun, thirty machine-guns, and about 1300 rifles.

On the 30th November His Majesty the King sent the following cable of congratulation to Gen. van Deventer:

> I heartily congratulate you and the troops under your command on having driven the remaining forces of the enemy out of German East Africa.

On the 6th December Gen. van Deventer answered his Majesty's cable in the following terms:

> I beg to tender the loyal and heartfelt thanks of the East African forces for your Majesty's most gracious message, which has given the liveliest satisfaction to all ranks, and has more than compensated us for the hardships and difficulties of the East African campaign.

On the 5th December Field-Marshal Sir Douglas Haig wired to Gen. van Deventer:

> On behalf of the British Armies in France I send you and the gallant troops under your command our heartiest congratulations on having completed the conquest of the last German colony. The perseverance, patience, and determination required for this achievement are fully realized by all of us here in France, and command our admiration.

Gen. van Deventer's answer to this wire was greatly appreciated, and endorsed by the whole of the Nigerian Brigade:

> I thank you most sincerely for your congratulations. We follow the splendid achievements of the British Armies in France with the greatest interest and admiration, and are proud to think that the East African force has played its part, however small, in the great struggle.

An attempt was now made to catch up von Lettow. Col. Breytenbach's mounted column was at this time on the banks of the Rovuma. A 25th Cavalry patrol had actually gained touch with von Lettow's rearguard under Klinkhardt. This officer had remained on the Rovuma as long as he dared in order to cover Tafel's crossing when he should arrive, and he was therefore some distance behind von Lettow's main body. The patrol, thinking that they were in touch with a big force, withdrew. It seems, however, unfortunate that they were not greatly reinforced, for had they continued to trouble Klinkhardt that officer would most probably have been forced to surrender. He had with him only eighty Askaris, who were greatly hampered by having with them a large amount of heavy baggage, which included von Lettow's own private kit and papers. The porters carrying these loads were exhausted, and all were very short of supplies.

Klinkhardt a few days later gave himself up on account of ill-health. He stated after his capture, that if all this baggage had been lost, very likely von Lettow would have been forced to surrender, and in any case most of his European followers would have done so.

We must now turn our attention to von Lettow. After he had fought the Portuguese at Ngomano he marched south. The nearest British troops to him were the Nigerian Brigade at Gongonuchi, 55 miles by road to Ngomano. All other British troops were well to the east, on the look-out for Tafel. Von Lettow at the worst could count on two clear days' start of any pursuing troops. His force was, however, very short of food and ammunition, even taking into account that which they had seized from the Portuguese. On or about the 8th December the Germans attacked a Portuguese post on the Ukula mountains. This post had moved out from Nanguri Fort a few days previously, leaving behind them at that place only a small guard over a very big *dump* of supplies and ammunition. The Portuguese force on the Ukula surrendered after a stiff fight. All the Europeans of this force were immediately set at liberty after giving their parole that they would not fight against the Germans again in Africa. After this surrender the Germans marched to the Nangoar Fort, which place they took unopposed on the 12th December. Here they captured 100,000 rations and vast stores of ammunition. This Portuguese fort was a well-built redoubt standing in the centre of a huge clearing. The Lujenda river flowed within a mile of the fort. It is therefore rather hard to understand why these supplies and ammunition were not thrown into the river before the arrival of the Germans.

At Nangoar fort the German force broke up into two parties, one marching towards Port Amelia and occupying Medo Boma and Meza, and the other column continuing the march south along the Lujenda river, and eventually during the latter half of December, occupying Mwembe near the Mchinga Hills.

All this time the British forces were not by any means resting on the British border, but were actively trying to assist the Portuguese. The 1st and 3rd Nigeria Regiments crossed the Rovuma during the first week in December, and immediately commenced patrolling south in conjunction with the mounted column and the Intelligence Department scouts. An officer of the 3rd Battalion was sent to the Ex-Governor, von Schnee, under a flag of truce on the 4th December, with a letter from the British Commander-in-Chief informing the Ex-Governor that, as all the German troops had evacuated the German colony, that colony was formally annexed by the Allies. During the second week in December the Nigerian Brigade and the Kashmiri Battery got up a race-meeting for two silver cups presented by Brigadier-General Mann and Colonel Badham. I should imagine that it was the first time in history, and probably the last for many decades to come, that a race-meeting of this sort had taken place on the German-Portuguese border of East Africa. There were in all three races—a flat race, a steeplechase, and a mule race for the natives. The last was the most amusing to watch, for most of these diabolic animals behaved just as they wished, and went where the spirit moved them. The whole country for some acres round was covered by native Indians and Nigerians who had been forced to give up the uneven contest. After a day or two most of the mules were collected, but not more than two or three mules ever finished the race.

The ration question during the early weeks on the Rovuma was not too satisfactory. Early on Christmas morning parties were sent out from each company of the 4th Battalion to shoot for *the pot*. The hunter of 16 Company distinguished himself by shooting an M.I. horse in mistake for an antelope, much to the annoyance of the M.I. Mills' bombs proved themselves most useful in lieu of dynamite for killing fish in the river. A bush pig and a pigeon constituted the total bag of the combined efforts of all companies, not to mention the horse. Very late on Christmas Day 16 Company's hunter re-established his popularity by bagging two buck. The Christmas dinner was not a great success in spite of all that was done to try to make things go off well. One could not help looking round the table and thinking of the jolly crowd that spent Christmas Day together in 1916, at Tulo. Only eight of the original officers of the 4th Battalion were present on both Christmas Days. No less than twenty-two Europeans in this battalion, out of the original contingent, had either made the extreme sacrifice, been wounded, or fallen a victim to the many diseases which affect that distressful country; but the 4th Battalion was a great deal better off than most of the other battalions in this respect.

Some weeks before Christmas the Gold Coast Regiment had been sent round by sea to Port Amelia, whilst Gen. Northey had moved south, and by this time had a strong force operating against von Lettow through Nyasaland. On the 12th January all the British troops operating from the Rovuma, except the I.D., began to evacuate Portuguese territory owing to the rains having commenced, thus making the Rovuma dangerous for crossing.

This sees the end of the campaign as far as the Nigerian Brigade was concerned, and all the battalions were gradually withdrawn to Mtama. There cannot be a worse country to be found in Africa than that in which the Nigerians operated from the Rovuma into Portuguese East Africa. It is most unhealthy, uninteresting, and devoid of all native population. No desert could produce less than this country did during the Nigerian occupation of Portuguese territory. When the Nigerians were withdrawn, two strong columns were in the act of operating from Port Amelia and Nyasaland, whilst a brigade of King's African Rifles were placed in a good central position commanding the line of the Rovuma.

CHAPTER 18

Envoi

With the crossing of von Lettow into Portuguese territory the enemy lost their last colony, and now not one square mile of territory outside Europe does Germany hold. In 1913 she was the third greatest colonizing power after Britain and France. Whatever will be the final result of the Great War, Germany will have to rebuild her Colonial Empire once again from the bottom. At all costs Germany should never be allowed to hold one yard of territory in Africa, for this we owe to ourselves as well as to the native populations of the late German states.

The African native has proved himself to be made of first-class fighting material—just as good as the best Indian soldier when properly trained and officered. The British Government cannot afford to open to the Prussian General Staff this vast recruiting ground from which tens of thousands of the best trained negro soldiers could operate against Europe or our Asiatic or African possessions. Gen. von Freytag, for some time Deputy Chief of the German General Staff, has lately published a book entitled *Deductions of the World War.* In it we learn that if his deductions are correct, the Union Forces of South Africa will be powerless against the German-trained hordes of Africans to be, and the conquest of North Africa and Egypt will follow the fall of South Africa. This, the General maintains, will be accomplished without the deflection of any white troops from Europe; and further, a great army will be planted on the flank of Asia, the influence of which will be felt throughout the whole of the Middle East as far as Persia and beyond. From these facts, as seen by the Germans, it is self-evident that the civilization of the African native and the economic development of the whole of this vast continent, will at all times take a second place to the German schemes for world power and world conquest. The African native will be used in future, if the Germans have their way, as a tool in the hand of German Militarism. For over three years negro troops under white officers have kept employed a vast British and Allied army. This fact alone proves what could be done with a greater and better-equipped negro force. It is wonderful to think how von Lettow has managed to hold his force together in spite of privations of every kind, shortage of ammunition, and a constant state of being driven from one place to another. Through all this the German native soldier has served his master most faithfully. I doubt if any other soldier than an African would have put up with so much discomfort for so many months. If the Germans ever get back their lost colonies we and the rest of the world are courting disaster; for the German, having found out what a wonderfully fine soldier the negro makes, will at the first opportunity form a vast colonial black army, which will be a menace, not only to the rest of Africa, but to the whole of the world.

Without the aid of negro troops the Allies would never have been able to drive von Lettow out of German East Africa. The Empire owes more recognition than has up to date been given to the negro soldier for all that he has had to endure and all the appalling hardships in East Africa and the Cameroons he has gone through for the sake of the Empire. Their deeds have not been done in the limelight, and the public have heard very little of their doings. None of the battles fought by them will ever be really famous in the world's history, as many lesser battles in the past have been, but, my reader, they have fought and conquered, suffered and died, for the British Empire. "There be of them that have left a name behind them that their praises might be reported, and some thereby which have no memorial, who are perished as though they had never been born." I sincerely hope that all the negro has done for the British race will not be forgotten, and that the welfare of the African will be one of Britain's first considerations after the war; to continue in the words of the *Book of Ecclesiastics*, let it be that "their seed shall remain for ever, and their glory shall not be blotted out."

The Brigade eventually embarked for West Africa on the *Saxon*, the *Briton*, and the *Kinfauns Castle* during the second week of February 1918. All these ships arrived, after a comfortable but uneventful voyage, at Lagos on the 16th March. The Overseas Contingent had a tremendous reception, headed by the Governor in person, on their arrival back in their native land. Our send-off from Nigeria had been lacking somewhat in enthusiasm, the home-coming was the very reverse. Wherever the different units of the Overseas Contingent went after landing they were received with open arms by the people, both black and white, of Nigeria, who did all in their power to show their appreciation of the regiment that bears the name of their colony.

The enemy's stubborn defence of his last colony has been a great military feat, and Nigerian soldiers are the first to admire their pluck and endurance, but I think I shall be voicing the opinion of all Nigerians if I express a fervent hope that German East Africa, a land where so many of our best of both colours have lost their lives or their health, might never be allowed to become a menace to our Empire in future by being prematurely or unwisely returned to its late German owners. I hope this account has given my reader a little insight into the nature of the Nigerian soldier. He is one of the best fellows on earth when properly handled. His loyalty to his officers is profound; he is no saint, but then what other soldiers are saints? In many ways he is utterly childish, and can only be treated as an overgrown child. To know him is to love him in spite of all his bad habits. He is a born gambler, and cannot help playing *char-char* (gambling) whenever he has any money, but he is generous to the point of foolishness, for he is willing to share his last shilling with a friend or fellow-countryman at any time.

There is no doubt that the East African Campaign has been a great education to the native Nigerian. He has seen much in East Africa, Durban, and Cape Town that he will never forget, the most important being the tremendous power and resources of the British Empire. His mind is no longer bounded by the sea, bush, and desert of Nigeria; he is an older, but a much wiser, soldier now, on his return from the East African Campaign, than he was when he embarked for that country.

Nigeria has proved that, besides producing palm oil and ground nuts, she can produce Men. It remains to be seen if she is going to make the best use of this—the world's most valuable product—but now is her opportunity. Never before in the history of the world has man-power been at so high a premium as it is at present.

May the lives of all those that have fallen in German East Africa not have been given in vain, but by their sacrifice shall yet another great tropical country be added to our vast Empire. May Prosperity and Peace reign in the future in this our youngest Colony as they have done in the past in all other British possessions throughout the world. I would conclude this book in the words of Rudyard Kipling's poem, *The Settler*,[1] written at the end of the Boer War:

> *Here, where my fresh-turned furrows run,*
> *And the deep soil glistens red,*
> *I will repair the wrong that was done*
> *To the living and the dead.*
> *Here, where the senseless bullet fell*
> *And the barren shrapnel burst,*
> *I will plant a tree, I will dig a well,*
> *Against the heat and the thirst.*
>
> *Earth, where we rode to slay or be slain,*
> *Our life shall redeem unto life;*
> *We will gather and lead to her lips again*
> *The waters of ancient strife.*
> *From the far and fiercely-guarded streams,*
> *And the pool where we lay in wait,*
> *Till the corn cover our evil dreams*
> *And the young corn our hate.*

---

1. From *The Five Nations* (Methuen).

Bless then our God, the new-yoked plough,
And the good beasts that draw,
And the bread we eat in the sweat of our brow
According to Thy Law!

After us comes a multitude—
Prosper the work of our hands,
That we may feed with our land's food
The folk of all our lands!

Ne unquam virtus fereant animusque Nigeriensis!

An Epilogue

Since completing this book in the spring of 1918 many changes have taken place in Nigeria.

From the ashes of the old Nigerian Brigade which had seen service in Togoland, the Cameroons, and East Africa, a new Brigade had been born and in turn has passed away. On the 1st June 1918 this new unit came officially into being under the title of the 1st (Nigerian) West African Frontier Force Service Brigade; at the same time the 2nd West African Frontier Force Service Brigade was formed in the Gold Coast Colony. It was hoped that the 3rd (Nigerian) W.A.F.F. Service Brigade would be formed at a later date. On the completion of the 3rd Brigade, British West Africa would be in possession of a Service Division. It must be remembered that in addition to these service troops the garrison of the various Colonies had to be maintained. The 1st (Nigerian) W.A.F.F. Service Brigade, known locally as the 1st West African Service Brigade (1st W.A.S.B.), was placed under the command of Brigadier-General F. H. G. Cunliffe, C.B., C.M.G. His Staff consisted of: Captain A. C. Milne-Home, M.C., Brigade Major; Captain J. H. Naumann, Staff Captain; Lieut. W. E. Burr, Staff Quartermaster; Captain H. Bourne, Paymaster; Lieut. A. C. E. Darke, D.C.M., Officer in Charge of Records; Lieut. B. R. Harrison, in Charge of the Clearing Depot; with Lieut.-Col. T. M. R. Leonard, D.S.O., as Principal Medical Officer. The Battalion Commanders were: 1st Battalion—Lieut.-Col. C. E. Roberts, M.C.; 2nd Battalion—Lieut.-Col. G. L. Uniacke, D.S.O.; 3rd Battalion—Lieut.-Col. J. A. Stewart; 4th Battalion—Lieut.-Col.

J. Sargent, D.S.O. The other Unit Commanders were: Major T. A. Vise, M.C., R.A. Battery Commander; Captain C. G. Evans, in Command of the Pioneer Company; Captain E. F. Carson, Stokes Gun Battery Commander; Major W. D. Downes, M.C., in Command of the Brigade Machine Gun Company.

Of these officers all had been with the old Nigerian Brigade in East Africa, and many of their names already figure in the foregoing narrative, with the exception of Lieut.-Col. Stewart, who up to this time had been Commanding a Training Centre in Nigeria.

In addition to all these various units there was an Overseas Depot of 1800 native rank and file under the command of Major F. H. Hawley, composed of recruits who had passed through the Training Centres, and the Training Centres themselves, which were all placed under the command of Lieut.-Col. E. C. Feneran.

The old single-company system which had been in vogue since the formation of the W.A.F.F. now disappeared, and its place was taken by the double-company system, as in the army at home.

Bombing, trench warfare, scouting, machine and Lewis gunnery, double company drill, etc., occupied the time of every one from the day of the return of the Brigade from East Africa until the outbreak of the Egba rising in June. It is quite impossible to write here of all that befell the W.A.S.B. during this expedition in the forest country of Southern Nigeria, as this would necessitate a volume to itself.

During this expedition the battalions were more or less split up, and companies operated individually. The Brigade suffered the better part of one hundred casualties whilst enforcing law and order on the unruly people of the Egba Province.

The natives of this country chiefly contented themselves in pulling up long stretches of the permanent way of the Nigerian Government Railway, cutting telegraph wire, and destroying the property of European traders. The work of the troops was strenuous, but the Brigade lived up to its reputation of efficiency and discipline.

At last the rebels were forced into subjection early in August, and the various units of the Brigade returned to their training stations.

From this time onwards the most vigorous training was carried out by all ranks, so that by the end of September the Brigade had arrived at a very high state of efficiency, and was fit for service in any theatre of operations to which it might be required to proceed. About this time definite orders were received for the 1st W.A.S.B. to proceed to Egypt; but, alas, fate was against this! Two transports out of the five which had been allotted by the shipping controller to move the Brigade east arrived off Lagos during the last week of September. Just before their arrival the epidemic of Spanish influenza, which had invaded two-thirds of the globe, crept down the West Coast to Nigeria. The troops and civil population went down like ninepins before it, and within a few days of the commencement of the epidemic in Nigeria over half of the W.A.S.B. were in hospital. The epidemic was no respecter of persons. Europeans and natives went down similarly before it. The medical authorities of Nigeria pronounced that it was quite impossible for the Brigade to embark. Thus the transports continued their journey south to Cape Town without the troops.

The move to Egypt was postponed for a month. In the meantime the Allies had signed an Armistice with Bulgaria, Turkey, and Austria. Early in November the move to Egypt was definitely cancelled, and preliminary orders for the demobilization of the Service Troops of West Africa were received.

The last day of 1918 saw the end of the 1st W.A.S.B. On the 1st January 1919 this fine body of men ceased to exist.

This is nearly the end of the story of the doings of the Nigerians in the Great War, but my account would not be complete if I did not quote the Brigade Order which was published on 16th December 1918 by Brigadier-General F. H. G. Cunliffe, C.B., C.M.G.:

> Before the demobilization of the 1st (Nigerian) W.A.F.F. Service Brigade is completed, the Brigadier-General Commanding wishes to bid farewell to all ranks.

Whereas none can but feel relief that hostilities are ended, yet there cannot but be a sense of personal disappointment that such a fine body of men as the Service Brigade contains did not get the opportunity of helping to administer the *coup de grâce* to the enemy in the field.

As is now known, the Brigade was destined for the Egyptian Expeditionary Force with a view to operations in Palestine under General Allenby, to whom a very high recommendation of the Nigerian Brigade was dispatched.

To all Units, Departments, and Individuals of the Brigade who have assisted to bring the Brigade to the high state of efficiency to which it has undoubtedly attained, the Brigadier-General wishes to tender his deepest gratitude. He wishes to take this opportunity of expressing his sympathy with the relatives of those who have given their lives for their country while serving with the Overseas Contingent and the Service Brigade, and with those who from wounds or sickness are likely to suffer from lasting effects, and he wishes to offer his heartiest congratulations to all who have been granted awards or mentions in dispatches. He wishes the best of luck to all ranks into whatever sphere of fife they are about to enter, whether the Army, the Civil Service, or private employments, and finally hopes that all will spend a happy Christmas and many prosperous New Years.

Before finally putting down my pen and writing the words "The End" I should like my reader to turn to East Africa once again. There are some men in this world whom one is compelled to admire, be they friend or enemy. General Von Lettow Vorbeck is such a one.

When the Nigerians left Portuguese East Africa and returned to Lindi, they left Von Lettow with a handful of men in a desolate, swampy country south-west of Port Amelia, with the rainy season in front of him.

His native troops were far away from their own country. He had seen his force dwindle from an army in being to a handful of outcasts in a strange land.

On the 16th February 1918, as we, on board the Union Castle steamer the *Briton*, watched the low shores of East Africa sink away below the horizon, we were tempted to believe that Von Lettow's days were numbered and that the tragedy of a brave leader's defeat was all but completed. To the amazement of ourselves and the world in general, a few months later Von Lettow led his handful of men back across the Rovuma and marched north again through what had once been a German colony. When last heard of he was marching towards Tabora, but when he gave himself up, on 14th November 1918, he was south of Kasama, in Northern Rhodesia. His end only came with the fall of the German Empire. In the Allies' terms of the Armistice with Germany Von Lettow was honoured with a clause all to himself, in which he was allowed a month to give himself up. I do not think that in the whole history of the war there has ever been a more striking character than General Von Lettow Vorbeck. He was a genius in the art of bush warfare, a man of indomitable spirit—a most remarkable leader of men, who did not know what it was to be beaten. To him discomfort, hunger, heat, shortage of ammunition and supplies were all as nothing. He had one object in life only, and that was never to be taken by the British. He has at least earned for himself undying fame for being a brave man and a worthy enemy.

This is the end—Armageddon has been fought and won—the British Empire has made good! It has proved once again in history that it is invincible and can never be broken into from the outside as long as it stands together. It is as the City of Mansoul referred to in John Bunyan's *Holy War*, which could only be broken into at the will of the townsmen:

> For here lay the excellent wisdom of him that built Mansoul, that the walls could never be broken down nor hurt by the most mighty adverse potentate unless the townsmen gave consent thereto.

Appendix A

List of Fighting Troops in the Field at the End of 1916

2nd L.N. Lancs.
25th Royal Fusiliers
2nd Rhodesian Regt.
5th S.A. Infantry
6th S.A. Infantry
7th S.A. Infantry
8th S.A. Infantry
10th S.A. Infantry
98th Infantry
63rd P.L.I.
61st Pioneers
57th Rifles
129th Baluchis
40th Pathans
Indian Vol. Maxims
17th Indian Infantry
30th Punjabis
130th Baluchis
2nd Kashmirs
3rd Kashmirs
Bharatpar Infantry
3rd Gwaliors
Jhind Infantry
Kapurthala Infantry
Rampur Infantry
5th Light Infantry
1st Nigeria Regt.
2nd Nigeria Regt.
No. 13 S.A. Field Battery

3rd Nigeria Regt., W.A.F.F
4th Nigeria Regt., W.A.F.F
Gold Coast Regt.
1/2 K.A.R.
1/3 K.A.R.
2/3 K.A.R.
2/2 K.A.R.
2/4 K.A.R.
5th K.A.R.
African Scout Battalion
Cape Corps
2nd W.I. Regt.
British W.I. Regt.
4th S.A. Horse
7th S.A. Horse
9th S.A. Horse
K.A.R., M.I.
No. 1 S.A. Field Battery
No. 2 S.A. Field Battery
No. 3 S.A. Field Battery
No. 4 S.A. Field Battery
No. 5 S.A. Field Battery
No. 6 S.A. Field Battery
No. 7 S.A. Field Battery
No. 8 S.A. Field Battery
No. 12 S.A. Field Battery
W.A.F.F. No. 12
(Howitzer Battery.)
No. 27 Mountain Battery

No. 14 S.A. Field Battery
No. 15 S.A. Field Battery
(Heavy Battery.)
No. 16 S.A. Field Battery
Kashmir Mountain Battery
No. 22 Mountain Battery

No. 28 Mountain Battery
134th Howitzer Battery
Naval Gun Detachment
Gold Coast Regt. Battery
Nigerian Battery

APPENDIX B

SUMMARY OF STRENGTHS OF INFANTRY BATTALIONS IN GERMAN EAST AFRICA, 1917, ESTIMATED ON THE BASIS OF MAXIMUM " EFFECTIVE " STRENGTH

1. *European Battalions:*

25th Royal Fusiliers	. 200	⎫ 870—of whom 400 permanently, and 200 (6th S.A.I.) mostly, were on L. of C.
259th M.G. Coy. .	. 70	
6th S.A.I. . .	. 200	
7th S.A.I. . .	. 200	
8th S.A.I. . .	. 200	⎭

2. *Indian Battalions:*

   (a) *Imperial:*

   5th L.I.
   30th Punjabis
   17th Infantry (The Loyal Regt.)
   33rd Punjabis
   40th Pathans
   55th (Coke's Rifles)
   57th (Wilde's Rifles)
   127th Baluchis
   129th Baluchis
   61st K.G.O. Pioneers

   Maximum average effective strength, 450. 10 Battalions = 4500.

   (b) *Imperial Service:*

   Bharatpur Infantry
   Gwalior Infantry
   Jhind Infantry
   Kapurthala Infantry
   Rampur Infantry

   Maximum average effective strength, 400. 5 Battalions = 2000.

3. *African Battalions*:

    K.A.R., 20 Battns. at . . 500 ⎫
    N.R., 4 Battns. at . . . 500 ⎪
    Gambia Company . . . 100 ⎬ 14,400
    Gold Coast Regt. . . . 700 ⎪
    Cape Corps . . . . 1600 ⎭

4. *West Indian Troops*:

    W.I. Regt. ⎫ 600. Both on L. of C.
    B.W.I. Regt. ⎭   latterly.

        TOTAL STRENGTH—21,770

  European Battns. 4.0% ⎧ European and ⎫
  Indian Battns. 29.8% ⎨ quasi-Euro- ⎬ 6.8%
                      ⎩ pean   ⎭
  African Battns. 63.4% ⎧ Natives pure ⎫
  W.I. Battns. 2.8% ⎩ and simple ⎭ 93.2%

5. *Mounted Troops*:

    1. Europeans, 10th S.A.H., 200 ⎫   Europeans, 34%
    2. Indians, 25th Cavalry, 300 ⎬ Total, 600 Indians, 50%
    3. African, K.A.H., M.I., 100 ⎭   Africans, 16%

6. *Artillery*:

    (1) Europeans—
      No. 3 S.A.F.A.   ⎫
      No. 5 S.A.F.A.   ⎪   Percentage of
      No. 15 R.M.A.H.B. ⎬ 5 Batteries Batteries, 45.4
      Cornwall H.B.   ⎪ 14 Guns   Percentage of
      Hull H.B.   ⎭   Guns, 36

    (2) Indians
      22nd M.B.   ⎫
      24th M.B.   ⎪   Percentage of
      27th M.B.   ⎬ 5 Batteries Batteries, 36.3
      29th M.B.   ⎪ 20 Guns   Percentage of
      K.M.B.   ⎭   Guns, 42

(3) Africans—

Nigerian Battery { 2 Batteries } Percentage of Batteries, 18.3
Gold Coast Battery { 8 Guns } Percentage of Guns, 22

    Percentage of Batteries—European . 45.4
                                 Native   . 54.6
        Percentage of Guns—   European . 33.33
                                 Native   . 66.66

7. *Technical Troops :*
   (1) Indian—Faridhkot Sappers and Miners, and one other unit.
   (2) African—E.A. Pioneers (2 sections), Road Corps (2), Nigerian Pioneers (1 Coy.).
   (3) European—Nil.

8. *Administrative Services (non-combatants) :*

   A.S.C., S.A.S.C., R.A.M.C., E.A.M.S., W.A.M.S., S.A.M.C., Transport and Supply Departments, G.H.Q., Staffs, Signals, etc.—almost entirely European.

APPENDIX C

AWARDS TO THE NIGERIAN BRIGADE FOR SERVICE IN GERMAN EAST AFRICA

In the following list of awards, the narratives concerning each award have been taken from the records of the Nigeria Regiment. They, therefore, will not agree word for word with the narratives published in the *London Gazette*. In many cases individuals have been recommended by their Commanding Officers for an award on more than one occasion. It is quite impossible to state for which recommendation an award was granted. In several actions out of which these recommendations arose individuals have earned an award apparently for no particular action, but seem to have been given the award for the sum total of these recommendations. Therefore all recommendations before an award was actually granted are given in the following list:—

Brevet Rank

Name.	Rank.	Unit.	Date of Award.	Remarks.
BADHAM, J. F.	Major, T. Lt.-Col.	3rd N.R.	New Year Honours List, 1918	To be Brevet Lt.-Col. for continual good service in the field, when commanding a Battalion.
MANN, G. D., D.S.O.	Major, T. Lt.-Col.	Brig. H.Q.	27.7.18	To be Brevet Lt.-Col. for valuable services rendered when acting as Brig.-Gen. of the Nigerian Brigade.
SARGENT, J., D.S.O.	Major, T. Lt.-Col.	4th N.R.	27.7.18	To be Brevet Lt.-Col. for good services rendered when acting as G.S.O.1 of the Lindi Force.

Order of St Maurice and St Lazarus

CUNLIFFE, F. H. G., C.B., C.M.G.	BrGen.	..	26.5.17	Award of the above order, officers' class, for distinguished service during the campaign.

Croix de Guerre

FENERAN, E. C.	Major, T. Lt.-Col.	1st N.R.	26.5.17	Good services as a Battalion Commander.
CRICHTON, Hon. J. A., D.S.O.	Capt.	Brig. H.Q.	26.5.17	Good work on the Staff of the Brigade.
LEONARD, T. M. R.	T. Lt.-Col.	W.A.M.S.	26.5.17	Good work as P.M.O. to the Brigade.

D.S.O.

SARGENT, J.	Major, T. Lt.-Col.	4th N.R.	Birthday Honours, 1917	Skilfully handled two Companies of the 4th N.R. at NGWEMBE, on the 24th Jan. 1917, when in support of the 3rd N.R. so as to cover the retirement of that Battalion, which was being closely pressed by the enemy. He personally took over the command of the rear-guard, and by bold and skilful handling of his troops saved a very critical situation and enabled the retirement to be carried out in safety.
UNIACKE, G. L.	Br.-Maj., T. Lt.-Col.	2nd N.R.	29.10.18	Continuous good work throughout the campaign and skilful leadership since being promoted to the command of a Battalion.
BADHAM, J. F.	Br.Lt.-Col.	3rd N.R.	27.7.18	Continuous good work throughout the campaign and skilful leadership in the field whilst serving in Brig.-Gen. O'Grady's column in the LINDI AREA.

D.S.O.—continued

Name.	Rank.	Unit.	Date of Award.	Remarks.
LEONARD, T. M. R.	P.M.O., T. Lt.-Col.	W.A.M.S.	27.7.18	Continuous good work as P.M.O. throughout the campaign.
CRICHTON, Hon. J. A.	Capt.	Brig. H.Q.	27.7.18	Continuous good work on the Staff. Most marked when on the RUFIJI when that river was in flood. At MAHIWA, from the 15th to 18th Oct. 1917, he displayed marked coolness in action and devotion to duty, personally superintending the distribution of ammunition under very heavy fire. In spite of ill-health he has at all times shown the greatest devotion to duty.

Bar to D.S.O.

Name.	Rank.	Unit.	Date of Award.	Remarks.
UNIACKE, G. L., D.S.O.	Br.-Maj., T. Lt.-Col.	2nd N.R.	New Year Honours List, 1918	Conspicuous gallantry at BWEHO-CHINI on 22nd Sept. 1917 when in command of his Battalion.

Bar to the Military Cross

Name.	Rank.	Unit.	Date of Award.	Remarks.
PRING, F. J. H, M.C.	Capt.	1st N.R.	Jan. 1917	Displayed great initiative and judgment under heavy fire at MKINDU on the 18th Jan. 1917. Owing to his correct appreciation of the situation the position was taken with only slight loss to the attackers.

GARDNER, A., M.C.	Capt.	2nd N.R.	29.10.18	Displayed the greatest gallantry at BWEHO-CHINI on the 22nd Sept. 1917. This officer, with Capt. Fowle, M.C., held the left flank during repeated and most determined attacks. His company charged the enemy during the most critical time, and inflicted heavy loss on them with the bayonet.
HAWKINS, A. S. G., M.C.	Lieut.	3rd N.R.	24.12.17	Displayed the greatest gallantry and devotion to duty at MKWERA on the 8th Nov. 1917.
COLLINS, J. G., M.C.	Capt.	3rd N.R.	15.1.18	Conspicuous gallantry at NYENGEDE on the 30th Sept. 1917, where he was wounded.
WATERS, C. L., M.C.	Capt.	1st N.R.	15.1.18	Conspicuous gallantry and devotion to duty at MAHIWA, 15th to 18th Oct. 1917.
FOWLE, C. H., M.C.	Capt.	2nd N.R.	27.7.18	Has at all times displayed marked coolness and gallantry in action, and has been a most reliable officer throughout the campaign. At BWEHO-CHINI, on 22nd Sept. 1917, he commanded his Company with the greatest ability, helping to repulse several most determined attacks. Owing to his fine personal leadership his men have the greatest confidence in him.

Military Cross

GARDNER, A.	Capt.	2nd N.R.	4.1.17	Displayed fine initiative, 1st Jan. 1917, at TSCHIMBE, when he led a charge resulting in the capture of an enemy's howitzer and several prisoners.
ARMSTRONG, H. W. R.	Capt.	3rd N.R.	10.6.17	When under very heavy fire assisted No. 5701 Pte. Olubi Ijero (since died of wounds) to carry Sergt. Dixon, who had been wounded, out of action at NGWEMBE on the 24th Jan. 1917. He subsequently held on with a section under very

Military Cross—continued

Name.	Rank.	Unit.	Date of Award.	Remarks.
ROBINSON, A. C.	Capt.	3rd N.R.	10.6.17	Handled his Company with the greatest judgment and coolness at NGWEMBE on the 24th Jan. 1917. His action kept the enemy in check at a most critical period until reinforced, thus enabling the main body and guns to get clear.
WINTER, N.	Lieut.	4th N.R.	10.6.17	Skilfully handled his men under heavy fire at NGWEMBE on the 24th Jan. 1917, where by his personal example and skilful fire control, caused the enemy to withdraw their attack against the Nigerian right flank.
BURNEY, G. T.	Capt.	1st N.R.	29.10.18	Continual good work as Adjutant of his Battalion and great devotion to his work, also conspicuous gallantry in the action at BWEHO-CHINI on 22nd Sept. 1917.
WATERS, C. L.	Capt.	1st N.R.	29.10.18	With the greatest skill frequently commanded patrols. Also, at the capture of MKINDU on the 18th Jan. 1917, was in command of the supporting Company, where his skilful leadership and fire control greatly aided in the capture of the position. Gallantry at BWEHO-CHINI on 22nd Sept. 1917.
STUDLEY, G.	Lieut.	2nd N.R.	29.10.18	Conspicuous gallantry in the action at BWEHO-CHINI on the 22nd Sept. 1917. He defended 30 yards of front in a most exposed position with a Lewis gun, and in this way stopped two most determined attacks

heavy fire so as to allow the wounded to be brought in.

COLLINS, J. G.	Capt.	3rd N.R.	5.11.17	Continued good work as Adjutant of his Battalion and gallantry at NGWEMBE.
SOUTHBY, R.	Lieut.	3rd N.R.	5.11.17	Conspicuous gallantry during the action at NYENGEDI, 30th Sept. 1917, when he repelled two very determined counter-attacks.
HETLEY, C. R.	Capt.	4th N.R.	26.11.17	When in command of a reconnaissance near MAHIWA, on the 15th Nov. 1917, which had been sent forward to report upon the enemy's position, he was heavily attacked on all sides by greatly superior numbers. He displayed the greatest skill in extricating his Company from a most difficult position. His coolness and courage during a period of great stress, when all his officers and many rank and file had become casualties, set a fine example to his Company, and was undoubtedly the principal element which enabled the withdrawal to be successfully accomplished without the loss of either machine or Lewis guns.
HART, J. J.	Lieut.	1st N.R.	26.11.17	Most gallant conduct under most heavy fire at BWEHO-CHINI on the 22nd Sept. 1917, when he bandaged a shattered leg of a brother officer and later carried him back to cover, thereby narrowly escaping capture himself. Afterwards he greatly helped to steady and rally his section by his fine example under a very heavy cross fire.
HAWKINS, A. S.C.	Lieut.	3rd N.R.	26.11.17	At MAHIWA, on the 18th Oct. 1918, displayed great gallantry. He took charge of a Lewis gun under very heavy fire, and by his steady and accurate firing silenced one of the enemy's machine guns, thereby enabling a section which had been detached on the enemy's flank to disengage from the action and withdraw without casualties. He has in several previous engagements displayed the greatest gallantry in action.

Military Cross—continued

Name.	Rank.	Unit.	Date of Award.	Remarks.
FELL, M. E.	Capt.	2nd N.R.	27.12.18	Conspicuous gallantry and coolness in handling his Company at BEHO-BEHO on 3rd Jan. 1917. Again, at BWEHO-CHINI on 22nd Sept. 1917 showed the greatest gallantry by his total disregard for personal danger under very heavy fire. In this action he kept his men absolutely steady by his example of coolness under fire. Again, at MAHIWA on 16th October 1917 his good leadership was most marked when he personally led a section of his Company to reinforce a part of the 4th N.R. trench line, which was being heavily shelled by the enemy's artillery.
FINCH, H. S.	Capt.	3rd N.R.	27.12.18	At MAHIWA on the 18th Oct. 1917 displayed great devotion to duty throughout the day, when under heavy fire he carried orders to the firing line, and arranged the replenishment on ammunition and the supply of water to the men in the front line.
FOX, D. B.	Lieut.	4th N.R.	27.12.18	Showed the greatest pluck and devotion to duty when in command of the vanguard on the 7th June 1917. He showed the greatest skill in handling his men, and in the fight that followed on this day did some most useful work with a machine gun. Again, at MAHIWA on the 15th October 1917, when his Company were making a reconnaissance, he handled his half-company

MacLean, G. D. M.	Lieut.	Attached Gambia Company, 1st N.R.	27.12.18	with the greatest skill during the retirement, and displayed the greatest coolness and courage, setting a very fine example to his men. Later in the retirement, after he himself was wounded, he worked a Lewis gun under the most heavy fire with the greatest skill, and so enabled a portion of his Company, that were almost surrounded, to retire.
Maxwell, J. E. H.	Capt.	4th N.R.	27.12.18	Showed conspicuous gallantry at Mahiwa on 16th October 1917. During the action he set a magnificent example of coolness and resource to his men at a most critical time, when ammunition had almost run out. Again, at Mahiwa on 18th Oct. 1917 he distinguished himself by his stamina and endurance under the most trying circumstances. Rendered much useful service in command of a Company; he has always displayed a marked coolness and disregard of personal risk in action. His personal example and quiet manner of control in action have been most beneficial to his Company. At Mahiwa on 15th October 1917 he was in command of the vanguard; the manner in which he handled his Company during a very anxious and trying day reflects the greatest credit on his skill and leadership. His personal courage and example in this action had a most steadying effect on all ranks.
Vise, T. A.	Capt.	A.N.R.	New Year Honours List, 1918	Displayed the greatest promptness and coolness on the Mkindu-Mpangas Road on 14th March 1917 by bringing his guns into action at point-blank range. His action contributed largely to the enemy being repulsed after they had arrived to within 100 yards of the guns.

281

Military Cross—continued

Name.	Rank.	Unit.	Date of Award.	Remarks.
WEBB, S. N. C.	Capt., A. Major	4th N.R.	New Year Honours List, 1918	When in command of the 4th N.R. from 27th May to 23rd June 1917, rendered most valuable assistance to the Column Commander, particularly at the crossing of the Sibiti River, when he commanded the advanced troops. Also for continued good work as Adjutant of his Battalion and devotion to duty at all times.
BARBER, L.	Lieut.	2nd N.R.	27.12.18	Conspicuous bravery in action when he made a sketch of the enemy's position under heavy fire at BEHO-BEHO on 3rd Jan. 1917. Also at MAHIWA on 17th October 1917 he showed the greatest bravery by making his way round the German line and gaining touch with the 3rd N.R. with the idea in view of obtaining ammunition for the 2nd and 4th N.R., which were rapidly running short of ammunition.
BLACKMORE, C. W. P.	Lieut.	A.N.R.	27.12.18	Devotion to duty on all occasions, and for his gallantry and courage in action, has at all times been of the highest order. At MAHIWA on the 16th Oct. this officer brought both his guns into action, firing with fuse "O." One gun was put out of action, but the remaining gun was moved in order to help the infantry on the right flank; after two rounds were fired the entire gun crew became casualties and the position became untenable. This officer did all in his power to save the gun, at the greatest danger to himself, and behaved in a most gallant manner at a most trying time.

BUDGEN, T. A.	Capt.	1st N.R.	27.12.18	Gallant conduct and coolness under very heavy fire at BHEWO-CHINI on the 22nd Sept. 1917. He continued to work his machine gun with the greatest effect until he himself was wounded.
CROWE, D. M.	Lieut.	4th N.R.	27.12.18	Gallantry in action at MAHIWA on 16th Oct. 1917. When the portion of the trench line under this officer's command was compelled to withdraw owing to heavy shell fire he set a very fine example by his personal courage. He also displayed great initiative in re-occupying the trench line immediately the shell fire ceased and the enemy attack commenced. His promptness and bravery successfully countered a very critical period.
BECK, D. M. H.	Lieut.	1st N.R.	24.12.17	Most conspicuous gallantry in action at MAHIWA, on 16th Oct. 1917, covering the retirement of his Company with his section, until he was left with only six men unwounded.
CATT, A. W.	Lieut.	3rd N.R.	24.12.17	Conspicuous gallantry at MAHIWA on 8th Nov. 1917.
AMBROSE, W. G.	Capt.	3rd N.R.	New Year Honour, 1918	Gallantry in action at ITETE RIVER on the 26th July 1917.
BUCHANAN-SMITH, W.	Lieut.	3rd N.R.	Do.	Conspicuous gallantry on the MKINDU-MPANGAS ROAD on the 14th March 1917 when in command of a small advanced guard. He only fell back on the main body when all his party except one had become casualties. It was greatly due to his personal gallantry that the main body were able to have time to deploy and so save the guns from being captured by the enemy. Also at NYENGEDI on 28th Sept. 1917, when, after being severely wounded, assisted in driving off a superior enemy's force.

Military Cross—continued

Name.	Rank.	Unit.	Date of Award.	Remarks.
DOWNES, W. D.	Capt.	4th N.R.	New Year Honour, 1918	When in command of an advanced detachment from 5th to 7th June 1917 displayed great determination and dash in the handling of his command. His resolute action and skilful leadership against the enemy's rear-guard kept him on the run and prevented him occupying a stronger and more favourable position. Again, during the action at MAHIWA on the 16th Oct. 1917 it was greatly to this officer's credit that, after his Company had been forced to retire from their trench line, owing to the enemy's artillery enfilading his line and causing very heavy casualties, that he was able to re-form his somewhat shaken troops in the open, and later, when the enemy delivered an infantry attack, was able to lead them back to their old trenches and successfully repulsed the attack.
ROBERTS, C. E.	Major	4th N.R.	Do.	Consistent good work during the campaign, devotion to duty, and gallantry in the field at NGWEMBE on the 24th Jan. 1917, and coolness at all times in action.
ROBINSON, F. W. H.	Lieut.	3rd N.R.	Do.	Gallantry in action at ITETE RIVER on the 26th July 1917.
STRONGE, H. C.	Capt.	2nd N.R.	Do.	Conspicuous good service as Adjutant of his Battalion, showing the greatest coolness and pluck in every action his Battalion took part in, which was most marked at MAHIWA on 16th Oct. 1917.

MILNE-HOME, A. C.	Capt.	3rd N.R.	27.12.18	Has rendered general good work throughout the campaign, and shown at all times the greatest devotion to duty. At NGWEMBE on the 24th Jan. 1917 he showed the greatest coolness, and rendered great service to his Battalion by his marked ability in leading his Company.
O'CONNELL, H. G.	Capt.	3rd N.R.	27.12.18	Displayed great coolness at MAHIWA on 18th Oct. 1917 when ordered to take over a portion of the firing line which had been previously occupied by other troops. He carried out this most difficult work under very heavy fire. Later, when heavily attacked in his new position his personal example inspired his Company to remain perfectly cool. During the action he was twice wounded, but remained at his post throughout the day.
RABY, H. S. V.	Lieut.	1st N.R.	27.12.18	At BWEHO-CHINI on 22nd September 1917 his conduct was most fearless under very heavy fire and his control over his section was most marked. When out in the open he showed utter disregard of the enemy fire and kept his men steady by his personal example. When back in the trench he repeatedly left his cover in order to put either a Lewis or machine gun in order. Also at MAHIWA on 16th Oct. 1917 he showed the most conspicuous gallantry and devotion to duty. It was entirely due to his coolness, after his Captain was killed, that all his Company machine guns were saved.
RUMBOLD, W. R.	Lieut.	Pioneer Section and 3rd N.R.	27.12.18	Devotion to duty when in command of the Pioneer Section during 1917. He rendered valuable service to the Brigade in road-making and bridging during the advance, when he generally accompanied the advanced guard. At all times he displayed marked coolness under fire.

Military Cross—continued

Name.	Rank.	Unit.	Date of Award.	Remarks.
SHAW, M.	Lieut.	Stokes Gun Battery and 4th N.R.	27.12.18	Devotion to duty when in command of the Stokes Gun Section at MAHIWA from 15th to 18th Oct. 1917; he fought his gun under heavy fire with great credit. Again, at MKWERA on 8th Nov. 1917 he handled his Stokes guns with much skill and inflicted many casualties on the enemy. Also in LUCHIMI VALLEY on the 16th and 17th Nov. 1917, under very heavy fire, he rendered invaluable assistance to the infantry.
STEED, R.	Lieut.	2nd N.R.	27.12.18	Displayed marked ability and coolness when commanding a Company at MAHIWA from 15th to 18th October 1917. He has at all times shown gallantry and devotion to duty throughout the campaign. At BWEHO-CHINI on 22nd Sept. 1917 he rendered most valuable service by his skill in using a machine gun, which he continued to serve long after he had been wounded himself.
WOOD, L. C.	Lieut.	2nd N.R.	27.12.18	Has at all times shown the greatest devotion to duty and gallantry in the field. Though suffering continually from bad health, he has cheerfully carried on with his work, and shown the greatest initiative and ability in leading his men in action.
GIBSON, E.	Capt.	W.A.M.S.	27.12.18	Good service throughout the campaign.
MOREHEAD, H. R.	Capt.	W.A.M.S.	27.12.18	Conspicuous devotion to duty and gallantry in action, especially at NYENGEDI on 30th Sept. 1917.
SANDEMAN, T. R.	Capt.	W.A.M.S.	27.12.18	Conspicuous devotion to duty and gallantry in action. He was present with his Battalion at every action in which they took part.

Officers mentioned in Dispatches

Name.	Rank.	Unit.	Date.	In whose Dispatch.
CUNLIFFE, F. H. G., C.B., C.M.G.	Brig.-Gen.	H.Q.	11.10.17	Lieut.-Gen. Sir J. L. Van Deventer, K.C.B.
SARGENT, J.	Major, T. Lt.-Col.	4th N. R.	14.3.17	Maj.-Gen. A. R. Hoskins, C.M.G., D.S.O.
LEONARD, T. M. R.	T. Lt.-Col.	P.M.O.	11.10.17	Lieut.Gen. Sir J. L. Van Deventer, K.C.B.
MANN, G. D.	Major, T. Lt.-Col.	H.Q.	30.5.17	Maj.-Gen. A. R. Hoskins, C.M.G., D.S.O.
UNIACKE, G. L.	Bt.-Maj., T. Lt.-Col.	2nd N.R.	30.5.17	Do.
BADHAM, J. F.	Major, T. Lt.-Col.	3rd N.R.	30.5.17	Do.
GIBB, C.	Major	4th N.R.	21.1.18	Lieut.-Gen. Sir J. L. Van Deventer, K.C.B.
GREEN, C. H.	Major	3rd N.R.	21.1.18	Do.
PARR, B. C.	Major	2nd N.R.	11.10.18	Do.
WEBB, S. N. C.	Capt., T. Major	4th N.R.	30.5.17	Maj.-Gen. A. R. Hoskins, C.M.G, D.S.O.
HETLEY, C. R.	Capt.	4th N.R.	30.5.17	Do.
Do.	Do.	Do.	11.10.17	Lieut.-Gen. Sir J. L. Van Deventer, K.C.B.
MAXWELL, J. E. H.	Capt.	4th N.R.	30.5.17	Maj.-Gen. A. R. Hoskins, C.M.G., D.S.O.
MILNE-HOME, A. C.	Capt.	3rd N.R.	30.5.17	Do.
BURNEY, G. T.	Capt.	1st N.R.	30.5.17	Do.
BARCLAY, C. E.	Capt.	4th N.R.	30.5.17	Do.
COLLINS, J. G.	Capt.	3rd N.R.	30.5.17	Do.
FELL, M. E.	Capt.	2nd N.R.	30.5.17	Do.
SANDEMAN, T. R.	Capt.	W.A.M.S.	30.5.17	Do.
STRONGE, C. T.	Capt.	2nd N.R.	30.5.17	Do.
Do.	Do.	Do.	11.10.17	Lieut.-Gen. Sir J. L. Van Deventer, K.C.B.

Officers mentioned in Dispatches—continued

Name.	Rank.	Unit.	Date.	In whose Dispatch.
WATERS, C. L.	Capt.	1st N.R.	30.5.17	Maj.-Gen. A. R. Hoskins, C.M.G, D.S.O.
MIGEOD, G. E. A.	Capt.	C.S. and T.O.	30.5.17	Do.
ARMSTRONG, H. W. R.	Capt.	3rd N.R.	11.10.17	Lieut.-Gen. Sir J. L. Van Deventer, K.C.B.
BUDGEN, T. A. G.	Capt.	1st N.R.	Do.	Do.
CRICHTON, The Hon. J. A.	Capt.	H.Q.	Do.	Do.
MURRAY, G. G.	Capt.	2nd N.R.	Do.	Do.
PRING, J. H.	Capt.	1st N.R.	Do.	Do.
ROBINSON, A. C.	Capt.	3rd N.R.	Do.	Do.
VISE, T. A.	Capt.	A.N.R.	30.5.17	Maj.-Gen. A. R. Hoskins, C.M.G, D.S.O.
STRETTON, A. L. de C.	Capt., M.C.	1st N.R.	21.1.18	Lieut.-Gen. Sir J. L. Van Deventer, K.C.B.
VICARS, W. G.	Capt.	Record Office	Do.	Do.
TAYLOR, R. R.	Capt.	3rd N.R.	Do.	Do.
GARDNER, A.	Capt., M.C.	2nd N.R.	11.10.17	Do.
BUCHANAN-SMITH, W.	Lieut.	3rd N.R.	30.5.17	Maj.-Gen. A. R. Hoskins, C.M.G, D.S.O.
BARBER, L.	Lieut.	2nd N.R.	Do.	Do.
CATT, A. W.	Lieut.	3rd N.R.	Do.	Do.
STOBART, E. M. St C.	Lieut.	H.Q.	Do.	Do.
Do.	Do.	Do.	21.1.18	Lieut.-Gen. Sir J. L. Van Deventer, K.C.B.
FOX, D. B.	Lieut.	4th N.R.	11.10.17	Do.
WINTER, N.	Lieut., M.C.	4th N.R.	Do.	Do.
BURR, W. E.	Lieut.	H.Q.	21.1.18	Do.
CAVANAGH, B. G.	Lieut.	3rd N.R.	Do.	Do.
ELLIOTT, D.	Lieut.	2nd N.R.	Do.	Do.
KILBY, R. N.	Lieut.	1st N.R.	Do.	Do.
WHETTON, F. H.	Lieut.	4th N.R.	Do.	Do.

Bar to D.C.M.s. (*Europeans*)

Name.	Rank.	Unit.	Date of Award.	Remarks.
ELEMENT, R.	Sgt.	4th N.R.	3.10.18	Devotion to duty and coolness and courage in action. Most marked was his gallantry at MAHIWA on 15th Oct. 1917 and at NGWEMBE on 24th Jan. 1917.

D.C.M.s. (*Europeans*)

Name.	Rank.	Unit.	Date of Award.	Remarks.
TANTI, J.	T. Sgt.	2nd N.R.	29.10.18	Conspicuous gallantry at BWEHO-CHINI on 22nd Nov. 1917.
BADGER, C.	Sgt.	2nd N.R.	29.10.18	Showed great coolness at BWEHO-CHINI on 22nd Nov. 1917 in the handling of a Lewis gun under very heavy fire.
FRASER, J. H.	O.R.S.	2nd N.R.	New Year Honours, 1918	Devotion to duty and steady good work throughout the campaign.
HUNSWORTH, W.	C.-Sgt.	2nd N.R.	Do.	Gallantry at BWEHO-CHINI on the 22nd Nov. 1917. After being slightly wounded himself he remained at his post all day under very heavy fire and performed most useful work with his machine gun.
RUSSELL, C.	Sgt.	3rd N.R.	Do.	At KIBONGO on the 21st Jan. 1917 conspicuous gallantry when on patrol he sighted an enemy party of unknown strength and rushed them with one native soldier, capturing one German European and three Askaris.

D.C.Ms. (Europeans)—continued

Name.	Rank.	Unit.	Date of Award.	Remarks.
Darke, B. J.	Sgt.	3rd N.R.	3.10.18	Conspicuous gallantry in action at Nyengedi, 28th to 30th Sept. 1917.
Empringham, H.	Sgt.	4th N.R.	3.10.18	Rendered most useful service when in charge of a machine gun at Mahiwa on 16th Oct. 1917. In this action he displayed great pluck and devotion to duty; when severely wounded in the hand and unable to work the gun himself, he continued to supervise the firing and remained at his post until the enemy retired in the evening. After having his wound dressed he returned to his post and remained with his gun during the rest of this critical period.
Hawes, A. R.	Sgt.	2nd N.R.	3.10.18	Devotion to duty and steady good work in his Company. He rendered valuable service at Bweho-Chini on 22nd Sept. 1917.
Sanders, W. T.	Sgt.	2nd N.R.	3.10.18	At Bweho-Chini on 22nd Sept. 1917 he defended 30 yards of front with a Lewis gun in a most exposed position. By his courage and resource he stopped two most determined attempts of the enemy to break through the trench line.
Tasker, P. T.	Sgt.	1st N.R.	3.10.18	Showed great gallantry at Mahiwa on the 16th Oct. 1917 by keeping the enemy off with a Lewis gun whilst an officer and a few unarmed carriers were able to get away a gun, which was in great danger of falling into the enemy's hands, as all the gun team were casualties.

WATKINS, J. H.	Sgt.	1st N.R.	3.10.18	Showed at all times marked ability in leading his Company scouts. At BWEHO-CHINI on the 22nd Sept. 1917, when in charge of the scouts, he held the enemy's screen for three hours, enabling his Company to engage the enemy on their whole front and break up their attack when they attempted to deliver a charge.
GILLAN, A.	Bat. S.M.	A.N.R.	9.12.18	Showed at all times the highest devotion to duty and the greatest courage in the field. He had a most inspiring effect on the men of his Battery during the battle of MAHIWA, 15th to 17th Oct. 1917.
PAYNE, C. W.	Sapper	R.E. wireless, attached Nigerian Brigade	29.10.17	Gallantry and devotion to duty at BWEHO-CHINI on 22nd Nov. 1917 when on wireless duty.
BOTHA, J. H.	Sgt.	S.A. Inf., attached Nigerian Brigade	24.12.17	Gallantry and devotion to duty at MAHIWA on 16th Oct. 1917.
BOYD, W. J.	Sgt.	Do.	24.12.17	Gallantry and devotion to duty at MAHIWA on 16th Oct. 1917.

Military Medal (*Europeans*)

DIXON, F. J.	Sgt.	3rd N.R.	30.3.17	Gallantry at NGWEMBE, 24th Jan. 1917. Although severely wounded and closely pressed by the enemy, he directed the removal of his machine gun and S.A.A. boxes, and then told the gun team to leave him.
HUNT, A.	Sgt.	4th N.R.	26.11.17	Gallantry at MAHIWA on 16th Oct. 1917. When his Company was forced to evacuate their trench, owing to heavy shell fire, he rendered great

Military Medal (*Europeans*)—continued

Name.	Rank.	Unit.	Date of Award.	Remarks.
MacEwen, W. P.	Sgt.	S.A. Inf., attached Nigerian Brigade	24.12.17	assistance in restoring order by his personal example. He led the men back himself to reoccupy their trench when the German Infantry attacked, and carried a machine gun back himself at this most critical time. Gallantry at Mahiwa on the 8th Nov. 1917 when in charge of a machine gun.

Italian Bronze Medal

Name.	Rank.	Unit.	Date of Award.	Remarks.
Newbrook, H. (8649)	C.-Sgt.	1st N.R.	15.5.17	Showed great courage and initiative in handling his machine gun at Mkindoo on the 18th Jan. 1917.
Badger, C. W. (2735)	Sgt.	2nd N.R.	15.5.17	During the actions that his Battalion has been engaged in during June 1917 he has been most noticeable for his initiative and dash.
Woolley, C. (6004)	Sgt.	3rd N.R.	15.5.17	At Ngwembe on 24th Jan. 1917, when he was lying on the ground badly wounded, he ordered No. 4535 L.-Cpl. Akande Ilorin to get the machine gun away and leave him on the ground. Akande Ilorin wished to carry this B.-N.C.O. back to a place of safety. Thus he allowed himself to be taken prisoner in order that his gun might be saved.
Tanner, W. (10940)	Sgt.	4th N.R.	15.5.17	General meritorious service in the operations of 1st, 2nd, and 24th Jan. 1917.

Mentions in Dispatches

Name.	Rank.	Unit.	Award.	In whose Dispatch.
BAIGENT, H.	S.-Sgt.	R.A.M.C., attached 4th N.R.	30.5.17	Maj.-Gen. A. R. Hoskins, C.M.G., D.S.O.
CARFRAE, W.	C.S.M.	Nig. Sig. Sec.	Do.	Do.
CATT, A. W.	Q.M.S.	3rd N.R.	Do.	Do.
KELLIHER, J. C.	Sgt.	1st N.R.	Do.	Do.
LAMB, F. E., D.C.M.	Sgt.	4th N.R.	Do.	Do.
O'BERGIN, C. M. D.	Sgt.	3rd N.R.	Do.	Do.
RUSSELL, G., D.C.M.	Sgt.	3rd N.R.	Do.	Do.
SCOTT, J.	Sgt.	Nig. Sig. Sec.	Do.	Do.
WILTON, E.	C.S.M.	1st N.R.	Do.	Do.
VICARS, W. G.	S.S.M.	Record Office	Do.	Do.
BADGER, C. W., D.C.M.	Sgt.	2nd N.R.	11.10.17	Lieut.-Gen. Sir J. L. Van Deventer, K.C.B.
BLAIR, H.	Sgt.	Attd. H.Q.	Do.	Do.
DIXON, F. J., M.M.	Sgt.	3rd N.R.	Do.	Do.
NEWBROOK, H.	Sgt.	1st N.R.	Do.	Do.
RUFFELL, F.	Sgt.	2nd N.R.	Do.	Do.
TANNER, W.	Sgt.	4th N.R.	Do.	Do.
WOOLLEY, C.	Sgt.	3rd N.R.	Do.	Do.
HUNT, A., M.M.	Sgt.	4th N.R.	21.1.18	Do.
KERRY, A.	Sgt.	1st N.R.	Do.	Do.
WALTER, F. B.	Sgt.	Record Office	Do.	Do.

Awards to Native Rank and File

2nd Bar to W.A.F.F. D.C.M.

No.	Rank.	Name.	Unit.	Date of Award.	Remarks.
3087	C.S.M.	Sumanu, D.C.M.	3rd N.R.	10.10.18	At Nyengedi on the 30th Nov. 1917 he showed most conspicuous gallantry, and in order to save him from receiving further wounds protected him by his own body and in doing so was wounded himself. His conduct has at all times been of a very high order.

1st Bar to W.A.F.F. D.C.M.

No.	Rank.	Name.	Unit.	Date of Award.	Remarks.
6410	C.M.S.	Momadu Kukawa, D.C.M.	2nd N.R.	15.1.18	Most conspicuous gallantry at Behobeho on 3rd Jan. 1917. Continual good patrol work, especially between 21st and 25th Aug. 1917 when in charge of the Lupengo patrol. His information was clear and concise.
4245	C.S.M.	Momadu Bauchi, D.C.M.	4th N.R.	10.10.18	Continuous devotion to duty and gallantry in the field throughout the campaign. He served his Company at all times most faithfully under rather trying circumstances, as he succeeded a C.S.M. with a very fine record and was himself a newcomer to his present Company. He established himself by constant disregard of personal risk and continual hard work.

3780	Sgt.	Audu Katsena, D.C.M.	4th N.R.	10.10.18	Conspicuous gallantry at Mkwera on the 8th Nov. 1917. When under most heavy fire, and when the enemy were within 150 yards, he twice went back for ammunition and distributed it to the men of the 3rd N.R., who had run out of it. His coolness under the heaviest fire is remarkable. He has always exhibited the highest courage and devotion to duty. He has not missed a day's duty during the campaign.

W.A.F.F. D.C.M.

4535	L.-Cpl.	Akande Ilorin	3rd N.R.	7.4.17	Gallantry at Ngwembe on 24th Jan. 1917, where he succeeded in saving his machine gun and ammunition from capture, having to make three journeys for the same under a most heavy fire.
6384	C.S.M.	Garuba Mandara	1st N.R.	29.10.17	Conspicuous gallantry at Bweho-Chini on the 22nd Nov. 1917.
4699	C.S.M.	Momadu Kukawa	2nd N.R.	29.10.17	Gallantry and coolness at Bweho-Chini on 22nd Sept. 1917. At retirement his trench was exposed to heavy reverse fire as well as frontal fire. During this critical time he kept his men in hand. Further, he continuously visited two picquets under heavy fire.
5861	C.S.M.	Manu Zozo	1st N.R.	29.10.17	Gallantry and devotion to duty at Bweho-Chini on 22nd Sept. 1917.
81	Gunner	Modi	A.N.R	24.12.17	Gallantry and devotion to duty at Mahiwa on 16th Oct. 1917, when he continued to work his gun under heavy fire until the rest of the gun team were either killed

W.A.F.F. D.C.M.—continued

No.	Rank.	Name.	Unit.	Date of Award.	Remarks.
					or wounded. Though wounded, he then assisted his officer in attempting to remove the breech block under very heavy flanking fire at close range. When he found this was impossible he damaged the breech block as much as possible, and only abandoned the gun to the enemy when ordered to do so by his officer, when the enemy were within 25 yards.
Tx 3	C.S.M.	SAIDU	1st N.R.	24.12.17	Gallantry and devotion to duty at MAHIWA on the 16th Oct. 1917.
5297	Acting L.-Cpl.	ALI ANGASS	1st N.R.	24.12.17	Gallantry and devotion to duty at MAHIWA on the 16th Oct. 1917. Being the only man left alive of a Lewis gun team, he did all in his power to help a British N.C.O. to save a Maxim gun.
6516	Pte.	BAKO BERNIN KEBBI	1st N.R.	24.12.17	Gallantry and devotion to duty at MAHIWA on the 16th Oct. 1917.
35	Bom'br.	BABALLI	A.N.R.	15.1.18	Gallantry and devotion to duty in the action on the MKINDU-MPANGAS ROAD on 14th March 1917, where, without orders or assistance, dressed all the wounded himself under heavy fire, and evacuated them in safety, thus possibly saving many lives. He has shown the greatest devotion to duty at all times.
16	Sgt.	A. I. KONTAGORA	A.N.R.	15.1.18	Devotion to duty in the action at MGETA RIVER, 1st to 3rd Jun. 1917, and again,

95	Cpl.	Osuman Badiri	A.N.R.	15.1.18	when with Col. Lyle's Column, from 5th to 17th Jan. He showed marked coolness and courage at Mahiwa on 16th Oct. 1917, when with Lt.-Col. Roberts' Column.
					Gallantry in action, when as a gunner he always accompanied the F.O.O., rendering him the greatest assistance at all times by his fearless conduct under fire. He displayed great devotion to duty in action on the Mkindu-Mpangas Road on the 14th March 1917.
6426	Cpl.	Mallam Duchi	1st N.R.	15.1.18	Gallantry and devotion to duty, both of which were most marked at Mkindu on the 18th Jan. 1917, where, without European supervision and under heavy fire, he covered the advance of his Company with a machine gun. He showed great skill and coolness in lifting his fire as his Company advanced, thereby greatly assisting in the capture of the position.
5574	Cpl.	Adamu Gwana	2nd N.R.	15.1.18	Displayed and set a fine example on a patrol encounter on the 15th July 1917.
7140	Sgt.	Moma Bauchi	2nd N.R.	15.1.18	Led his section most skilfully in the attack on Msswega on 26th May 1917.
5983	Cpl.	Awudu Kaduna	3rd N.R.	15.1.18	Displayed great pluck and dash on 7th June 1917 near Mkalama when leading his men forward under constantly heavy fire.
2238	Sgt.	Abe Ijesha	4th N.R.	15.1.18	
6153	Pte.	Salami Offa	4th N.R.	15.1.18	Gallantry and devotion to duty at the action at Mgeta River, 1st Jan. 1917, when, although wounded in the first advance, refused to leave the firing line and carried on throughout the day.

W.A.F.F. D.C.M.—continued

No.	Rank.	Name.	Unit.	Date of Award.	Remarks.
5395	C.S.M.	Morakinjo Ibadan	4th N.R.	15.1.18	Continuous good service and hard work throughout the campaign when acting as R.S.M.
2610	C.S.M.	Laleyee Ifon	4th N.R.	15.1.18	Continuous good service throughout the campaign.
26	Gun Carrier	Osuman Bauchi	A.N.R.	10.10.18	Conspicuous gallantry in action at Mahiwa on 16th Oct. 1917 when with Lt.-Col. Roberts' Column. During this action, when the guns were firing at fuse " O " he kept up the supply of ammunition under heavy fire. Finally, when most of the gunners were casualties, he took their places as they fell out, and ably assisted the working of the gun. When the gun was put out of action he picked up a dead gunner's rifle and used it.
7561	Cpl.	Sali Sokoto	Pioneers	10.10.18	Gallantry in action at Mahiwa on 16th Oct. 1917 when with Lt.-Col. Roberts' Column. He also showed marked gallantry at Kibongo when bridging the river. Throughout the campaign he has set a splendid example to the men of his unit.
6389	Pte.	Awudu Kano	Stokes Gun Battery	10.10.18	Continuous good work in keeping up the supply of ammunition in action and coolness under heavy fire.
Tx 1	C.S.M.	Garuba Kukawa	1st N.R.	10.10.18	Consistent good work under frequent difficult circumstances throughout the campaign. He showed great coolness and disregard

6429	L.-Cpl.	IMORU RAHA	1st N.R.	10.10.18	for personal danger at MAHIWA on 16th Oct. 1917. He carried messages continuously under heavy fire until badly wounded.
5665	Sgt.	MOMADU ZARIA	1st N.R.	10.10.18	Consistent good work throughout the campaign. He showed great pluck and determination as a patrol leader on many occasions.
7048	Pte.	WAHERIGA	1st N.R.	10.10.18	During the action of MAHIWA on 16th Oct. 1917 he assisted to carry back a wounded officer (Lieut. Schenkil) who was in danger of being captured. He has consistently shown devotion to duty under frequently difficult circumstances.
5900	L.-Cpl.	DOGON DOCHI	1st N.R.	10.10.18	Assisted No. 5655 Sergt. Momadu Zaria to carry back a wounded officer (Lieut. Schenkil) at MAHIWA on 16th Oct. 1917. At MAHIWA on 16th Oct. 1917 he went back for ammunition for his Company. Through his action the enemy's attacks on the right flank were beaten back.
7276	Acting L.-Cpl.	LEBBO YOLA	1st N.R.	10.10.18	Showed great gallantry at MAHIWA on 16th Oct. 1917. They were machine gunners, and after the remainder of their gun teams were shot down they continued to fire their guns, which enabled the Company to make a partial retirement.
7247	Pte.	BAKO	Do.	Do.	
4879	Sgt.	AGELA AYENA	2nd N.R.	10.10.18	Constant courage and coolness under fire and skill in handling his section, especially at MAHIWA on 15th Oct. 1917, when he was commanding a section of a half Company which was covering the retirement of a Company of the 4th N.R. He again showed great skill and courage on 16th Oct. 1917.

W.A.F.F. D.C.M.—continued

No.	Rank.	Name.	Unit.	Date of Award.	Remarks.
8125	Pte.	TANKO KATSENA	2nd N.R.	10.10.18	At MAHIWA on 16th Oct. 1917 they twice carried water to the firing line under intense fire from machine guns, previous attempts having failed. They were both little more than recruits at the time.
8145	Pte.	OSUMAN LAKAI	Do.	Do.	
35	M.G.C.	GARUBA BORNU	2nd N.R.	10.10.18	This carrier at BWEHO-CHINI on 22nd Oct. 1917 rescued a wounded man under heavy fire. He also ably assisted the supply of ammunition to his machine gun.
4655	Pte.	MOMADU GERI	2nd N.R.	10.10.18	Gallantry in action at BWEHO-CHINI, NA-HUNGU HILL, and MAHIWA.
4319	Pte.	MWA	2nd N.R.	10.10.18	Continually carried messages across a fire-swept zone heedless of danger at BWEHO-CHINI, 22nd Sept. 1917.
5528	Acting L.-Cpl.	MOMA ALBASSA	2nd N.R.	10.10.18	At BWEHO-CHINI on the 22nd Oct. 1917 he continued to serve his machine gun after he was wounded until he was relieved, in spite of having been ordered to go to the dressing station.
6453	C.S.M.	SUMAH KANO	2nd N.R.	10.10.18	Continuous devotion to duty and good service in the field throughout the campaign.
6955	Pte.	ABDU KANO	2nd N.R.	10.10.18	Conspicuous gallantry at BWEHO-CHINI on 22nd Oct. 1917, when under heavy fire he brought up ammunition and filled Lewis gun drums in the open.
5666	L.-Cpl.	MAZU DAMAGARA	2nd N.R.	10.10.18	Conspicuous gallantry and devotion to duty at BWEHO-CHINI on the 22nd Oct. 1917. When in charge of a picquet he remained at

5631	Pte.	AMADU GAIYA	2nd N.R.	10.10.18	his post until his object was achieved and after four out of the six men were casualties. He has at all times volunteered for risky patrol work, and has set an example of absolute fearlessness under fire.
					Conspicuous for his courage at all times, and has set a fine example to all ranks for his contempt of danger.
3/11/23	M.G.C.	ABUDU DUNGA	3rd N.R	10.10.18	At NYENGEDI on the 30th Sept. 1917 he displayed the greatest gallantry and devotion to duty. His own machine gun, being in the second line, was not in use, so he volunteered and carried ammunition to a gun in the front line and also distributed ammunition in the firing line under very heavy fire.
Tx 60	Sgt.	SALIHU BAUCHI	3rd N.R.	10.10.18	Conspicuous gallantry and devotion to duty at MAHIWA on 18th Oct. 1917, and again at MKWERA on the 8th Nov. 1917.
5995	L.-Cpl.	GRASS BALI	4th N.R.	10.10.18	Has shown the greatest devotion to duty and bravery in the field, setting a most admirable example to all ranks.
5039	Sgt.	SHEFU KATAGUM	4th N.R.	10.10.18	At MAKALAMA on the 7th June 1917, when in charge of flankers, he acted with pluck and boldness in leading his party over most difficult country, and so contributed largely to the defeat of the efforts of the enemy in delaying our advance.
33	Stretcher Bearer	LANGALA KATSENA	4th N.R.	10.10.18	Has consistently shown the greatest devotion to duty, taking forward with promptness his stretcher when required, and showing utter disregard for his own personal safety, even under the heaviest fire.

W.A.F.F. D.C.M.—continued

No.	Rank.	Name.	Unit.	Date of Award.	Remarks.
7432	Pte.	Hassan III.	4th N.R.	10.10.18	Has consistently shown the greatest devotion to duty and marked bravery and enterprise in the field. His conduct in the fighting on the 16th Oct. 1917 at Mahiwa was specially worthy of recognition.
3936	Cpl.	Idowa Ibadan	4th N.R.	10.10.18	Has consistently shown the greatest devotion to duty and bravery in the field. On 15th Oct. 1917 at Mahiwa he was in charge of the "point," showing great courage and steadiness under heavy fire within a few yards of the German entrenched position.
R 218	L.-Cpl.	Barbara Hadeija	3rd N.R.	10.10.18	Conspicuous gallantry in action at Mkwera on 8th Nov. 1917. Although wounded, and twice told to proceed to the dressing station, he remained in the firing line until his section Commander was wounded. He then carried him back under heavy fire to a place of safety and then returned and took charge of the section.

Military Medal (to Native Rank and File)

| 6741 | L.-Cpl. | Suli Bagerimi | 4th N.R. | 5.1.17 | When acting as N.C.O. in charge of scouts who forded the Mgeta River during the action on 1st Jan. 1917 he came under heavy machine gun fire. He acted with |

3428	Sgt.	Moma-na-Jegga	2nd N.R.	5.1.17	the greatest coolness. After locating accurately the gun position, he returned and reported to the artillery, which through his information put this machine gun out of action. Carrying out this duty his clothing was pierced by five bullets.
3954	C.S.M.	Sambo Bauchi	2nd N.R.	5.1.17	Showed great gallantry in action at Tschimbe on 1st Jan. 1917.
7256	Pte.	Awudu Bauchi	1st N.R.	28.1.17	Showed great gallantry in action at Tschimbe on 1st Jan. 1917.
					Conspicuous gallantry in action at Mkindu on 18th Jan. 1917, where he repeatedly took charge of parties of men, initiating and leading rushes on the enemy's position under heavy machine gun fire.
6471	Pte.	Belo Opoma	3rd N.R.	29.1.17	At Ngwembe on 24th Jan. 1917 he showed great gallantry in saving his machine gun, and later made great use of his gun against the enemy.
453	Sgt.	Musa Sokoto	3rd N.R.	29.1.18	Led his men with bravery in the attack, and was one of the first men in the German machine gun emplacements.
1359	C.S.M.	Tukeru Bauchi	4th N.R.	29.1.17	Displayed great pluck and coolness in transmitting orders under very heavy fire at Ngwembe on 24th Jan. 1917. His personal example had a most steadying effect on his Company.
5786	Pte.	Belo Ibadan	4th N.R.	29.1.17	At Ngwembe on 24th Jan. 1917 displayed great daring and initiative, by advancing to a mound 100 yards to his right and within 50 yards of the enemy, and so prevented them turning that flank as they were endeavouring to do.

Military Medal (to Native Rank and File)—continued

No.	Rank.	Name.	Unit.	Date of Award.	Remarks.
3	M.G.C.	AWUDU KATSENA	4th N.R.	29.1.17	Gallantry at NGWEMBE on the 24th Jan. 1917. When his Captain was wounded and being carried back, without orders he picked up a rifle and kept up a rapid fire at the advancing enemy, and so covered the stretcher party.
2897	C.S.M.	BELO AKURE, D.C.M. (with bar)	4th N.R.	7.4.17	Displayed courage and coolness in the defence of a post at KIBONGO on the 17th March 1917 when attacked by a much superior force. He displayed great bravery at KIBONGO on the 25th March 1917 in a patrol encounter, in which he captured an enemy European in spite of a determined attempt at rescue.
5489	C.S.M.	SALAMANO YOLA, D.C.M.	3rd N.R.	10.6.17	Behaved with great gallantry at NGWEMBE on the 24th Jan. 1917 during the German counter-attack. He also rallied the men of his Company on three occasions under heavy fire.
5890	Sgt.	MAFINDE SHEWA	2nd N.R.	29.10.17	Displayed the greatest gallantry at BWEHO-CHINI on 22nd Sept. 1917 when in command of 16 men he rushed an enemy post and captured a European and 29 boxes of ammunition. Again, later in the day, when his Company was heavily attacked and in danger of having a flank turned, he charged and drove them back with his section. He, by himself, chased a German

No.	Rank	Name	Unit	Date	Remarks
6982	Pte.	Tanko I.	1st N.R.	29.10.17	officer through the bush for 300 yards, and bayoneted him, notwithstanding the fact that the enemy were all round in strength. He then killed a German Askari, after he had been severely wounded himself. Displayed gallantry and great devotion to duty at BWEHO-CHINI on the 22nd Sept. 1917. He furnished valuable information about the position of enemy machine guns.
6426	L.-Cpl.	Mallam Duchi	1st N.R.	29.10.17	Displayed great gallantry at BWEHO-CHINI on 22nd Sept. 1917 in using his machine gun, which he continued to use under very heavy fire until it was put out of action and he himself was wounded. He then brought back his gun by himself and so saved it from being captured.
6117	Pte.	Moma Sokoto	1st N.R.	29.10.17	Displayed great gallantry at BWEHO-CHINI on 22nd Sept. 1917 when in charge of stretcher bearers. He was specially mentioned by the S.M.O. for the way he conducted stretchers up to the firing line across a fire-swept area and dressed his wounded comrades under heavy fire.
6326	Pte.	Alu Kuri	3rd N.R.	29.10.17	Displayed conspicuous gallantry at MSSWEGA on 26th July 1917.
3606	Sgt.	Damagara Argungu	3rd N.R.	5.11.17	These two displayed conspicuous gallantry at NYENGEDI in the action 28th to 30th Sept. 1917.
4312	Pte.	Afolabi Ibadan	Do.	Do.	
9001	C.S.M.	Alhagi	3rd N.R.	26.11.17	They displayed conspicuous gallantry at MAHIWA on 18th Oct. 1917.
5593	Pte.	Amadu Kara	Do.	Do.	At MAHIWA on the 15th Oct. 1917 showed most conspicuous gallantry in saving a Lewis gun, and bringing in wounded men and a wounded officer under heavy fire on
6834	Pte.	Jonathan Siloko	4th N.R.	26.11.17	

Military Medal (to Native Rank and File)—continued

No.	Rank.	Name.	Unit.	Date of Award.	Remarks.
1569	Pte.	Lowani Ede	4th N.R.	26.11.17	the occasion when his Company were engaged on reconnaissance, and were heavily attacked and pressed back with severe losses. Gallantry at Mahiwa on the 15th Oct. 1917. When little more than a recruit himself, and in his first action, collected magazines for a Lewis gun under very heavy fire, which magazines had been dropped in the bush by runaway and frightened carriers in action, thus enabling the gun to remain in action, covering the retirement of the Company.
2880	Sgt.	Adeyemi Ibadan	3rd N.R.	24.12.17	Displayed conspicuous gallantry and devotion to duty at Mkwere on 8th Nov. 1917.
4948	Sgt.	Maina	Do.	Do.	
7164	Cpl.	Moma Pica	Do.	Do.	
135	Sgt.	Adeyemi Ibadan	Do.		
5776	Pte.	Momadu Hadeija	4th N.R.	11.11.17	Displayed great initiative and courage near Malongu on 27th May 1917 when in charge of a patrol reconnoitring the railway. Seeing a large number of the enemy to his front, he guarded his left rear with four men, and proceeded with the remaining two to further investigate, when he caught sight of a group of German Europeans at close range. He opened rapid fire on them. Two were seen to fall. At the time he was within 50 yards of at least a company of the enemy.

No.	Rank	Name	Unit	Date		
5542	C.S.M.	Moma Dikoa	1st N.R.	11.11.18	Distinguished himself whenever he came under fire. At MKINDU on 18th Jan. 1917 he displayed great devotion to duty by continuing to perform his duties under heavy fire after he had been wounded. Later, when a convoy of wounded came under the enemy's fire he took command of the escort and conducted the defence.
5544	Sgt.	Dodo	3rd N.R.	11.11.18	Displayed conspicuous gallantry in the action at ITETE RIVER on 26th July 1917.
7097	Pte.	Gamba Keffi	Do.	Do.	

Meritorious Service Medal

5992	Pte.	Audu Illo	3rd N.R.	26.2.17	Gallantry in attempting to save life. When fully dressed he jumped into the RUFIJI RIVER on the 15th Jan. 1917, which at the time was in flood and the stream very strong and attempted to save the life of a comrade from drowning.

Mentions in Dispatches (Natives)

No.	Rank.	Name.	Unit.	Date.	In whose Dispatch.
Tx 1	C.S.M.	Garuba Kukawa	1st N.R.	11.10.17	Lieut.-Gen. Sir J. L. Van Deventer, K.C.B.
6429	Cpl.	Imoru Raha	Do.	Do.	Do.
5631	Pte.	Amadu Gaiya	2nd N.R.	Do.	Do.
4772	Sgt.	Moma Kano	Do.	Do.	Do.
5544	Sgt.	Dodo	3rd N.R.	Do.	

Mentions in Dispatches (Natives)—continued

No.	Rank.	Name.	Unit.	Date.	In whose Dispatch.
3087	C.S.M.	Sumanu, D.C.M.	3rd N.R.	11.10.17	Lieut.-Gen. Sir J. L. Van Deventer, K.C.B.
7097	Pte.	Garuba Keffi	Do.	Do.	Do.
5776	Pte.	Momadu Hadeija	4th N.R.	Do.	Do.
5039	Sgt.	Shefu Katagum	Do.	Do.	Do.
5542	C.S.M.	Moma Dikoa	Do.	Do.	Do.
Do.	Do.	Do.	Do.	30.5.17	Maj.-Gen. C. R. Hoskins, C.M.G., D.S.O.
6426	Acting L.-Cpl.	Mallam Duchi	1st N.R.	Do.	Do.
472	M.G.C.	Brimah	2nd N.R.	Do.	Do.
6410	C.S.M.	Momadu Kukawa	Do.	Do.	Do.
5983	L.-Cpl.	Audu Kaduna	3rd N.R.	Do.	Do.
5489	C.S.M.	Salumanu Yola	Do.	Do.	Do.
2610	C.S.M.	Laleye Ifon	4th N.R.	Do.	Do.
5395	C.S.M.	Morakinjo Ibadan	Do.	Do.	Do.
6153	Pte.	Salammi Offa	Do.	Do.	Do.
16	Sgt.	Ali Kontagora	A.N.R.	Do.	Do.
35	A. Bdr.	Babelle	Do.	Do.	Do.
95	Gnr.	Osuman Badra	Do.	Do.	Do.
5911	Sgt.	Abdu Sokole	1st N.R.	21.1.18	Lieut.-Gen. Sir J. L. Van Deventer, K.C.B.
6895	Sgt.	Moma Godia	Do.	Do.	Do.
48	Pte.	Maidugu	Do.	Do.	Do.
281	M.G.C.	Dan Sokoto	Do.	Do.	Do.
7082	Pte.	Ungulu Zaria	2nd N.R.	Do.	Do.
4656	L.-Cpl.	Awudu Kano	Do.	Do.	Do.
5619	Acting L.-Cpl.	Bake Telwa	Do.	Do.	Do.
6690	Sgt.	Jiddo Jebakki	Do.	Do.	Do.
2805	Sgt.	Osuman Kano	Do.	Do.	Do.

5709	Sgt.	Osuman Bauchi	2nd N.R.	21.1.18	Lieut.-Gen. Sir J. L. Van Deventer, K.C.B.
4685	Sgt.	Moma Argungu	Do.	Do.	Do.
5067	Cpl.	Sabo	Do.	Do.	Do.
5005	L.-Cpl.	Madi Shillem	Do.	Do.	Do.
6064	L.-Cpl.	Shaibu Keffi	Do.	Do.	Do.
6543	C.S.M.	Sumah Kano	Do.	Do.	Do.
4699	C.S.M.	Momadu Kukawa	Do.	Do.	Do.
5791	L.-Cpl.	Baba-na-Yola	3rd N.R.	Do.	Do.
5630	Cpl.	Kola Bida	Do.	Do.	Do.
5017	Pte.	Mande Zaria	Do.	Do.	Do.
7030	Pte.	Sambo Bauchi	Do.	Do.	Do.
108	Cpl.	Audu Kadan	A.N.R.	Do.	Do.
30	Tr'ptr.	Ibrahim	Do.	Do.	Do.
87	Gnr.	Garuba Kano	Do.	Do.	Do.
50	Bom'br.	Maikerifi II		Do.	Do.
B 26	Carrier	Serikin Sati	Pioneer	Do.	Do.
	Dresser	Olubi	W.A.M.S.	Do.	Do.
	Dresser	Johnson	Do.	Do.	Do.

APPENDIX D

CASUALTIES

BELOW is given the Roll of Honour of the Nigerian Overseas Contingent for the whole period that we were in East Africa:

Officers Killed in Action or Died of Wounds.

Major Green.
Capt. Barclay.
Capt. Cook.
Capt. Dudley.
Capt. Higgins.
Capt. Stretton, M.C.
Capt. Norton Harper.
Capt. Waters, M.C.
Lieut. Strong.
Lieut. Ewen.
Lieut. W. H. Harrison.
Lieut. F. Oliver.
Lieut. Joseland.
Lieut. Stevenson.
Lieut. F. H. Robinson.
Lieut. H. W. Robinson.
Lieut. Miller-Stirling.
Lieut. Ryan.
Lieut. Sutherland-Brown.

British Non-Commissioned Officers Killed in Action or Died of Wounds.

C.Q.M.S. Lamb, D.C.M.
Sergt. Spratt.
Sergt. Evans, D.C.M.
Sergt. Booth.
Sergt. Tomlin.
Sergt. Packe.
Sergt. Riley.

Officers Died of Disease.

Capt. the Hon. R. E. Noel.
Lieut. Huddart.
Lieut. Baker.
Lieut. Catt, M.C.

British Non-Commissioned Officers Died of Disease.

Sergt. Powter.
Sergt. S. Walker.
Sergt. North.
Sergt. Kelly.
Sergt. Whitaker.
Col. Sergt. Duggan.
Sergt. Major Dwyer.

Officers and British Non-Commissioned Officers Wounded and Prisoners of War (subsequently released unconditionally).

Major Gard'ner.
Lieut. Jeffries.
Col. Sergt. Speak.
Col. Sergt. Wroe.
Sergt. Wooley.

Officers severely Wounded.

Major Waller, D.S.O.
Capt. and Adj. Collins, M.C.
Capt. A. C. Robinson, M.C.
Capt. Carson.
Capt. O'Connell.
Capt. Budgen.
Capt. Allen (twice).
Capt. Armstrong, M.C.
Capt. Rickards.
Capt. Pring, M.C.
Capt. Gardner, M.C.
Capt. Finch.
Lieut. Newton.
Lieut. Young.
Lieut. Thompson.
Lieut. Winter, M.C.
Lieut. Mytton.
Lieut. Southby, M.C.
Lieut. Buchanan-Smith, M.C.
Lieut. Spaxman.
Lieut. Graydon.
Lieut. Fox.
Lieut. Kellock.
Lieut. Mulholland.
Lieut. Bovill.
Lieut. Cunningham.
Lieut. Hawkins.

Officers slightly Wounded.

Lieut.-Col. Feneran.
Lieut.-Col. T. M. R. Leonard.
Major Gibb.
Capt. O'Connell.
Lieut. Studley, M.C.
Lieut. and Adj. Winter, M.C.
Lieut. Steed.
Lieut. Grandfield.
Lieut. Hillman.
Lieut. Edwards.
Lieut. Snape.
Lieut. Jerrim.
Lieut. Dyer.
Lieut. Pomeroy.

British Non-Commissioned Officers severely Wounded.

Sergt. Reilly.
Sergt. Dixon.
Sergt. Care.
Sergt. Groom.

Sergt. Trandark.　　　　Sergt. Ward.
Col. Sergt. Kerry.　　　Sergt. Darke.
Col. Sergt. Watkins.　　Sergt. Manad.
Sergt. M'Knight.

British Non-Commissioned Officers slightly Wounded.

Col. Sergt. Hunsworth.　　Sergt. Hunt, M.M.
Sergt. Fraser.　　　　　　Sergt. Tanner.
Sergt. Booth.　　　　　　 Sergt. Empringham.
Sergt. O'Bergin.

Accidentally Wounded.

Capt. Drake.

Officers invalided out of German East Africa from Diseases contracted on Active Service.

Lieut. and Act. Adj. Travers.　Lieut. R. F. Forrest.
Lieut. H. de B. Bewley.　　　　Lieut. Rutland.
Capt. R. R. Taylor.　　　　　　Lieut. W. E. Burr.
Lieut. R. H. Wortham.　　　　　Lieut. W. B. Preston.
Capt. H. C. Faussett.　　　　　Lieut. Avary.
Capt. E. T. P. Ford.　　　　　 Lieut. Marlow.
Lieut. Harris, M.M.　　　　　　Lieut. Hobson.
Lieut. B. G. Cavanagh.　　　　 Lieut. Wood.
Lieut. Harrison.

British Non-Commissioned Officers permanently invalided out of German East Africa from Diseases contracted on Active Service.

B.S.M. Thorogood.　　　Sergt. Grinyer.
Armourer Sergt. Collins.　Sergt. Taylor.
Sergt. Pearce.

The following table gives the numbers of native rank and file killed or died of wounds, or died from the result of accidents incurred by Active Service conditions, died of disease, and wounded, during the whole campaign. In addition many deaths occurred during the return voyage to Nigeria, which are not included in this table. This list does not include deaths to men repatriated on account of wounds or disease, who died after leaving East Africa :—

Company.	Killed.	Died.	Wounded.
No. 1	38	10	52
,, 2	17	8	38
,, 3	15	16	63
,, 4	7	8	11
,, 5	7	12	47
,, 6	11	11	33
,, 7	13	14	24
,, 8	9	7	26
,, 9	35	5	76
,, 10	41	16	75
,, 11	16	10	24
,, 12	32	7	86
,, 13	22	15	38
,, 14	14	11	19
,, 15	13	18	26
,, 16	22	19	49
Battery	23	17	22
Pioneer Section	3	3	6
Drafts	12	56	31

Maps

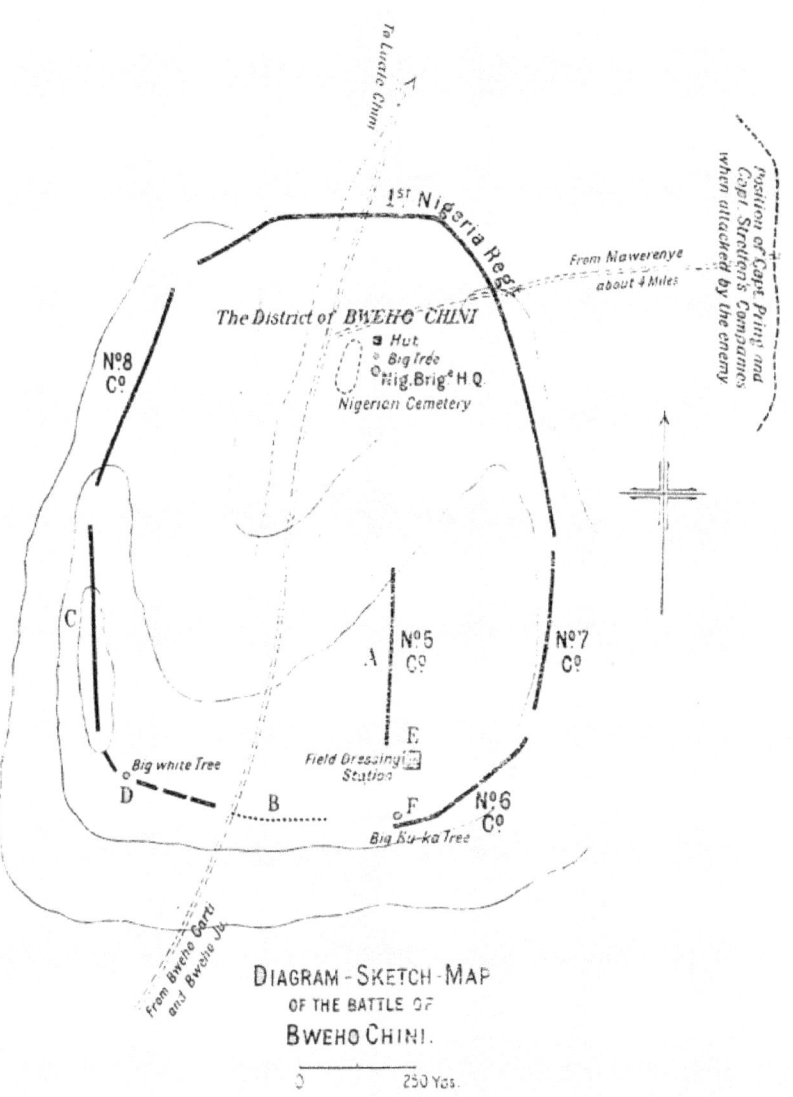

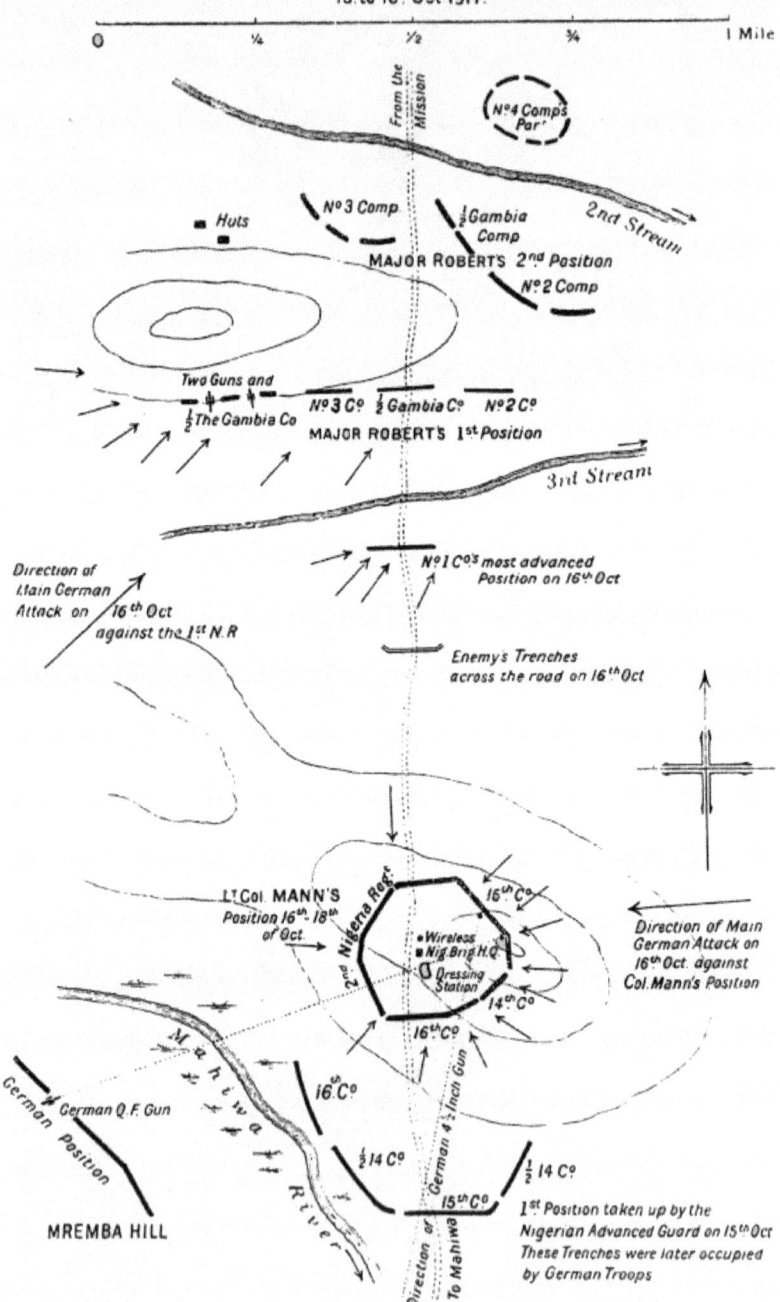

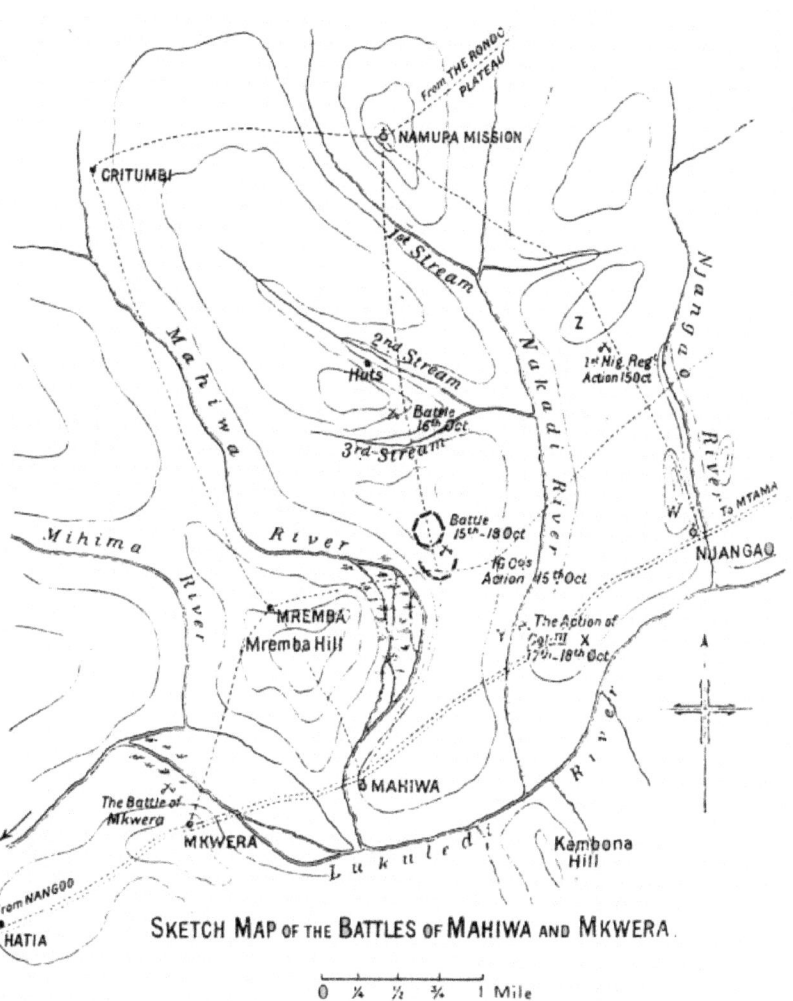

SKETCH MAP OF THE BATTLES OF MAHIWA AND MKWERA.

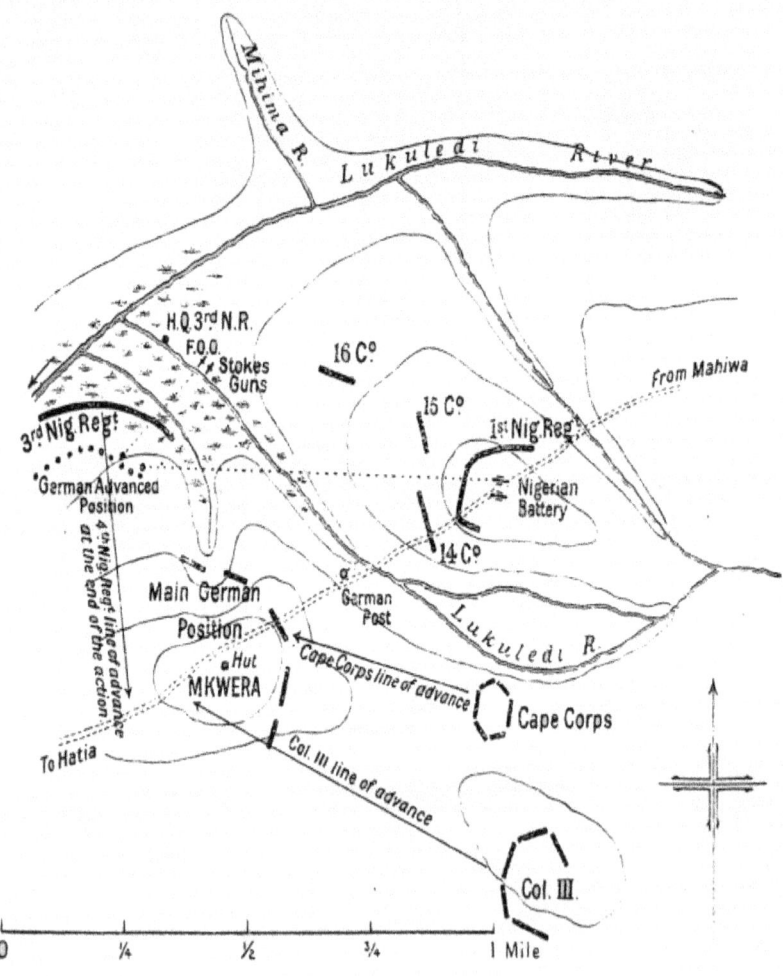

ALSO FROM LEONAUR
AVAILABLE IN SOFTCOVER OR HARDCOVER WITH DUST JACKET

DOING OUR 'BIT' by *Ian Hay*—Two Classic Accounts of the Men of Kitchener's 'New Army' During the Great War including *The First 100,000* & *All In It*.

AN EYE IN THE STORM by *Arthur Ruhl*—An American War Correspondent's Experiences of the First World War from the Western Front to Gallipoli and Beyond.

STAND & FALL by *Joe Cassells*—A Soldier's Recollections of the 'Contemptible Little Army' and the Retreat from Mons to the Marne, 1914.

RIFLEMAN MACGILL'S WAR by *Patrick MacGill*—A Soldier of the London Irish During the Great War in Europe including *The Amateur Army, The Red Horizon* & *The Great Push*.

WITH THE GUNS by *C. A. Rose & Hugh Dalton*—Two First Hand Accounts of British Gunners at War in Europe During World War 1- Three Years in France with the Guns and With the British Guns in Italy.

EAGLES OVER THE TRENCHES by *James R. McConnell & William B. Perry*—Two First Hand Accounts of the American Escadrille at War in the Air During World War 1-Flying For France: With the American Escadrille at Verdun and Our Pilots in the Air.

THE BUSH WAR DOCTOR by *Robert V. Dolbey*—The Experiences of a British Army Doctor During the East African Campaign of the First World War.

THE 9TH—THE KING'S (LIVERPOOL REGIMENT) IN THE GREAT WAR 1914 - 1918 by *Enos H. G. Roberts*—Like many large cities, Liverpool raised a number of battalions in the Great War. Notable among them were the Pals, the Liverpool Irish and Scottish, but this book concerns the wartime history of the 9th Battalion – The Kings.

THE GAMBARDIER by *Mark Severn*—The experiences of a battery of Heavy artillery on the Western Front during the First World War.

FROM MESSINES TO THIRD YPRES by *Thomas Floyd*—A personal account of the First World War on the Western front by a 2/5th Lancashire Fusilier.

THE IRISH GUARDS IN THE GREAT WAR - VOLUME 1 by *Rudyard Kipling*—Edited and Compiled from Their Diaries and Papers Volume 1 The First Battalion.

THE IRISH GUARDS IN THE GREAT WAR - VOLUME 2 by *Rudyard Kipling*—Edited and Compiled from Their Diaries and Papers Volume 2 The Second Battalion.

AVAILABLE ONLINE AT
www.leonaur.com
AND OTHER GOOD BOOK STORES

ALSO FROM LEONAUR
AVAILABLE IN SOFTCOVER OR HARDCOVER WITH DUST JACKET

ARMOURED CARS IN EDEN by *K. Roosevelt*—An American President's son serving in Rolls Royce armoured cars with the British in Mesopatamia & with the American Artillery in France during the First World War.

CHASSEUR OF 1914 by *Marcel Dupont*—Experiences of the twilight of the French Light Cavalry by a young officer during the early battles of the great war in Europe.

TROOP HORSE & TRENCH by *R.A. Lloyd*—The experiences of a British Lifeguardsman of the household cavalry fighting on the western front during the First World War 1914-18.

THE LONG PATROL by *George Berrie*—A Novel of Light Horsemen from Gallipoli to the Palestine campaign of the First World War.

THE EAST AFRICAN MOUNTED RIFLES by *C.J. Wilson*—Experiences of the campaign in the East African bush during the First World War

THE FIGHTING CAMELIERS by *Frank Reid*—The exploits of the Imperial Camel Corps in the desert and Palestine campaigns of the First World War.

WITH THE IMPERIAL CAMEL CORPS IN THE GREAT WAR by *Geoffrey Inchbald*—The story of a serving officer with the British 2nd battalion against the Senussi and during the Palestine campaign.

STEEL CHARIOTS IN THE DESERT by *S.C.Rolls*—The first world war experiences of a Rolls Royce armoured car driver with the Duke of Westminster in Libya and in Arabia with T.E. Lawrence.

INFANTRY BRIGADE: 1914 by *Edward Gleichen*—The Diary of a Commander of the 15th Infantry Brigade, 5th Division, British Army, During the Retreat from Mons

HEARTS & DRAGONS by *Charles R. M. F. Crutwell*—The first world war experiences of a Rolls Royce armoured car driver with the DuThe 4th Royal Berkshire Regiment in France and Italy During the Great War, 1914-1918.

TIGERS ALONG THE TIGRIS by *E. J. Thompson*—The Leicestershire Regiment in Mesopotamia During the First World War.

DESPATCH RIDER by *W. H. L. Watson*—The Experiences of a British Army Motorcycle Despatch Rider During the Opening Battles of the Great War in Europe.

AVAILABLE ONLINE AT
www.leonaur.com
AND OTHER GOOD BOOK STORES

www.ingramcontent.com/pod-product-compliance
Lightning Source LLC
Chambersburg PA
CBHW031615160426
43196CB00006B/145